Instagram:
CHUCKLEBERRIES,
Facebook: Jaycee Kesh

War, Momma, and

Me

Jaycee Kesh Akinsanya

Tim
Brother!
Here's to life.
Here's to memories and
the people we make them
with. Love is a verb-
an action verb.
Do it

Kesh-

i

Jaycee Kesh Akinsanya

ISBN- 978-1-7320-1130-4

Library of Congress Control
Number: 2018903731

Expert Gardener Publishing,
Whitewater, Missouri

You know, people in some countries look at others that way; like we've come to take something from them. What they should see is that we've come to offer them something. Every African, Indian, Chinese—most places you travel— the people are rich in culture; they show them how to live with each other. But we come to the melting pot with our ingredients, yet they don't allow us in their kitchen.

And in most cases, we're better cooks.

-Gloria A Bishop. 1950-2017

Dedication

To Gloria, my loving mother and friend; the day I forget you is the day I turn to dust, useless and taking up space. My value counts only when I remember that every fiber of my being was made possible because of you.

To "Mr. Olu," dear dad. I miss hearing you call me, "My brother."

To Aunty Olive, mommy to me in your own right.

To my loving siblings.

To the Bishop, Summerville and Akinsanya Families.

To Nikko, my Pokko Buzzfeed.

To civilians, especially the women who go unnoticed, enduring the damages of war; still loving, still nurturing.

Acknowledgement

I was born in the darkness of ignorance, but my spiritual preceptors opened my eyes with the torchlight of knowledge. I offer my respects to them.

A sincere thank you to all my friends and well-wishers who played a role in the manifestation of this memoir. There are too many of you to list here, but please know that I have, and still have the most amazing life because you are all in it.

They say a diamond never assumes its true form without some rough; to those who treated me with some kind of rough, I thank you too. I may be no diamond, but your rubbing against me abrasively only solidified my own self-worth.

To the editors and designers who helped make this book fit for publication, thank you.

Introduction

Why should I write a memoir? Who would benefit from it? These questions rattled around in my mind when I started this memoir back in 2008. I was on one of my travel journeys as a monk when the thought occurred to me. America had been sending troops to Iraq for about five years, and friends would try to engage me in discussions about the war. One crucial conversation that inspired this memoir began with a friend, Keagan, saying, "America is at war." I understood that he meant the troops were fighting in Iraq, but he said it as though the war was taking place right here on American soil. He spoke of taking safety precautions like buying enough canned goods and necessities. In Keagan's mind, an apocalypse could happen at any time, and he was preparing for it.

I chimed in that the American continent might never experience actual war like some of us had experienced. "You've experienced war, Kesh?" He asked. "When did you leave America and where was this war, did you fight as a soldier? You seem too young to still not be on duty. Dude, did you go AWOL and join the temple?" I told him that I was in fact not American, and wondered how he had not caught my accent all this time. Although it was very faint, my accent was easily recognizable. I explained that I was born in Liberia, and had experienced the first five years of the Liberian Civil War. It started the day before my 11th birthday, December 24th, 1989, and lasted for thirteen years. I shared some details of the war with him, and, in a state of amazement, he asked, "Dude, how did you survive? I mean, were you skinny and starving?"

"Actually," I told Keagan, "My mother took care of us. And she had a similar mentality as you have now. When we heard about the war, mom bought varieties of foods for storage. But when the actual war reached our part of town," I continued, "we had to leave our house, and most of the food went to the rebels." I told him about my mom, and about my family and said that I pray that present-day America never experiences war on its soil because people would go crazy. Excited fear, mixed with lack of conveniences and amenities would be the leading cause of war casualties. I described some conditions we lived under during the Liberian war and explained how dependent most people in America were on certain amenities such as microwave ovens and cell phones. He paid more attention when I gave an example of medical care: if a dangerous war happened, you couldn't call customer service to fix your prescriptions, or 9-1-1 for an emergency pick up. They too would be trying to stay close to their loved ones, and there would be no one to answer life or death questions. And what to speak of the most common amenities like electricity and running water; we didn't have those either. For now, war will be something filtered through a television screen for most Americans.

During conversations like these, someone would tell me, "Man, you should write a book!" I promised to do so one day when the time was right. I was leery of adding another "war survivor" story to bookshelves. I felt that there were enough stories of the atrocities of war, yet people never seemed to change. Something still triggered wars, and I wanted to know what it was. I thought I could write about the causes of conflict, and then people might detect those symptoms and try to prevent war. But I didn't know what caused my country's war, and other wars were still happening, so a book would have to wait until I had some clue.

Something else, which came up repeatedly with the mention of being a child who had experienced war, was the topic of a "ruined childhood." Most people would be right to conclude that the war situation ruined my ability to experience childhood. But I argued differently. I can still look back and say that I had a fantastic childhood experience. I was given a chance to experience first-hand emotions, process those emotions, and experience life in real time. Although I had seen the war first-hand, there was a veil of protection over me which shielded my innocence from effects like post-traumatic stress and psychological pain. That shield was my mother, one of the many women who endured and carried on their motherly duties when men were fighting each other for dominant positions. Some men who weren't fighting—men like stepfather—were targeted and harassed, and therefore, needed to keep low profiles to avoid death.

Before the war, I was given free reins to explore my surroundings and understand life that way. With my siblings, cousins, and friends, we played and daydreamed and made up fantasy worlds for ourselves. But we also did our duties like homework and house chores. During the war, I got to see, hear, and sometimes, question, certain incidents that I didn't understand. But the everyday duties remained. Schools were closed for some time, but daily education continued as I took advantage of the many books we had in our house. And after the war, I learned to adjust to life as it was then. Although the situations and environments changed around me, there were constants. Education was constant either in a school setting or in reading many books. Daily life activities like cleanliness and play time were steady as well, although sometimes adjusted due to the situation. The most constant of all was my mother's attitude as things around us changed. I felt that sticking to a continuous regimen, like chores and reading was a pivotal asset to helping us avoid future mental distress.

Through observing my mother, I learned to navigate my way through life changes in Liberia and abroad. As she would say when I tried to imitate her actions or attitude prematurely, "Monkey sees, monkey do." Her attitude was the first and foremost tool she used to play many roles: daughter, mother, wife, teacher, entrepreneur representing her country, and friend. She was fearless in the face of danger, practical in matters of faith, fair in her treatment of others, and had a heart of gold that tamed even soldiers in dangerous situations. She seemed to know how to properly blend concepts of religion, like the 23rd Psalm's "The Lord is my shepherd" into practical action when we needed higher intervention. She had a realistic outlook on life and used common sense as a guide in dealing with people or situations. She had a mystical side to her; something she shared with me in many conversations.

Mom's overall demeanor, as well as goal under any circumstance, was to stay relaxed. She was known in her later years for her most common sayings, "relaxing my mental tension," and, "don't let that disturb your mental tension." Previously, in her younger days, she had another famous saying, one she got from her favorite song, "A Charge to Keep I Have." She was often heard saying, when it came to being oneself, "I have my charge to keep, and my God to glorify, and you have yours." A lady with many witty remarks she claimed to have learned from the old people, she made concepts easily understandable through anecdotes and stories. Some of those stories became useful for me during the war.

I told friends that through my mother's expert guidance and love we survived the civil war. I then resumed attendance at school, although in a still unstable war situation. Searching for an understanding of the war situation, I took to reading many books. I wanted to help bring about a valuable solution that could at least slow down the pace of war. It seemed that every nation was on the brink of war, and I wanted to understand the whys behind it all. When a long period of stability arose, my father, who already lived in the U.S, brought me over to finish my education and continue living in a safer environment.

My first few years in America were a bit rocky as I tried to find where I fit in this new country. The lack of clear understanding of my place in America and my family's rudimentary knowledge of how the war had impacted my career drive caused a disconnect between my dad, my sister, and me. At one point, I moved to Minneapolis to live with my brother, and there, he gave me independence which helped me discover myself sexually and socially. It was in Minneapolis that I met my first core group of friends since leaving Liberia. Needing more autonomy, I again made another leap into the unknown. With a good friend, Brendan, I moved to Seattle, Washington on a one day truth or dare. Due to unforeseen circumstances, Brendan left Seattle shortly after we arrived, and I heard nothing from him again. I decided to one day write a memoir of my travels, so that if I were to meet Brendan again, we would sit and recount our different life adventures.

In Seattle, I opened myself to the possibilities life might offer, and got a chance to water my spiritual garden by living in a Krsna monastery. When I thought I had learned enough, I moved out of the monastery and lived in Seattle as a fashion model and continued to explore life. Because I had separated myself from my friends in Minneapolis and felt alone in Seattle, I traveled to India where I had a "quarter-life-crisis" experience. There I realized that I wouldn't feel satisfied, or "keep my charge," as mommy would say, unless I were involved in something that celebrated and cultivated the human spirit. I went back into the monastery in 2008, with the aim of working with some head monks to develop teaching techniques that would help new practitioners adjust to the Krsna culture, which is an ancient culture. People, I felt, needed the training to digest the kind of spiritual practice thoroughly, and at the same time, live daily lives in their own environments. After that second try of monastery living, still feeling unfulfilled working under the institutional structure of the monastery, I decided to travel a bit more independently. Traveling brought about some clarity, as well as time to reflect.

My reflections led to writing. I had written in diaries and journals all my life, but I wanted to write something more significant. Thus, my memoir was born. I still had no answers into the causes of wars which I thought would be written as a book. I did have, from some negative experiences while dealing with some leaders in the Krsna movement, insights into how people could become jaded and disenchanted in their spiritual search. I saw how, from my small experience, war could come about in more critical settings; somebody usurping a privileged position, and someone else plotting to take them out.

My memoir would be an excellent way to tell my story and caution others of what happens when people in influential positions fought. The people at the top who were fighting in my country didn't give a damn about me or any of the civilians. But the civilians were the ones who suffered the most. In Liberia, during the civil war, there was a saying: when two elephants fight, it's the grass that suffers. I wanted to alert the grass—hopeful students of spirituality, and civilians who only saw war via television—about the pitfalls of positions of power.

Good men went into influential positions with goals of making a real difference, and sometimes sold their values for higher ranks or emptier promises like the ones they make to their subordinates. But again, I didn't want to be a disgruntled whistleblower because I had experienced some negative aspects of the Krsna movement. Ninety percent of my experience was meeting and associating with highly realized spiritual people who imparted wisdom I still have yet to digest. I was also given freedom to travel as a monk and blossomed that way, which was one reason I had a friend like Keagan who wouldn't be caught dead around religious institutions. I got to study the Vedic books like *Bhagavad-Gita and Srimad Bhagavatam*, some of humankind's oldest scriptures. I traveled to different parts of the world and saw other humans exist with each other peacefully, with no scent of war lingering in the background. I wanted to share these experiences with people as well.

I had learned, from a friend named Leanna, the phrase, "Bloom where you're planted." In my book, I wanted to examine how I had "blossomed" where I was planted, especially periods like the war, my adjustment to American Life, and my life in the monastery. For most of my life, growth happened in periods—soils—of war and feeling like a misfit. Like a lotus which grows out of muddy waters, I had the seed of a flower deep within. Those murky wars and institutional situations caused me to take root and sprout. I am the child of a woman who had also been placed in dark circumstances but blossomed into a person who was admired and respected by her community. I too could rise above those incidents, as mom had taught me. I could make a difference in life without having to compete, fight, or hold a position of power.

I decided that this memoir would be about her as much as it was about me. My steps in life are only as sure or reliable as the foundation on which I walked. Mommy was a complex and fascinating woman who influenced and helped many, and I am her offspring. She was my foundation. I wrote this memoir as a self-examination, showing myself and others how much I had used mommy's wisdom to navigate life while I was away from her. Aside from my mother, my entire family, from my great-grandmother down, had a unique blend of respectful etiquette and abandoned familiarity, which gave us a kind of intimate closeness. The reader, I felt, should be able to enter into my story and experience instances where different conversations arose between my mother and me. They should be able to see how she gave wisdom in a way that cautioned without expectations.

As the years passed, I wrote bits and pieces, and I realized that my story was blossoming as I searched for my truth during pinching circumstances. Each traveling experience became something valuable to share as an example of how hard it can be when all you want to be is yourself, and how rewarding and sweet it can be when you find another piece of yourself. My friends were happy to hear that I had begun to write, but I was also still learning and experiencing some internal discord. I needed a project of my own to see if I could walk my walk.

Seeking to regroup, I traveled back to Liberia after seventeen years of absence, at a point when I needed to make a concrete decision in my life. Mommy was there to share more wisdom and empower me in a way that brought me back to America with renewed strength. I decided to live a secular life instead of a monastic life, and have more independence in how I presented what I had learned to others. I settled in Tucson, Arizona, where I met Nikko, my partner, after some foretelling incidences. Together with friends, we developed an excitement for organic farming and sustainability. The farming quest took Nikko and me on a journey around the U.S to our present farm situation.

For a while, I stopped writing my memoir but mystically began again on September 20th, 2017. That morning I wrote about mommy for four continuous hours. I appreciated the strength she had within her and my aspirations to come even close to her caliber. Later that evening I received news of mommy's hospitalization. Then, after mom's sudden passing, my grief flowed in the form of writing. It took me about a month to write almost 200 pages, as well as carry out my daily duties.

I hope that people will be inspired to take a glimpse at humanity from a different perspective—through my eyes—observing my mother and learning life lessons from her wisdom. Most especially, I wish that this memoir shows how she interacted with people and made them feel like they mattered. Every being matters and has a charge to keep on this journey through life. As for my spiritual quest, I aim to show the experiences I found as a seeker and the discernment I developed to know what practices were enlightening, and what actions were counterproductive. In life, we see that our values are often modeled after people we deem important in our development. Students imitate their professors; workers, their bosses; or followers, their leaders. For me, it is my mother who acts as the centerpiece of this memoir. At every stage in my life, I looked to her for guidance like an exploring child leaping in front of its mother, and at the same time, looking back to make sure she's still there watching and protecting. Her guidance for me was mostly subtle; she taught by example.

"Whatever action a great man performs, common men follow. And whatever standards he sets by exemplary acts, all the world pursues." Bhagavad-Gita.

War

Chapter One

Jaycee Kesh Akinsanya

The Lilliburlero

Watching war movies and playing soldier roles was a big part of our boy-hood. Many countries have their versions of Cops and Robbers, and we called ours, Police and Rogue. We played everywhere: in our rooms, the swamps, the schoolyard, or mommy's office. We fought wars and killed each other, and then five minutes later we were resurrected and played house or hopscotch. No one stayed dead in our wars. Wars were only a play where you would be killed one moment, and then the next moment, get back up for more games, or dinner. We pretended to be Rambo; we acted out characters like Charles Bronson, Chuck Norris, and Van Damme. These guys were invincible, and so were we. We had many other toys, but mom had to buy us toy soldiers again and again because those were the ones we played with the most.

We wanted to be heroes. We read many comic books and aspired to be like the superheroes. If one chose to live in the world, live in a world where Superman, Robin Hood, Green Lantern, Wonder Woman and the rest, lived. My brother Toye was an excellent artist and drew comic strips filled with heroes and villains. Back then, our consciousness was saturated with war and fast cars as I am sure it is in most places in the world where American culture entered. Every toy I recall had something connected with defense—our GI Joes, transformer cars, plastic soldiers—boys were meant to grow into strong men, and strong men became strong through fighting. Girls played with dolls and dollhouses, and a boy caught playing with girl toys was ridiculed.

Soon we would all come to find that in real wars, people died. They did not wake up for dinner, nor did they wake up to play the next game. War was not a game. In real wars friends became enemies, and such exposures, like death, hunger and human insanity, scenes for mature eyes, were displayed everywhere for all to see.

I sat on the doorstep of our home on the Old Road around a quarter to six in the evening. That was when my stepdad Rupert would sit outside and wait for the BBC World News at six o'clock on the radio. Rupert stood six-foot-one, was built like an athlete and had a beard that reminded me of Marvin Gaye. His favorite chair on the porch was the one closest to the street. Every evening he sat there with his small AM/FM radio and listened to the news of the world. Our house was next to the road, and the hanging flower pots filled with African Violets and other plants created a canopy-like privacy screen. Mom and her friends also sat on the porch almost every day after work, talking about the latest gossip. Today, there had been some unsettling, but unconfirmed rumors about a war outbreak near the Ivorian border in Nimba County. In the evening, we all gathered on the porch to confirm the rumors. Before this, I knew nothing of Liberian politics. I was a young boy, ten going on eleven, and had a wandering spirit which kept me out of the house on most days. If I was at home, I was absorbed in a mystery novel series like *Hardy Boys* and *Nancy Drew, or Aesop Fables* and other books. Now and then I heard a politician's name. Margaret Thatcher, Arafat, and Gorbachev were names that appeared in conversations between Rupert and his friends.

A month earlier, mommy gave birth to my baby sister Tashina, and nicknamed her Chee-Chee, after our Aunty Lois. Chee-Chee, who experienced some high fevers for a few days, had just been put to sleep. I was very inquisitive about the new baby and would try to be there next to mommy, learning everything I could about how to care for her. Mommy let me hold Chee-Chee when she was two weeks old, and also taught my brother Toye and I how to change her diapers. Being a big brother gave me a sense of responsibility, and when Chee-Chee would cry, I would go in and sing to her to put her to sleep. Mommy's friend Barbara, a Mormon lady from the U.S embassy gave me a few books about little babies months before Chee-Chee was born, and I read and asked mommy as many questions as I could about the baby in her womb. In her seventh month of pregnancy, while she drank her coffee one morning, I became curious and asked her if the hot coffee wouldn't burn the baby. Mom chuckled and told me that the baby was in a protected sac called a water bag. The baby wouldn't be burned because mommy only took a sip of coffee at a time. She said that by the time the coffee got to her stomach, the temperature would be colder and won't affect the baby.

After putting Chee-Chee to sleep, mommy came out to the balcony and sat closer to the door and lit her Benson & Hedges Menthol cigarettes. Mommy's face looked pensive, yet relaxed. She had a signature gaze—a poker face—that she wore, and no one could tell what was going on inside. Her left thumb had a bandage on it; a boil had developed at the tip of it a week after giving birth to Chee-Chee, and had now popped. Mom stood five-feet-two, but had a very authoritative presence that everyone noticed when she entered a room. The liveliness of her gait made for good joking remarks from Mary, our maid. Mary would say, "Look at Gloria Antoinette Bishop, walking like she owns the country." Mommy's voice had power to it, and when she tried to make a point in a conversation, she'd raise it a little bit; just enough to hush the other speaker. She laughed often, which would cause the dimples on her cheeks to deepen and all her "ninety-nine teeth" to be visible. Mommy was known for her joking remarks and playful jabs at people. "Ninety-nine teeth" was a phrase she would use for someone who smiled or laughed and displayed their pearly whites. "Look at him laughing, displaying all ninety-nine teeth God gave him," she would say. She was fond of adding lyrics and beat to a person's gait as they walked by our house: "Step Mr. President, step like a Billy Goat. Step Mr. President, step like a Billy Goat."

Some other neighbors also sat on the porch that evening waiting for the usual sound that announced the news hour. When it was one minute to six o'clock, Rupert told everyone to hush; the news was about to begin. A male voice began, "Eighteen hours Greenwich Mean Time, this is London. Here is the news." Next, a female reporter's voice, "You're tuned in to the General Overseas Service of the BBC. This is the British Broadcasting Corporation." Then a symphony rendition of *The Lilliburlero*, and finally, the news headlines.

A Birthday Halted

It was that hour when the beginning of the end of my boyhood arrived. It was a Sunday. Sunday, December 24th, 1989, the day before my eleventh birthday. News of insurgents on the northeastern side of the country was confirmed, and the men had something new for discussion. Charles Taylor, a former government official, entered Liberia via Ivory Coast, our neighbor country. He intended to topple the ruling administration led by Samuel Doe. Taylor, a former government official under Doe, had been removed from office for embezzlement and fled Liberia. Some say he went to Libya where he trained as a guerrilla fighter.

Mommy, Rupert, and our neighbor Steve talked about how this rebellion would be over in a matter of weeks. The Armed Forces of Liberia (AFL), would stop it, and all will be back to normal. They compared this new outbreak to the 1985 coup, led by Thomas Quiwonkpa who was captured, killed and his body left on display outside of President Doe's Executive Mansion as a warning to others. Rupert speculated that Taylor's entry into the country through Nimba had something to do with Quiwonkpa's death. Quiwonkpa was from Nimba County and was a Commanding Officer in Doe's army. In 1983, he was suspected of trying to stage a coup and overthrow President Doe but was discovered. He then fled into exile with some other military allies. In 1985, he returned but was ultimately caught. Parts of his body was mutilated and eaten, and then left out in front of the Executive Mansion on display. Quiwonkpa's village, Zuleyee, Nimba County was then harassed and ransacked by Doe's military forces. Doe's brutal actions caused a lingering grudge in the Gio and Mano tribes of Nimba County. Taylor knew the history and must have used the Gio and Mano as catalysts for his war.

It was exciting to hear of actual war, and we'd be there to see heroes and villains engage each other. When I asked mom what "rebel" meant, she said it was a person who went against authority. Charles Taylor, to me, was the villain; he had broken into the country and had rebels with him. Doe was the authority because he was the president in whose land Taylor had forcefully entered. In my mind, we would watch the battle on TV; it would take place at a stadium or someplace similar, and after the fighting, everything that was destroyed would be rebuilt, and life would go on. If Taylor won, he'd come riding victoriously into town and we'd all gather on Tubman Boulevard, the main road, and throw congratulatory rice grains at him. If Doe won, we'd do the same, and life would go on. Except mommy had a feeling that if Doe won, he'd go looking for those who supported Taylor, and kill them. People thought him uneducated and unpredictable.

But this also was the first time I felt invisible. Something else—someone else— had entered the minds of the adults there, and my birthday, Christmas day, no longer took precedence. From mommy, I was the third of my then four siblings: Cheryl, Toye, Jaycee (me), and Chee-Chee. When Cheryl left for America to finish school a few years earlier, mommy adopted a little girl, Serenna, to live with us. On my dad's side, I was his last child of six. Sheena, his eldest son, had just passed away in Nigeria earlier that year. The others were Sunde, Deji, Biodun, and my sister Yabo. Four of us were born on a holiday: Biodun, on New Year's Day, and Toye, on Liberia's Flag Day; I, on Christmas Day, and Chee-Chee, on President Tubman's Birthday.

I was conceived in London, while mommy was getting her Masters in Agriculture Science, and was due to be born on the twenty-seventh or twenty-eighth of December, but mom went into labor late in the evening of Christmas Eve. Dad somehow convinced her to have a C-section so that I could be born on Christmas Day. Mom agreed, and luckily it all went well; but when my other aunts and cousins would talk about it, it seemed like no one else was on board with such an idea. Some famous sayings surrounding my birth and the C-section were, "When Gloria was in love... hm!" Or, "How could Gloria have allowed Olu to convince her to have a C-section, Lord? Your mom was crazy, but we're glad you're here." To make matters more interesting, I heard that my dad wouldn't let anyone into the hospital room without a Bible because I was his special son, born on Christmas Day. Mommy named me Jaycee, and people jokingly called me "Jesus Christ."

My Dad, who everyone called Mr. Olu, migrated to the U.S in the early eighties for some civil engineering work. From what I remember about him, although I was only four or five years old, he was a well-respected man in the community. Dad stood five-eleven, and had a Santa Claus belly. He had a traditional Yoruba scar on his left cheek (he was born in Nigeria in 1934), and when he combed his hair, he parted the right side, which was a fashionable thing to do at the time. Dad worked for different government agencies in Liberia, like the Forestry Development Agency, and Public Works. He had a white Peugeot Sedan, and always sat, chauffeured, in the right back corner. He smoked cigars and, in the evenings, slowly sipped on a glass of brandy, and read his newspaper.

For the rest of the evening, I sat in the doorway listening to mommy, Rupert, and a few neighbors who stopped by to wish my family Merry Christmas. Everyone talked about the new events and had their opinion to give on the subject. Now and then someone would notice me and say happy birthday in advance, or ask what I was going to do for my party. But their focus, as the "Club Beer"—Liberia's local beer—emptied, one bottle after another, and their Benson and Hedges cigarettes burned, one stick after the other, was on the unfolding events.

Every guest at our house the next day had something to say about the rebel soldiers; who they were, where they came from, their leader, and his purpose. The focus was on removing President Doe from office. People said he was a dictator and had brought the morale of the country down. The rebel leader, Charles Taylor, was coming to rescue Liberia, and his speeches had people hopeful. Now and then mommy would make a joke about all the opinions being passed around the room: "The old people say opinions are like assholes; everybody has one. Now I have all these assholes here in my living room and on my porch." All I remember from that birthday was the movie Rupert rented for us to watch. It was called "*The Party*" and starred Peter Sellers. For days after, my friends and I would imitate the "birdie num-num" scene where Peter Sellers disturbs the whole party by speaking into the PA system.

Everything else now had the cloud of war over it. You'd hear shopkeepers tell you to buy more bread and condensed milk because the war was coming. Market women tried to sell you more of everything because "Wartime coming oh." None of us understood the gravity of war, and the events that were happening in the upper part of the country were just news that we thought would fade away soon. For months to follow, talk of this rebellion led by Charles Taylor's NPFL (National Patriotic Front of Liberia) filled the air. It became prominent—so fast. And all we heard was that the rebels would never get close to us because the AFL would get them before they got to the city. That was the confident estimation of my stepdad and his friends. They were the authorities on these matters. They had been to America and other

9

countries, and as kids, we thought anyone who had been to America automatically knew everything. Still, every evening at eighteen hundred Greenwich Mean Time we heard about the rebels and their conquests of different towns and counties. They were moving closer to the city, and with each move came a speech by the rebel leader gloating about victory for his forces. Such an address would be "counter speeched," as mommy put it, by President Doe.

A British Journalist, Elizabeth Blunt, described in detail the situation happening on the war front. We all sat around the radio and laughed at the way she talked about the food and the people. She described villagers digging up roots (cassava) to eat, or how they collected iron meat from the swamps for food (people collected a type of clam we called "suck-suck" or "kiss me"). It was indeed entertaining to hear local foods described in such a way by a foreign journalist. Cassava, known as yucca in other places, is one of the food staples in West Africa. Other roots include coco-yams, eddoes, and sweet potatoes. Suck-suck got its name from the way one had to suck this snail-like clam out of its shell. Most Liberians cook suck-suck in palm butter, a sauce made from the ripe red fruit on the palm nut tree. Palm oil comes from the same tree. Elizabeth Blunt became the voice we heard almost every day, giving us a glimpse into what was happening on the war front. I listened to the news for entertainment, mostly. I was eleven and had no grasp of the reality of the situation, and the woman I looked to for inspiration, mommy, had a turtle shell of a back that everything just seemed to roll right off. We waited each day for the time when the symphony theme of the BBC News would start, followed by "Eighteen hundred Greenwich Mean Time, this is BBC News."

Chapter Two

Jaycee Kesh Akinsanya

"It Shit Oh."

Within a few months, it was an apparent reality that the rebellion against the present government wasn't going to be "over in a few weeks." Refugees flocked to the city describing what they had seen. Rebel forces destroyed villages along the way and took hostages—young children especially—who were later drugged and forced to join the rebellion. Villagers fled in whichever direction they could. Some sought refuge in nearby Guinea, Ivory Coast, and Sierra Leone. Around the country, foreign businesses started closing up shop, and foreign governments began evacuating their citizens. When the American Embassy started evacuating their citizens, war became a definite reality. Mommy quickly prepared my brother Toye for evacuation; the lucky guy was born in Missouri while she was attending College there, and so he got to leave the country. A few days before his evacuation we all went to the city with mommy to get pictures taken.

The dress theme was blue: mommy wore a turquoise blouse with a matching skirt, and Toye had on a blue T-shirt and his favorite wrist wallet. I wore my favorite blue tank top with the words, "Surf and Sand," and Chee-Chee was dressed in a light blue dress. It was the last picture we took together and is one of the last remaining pictures we have in our pre-war album. Toye flew to the US and stayed with our Aunt Facia, who had also been living there for a few years.

Life went on side by side with the advancing of rebel forces. For a moment, mommy had to go to Israel and Egypt to attend a women's conference geared toward women entrepreneurs and was on one of the last flights back to Monrovia. At the time, she worked for the Ministry of Commerce, and it was common for her to travel to meetings in different places; Geneva, India, Las Palmas, Papua New Guinea, among others. My godmother, Esther, and mommy were among the first women in Liberia to hold degrees in Agricultural Science, and the responsibilities of work took them traveling. Shortly after mom's return to Liberia, the rebel forces captured the international airport, and no flights were able to leave or enter the country through that airport. A smaller airport in the city, Spriggs Payne Airfield, flew people to neighboring countries, but even that airport closed its doors when it became challenging to transport necessities like diesel for the planes.

With Toye gone and Mary, our maid, laid off to be close to her family during the uncertain times, I became mommy's right-hand man. My step-

13

brothers Chuckie and Robbie lived with us as well, and Robbie, the younger of the two, also helped in the management of the house. Mom taught us how to make market lists, ration out food, use water sparingly for washing dishes or clothes, and make sure our home was secure for the night before we settled in for bed.

Next to close were the local schools, as talk of the rebels coming closer, keeping families together, and gathering enough food and water barrels filled the air. As anticipated, the rebels took control of the water plant as well as one of the electric hydro dams. Workers were evacuated, killed, or recruited to fight, and there would be no electricity or running water for a while—perhaps until after the war. We had to go to the well down the hill for drawing water, and buy candles or kerosene for the oil lamps. Carrying well water became a talent for most of us. A skilled person could carry a bucket on his head, hands-free, and then one or two other buckets in each hand. The way back home wasn't an easy walk on a flat plane either. If you decided to carry water hands-free, it meant stepping over large tree stumps and climbing natural steps dug into the side of the hill by the well. In the beginning, there were accidents; your bucket would fall off your head and you'd have to go back and refill.

We had a few fifty-gallon polyethylene drums set in specific parts of the house; one in mom's bathroom, one in our bathroom, two in the kitchen, as well as a few five-gallon containers. We'd fill all these containers with water and mom would add an appropriate amount of chlorine to each tank to keep the water from developing algae. Depending on how much water we used each day, drawing water could be a daily task, which meant multiple trips to the well. Becoming an expert at carrying two or more buckets of water was hugely beneficial. Gathering water like this was nothing new either; most neighborhoods had wells because some people had no running water in their houses. For them, this was life as usual. It was the more "civilized" people who needed to learn this skill. But, as I recall, the energy in the air was never a frantic or fearful one; life had shifted gears, and this was our new reality.

No electricity meant that we couldn't freeze foods for long-term storage, so mom would buy fresh fish every day, and we would smoke and dry them for long-term preservation. The drying process was also a common practice in our neighborhood. Liberians love their dried meats and fish; now we just had to dry them for longer storage. A large metal barrel, perhaps one used for transporting oil or other liquids, was transformed into a smoker with shelves set up about two feet above the fire. You'd place the fish or meat on a metal rack, like one found in an oven, and place the tray on the drying shelves. The secret was to make sure the wood gave a lot of smoke and not so much fire as to overcook the food. Some expert food dryers would even season the meats or fish before placing them in the dryer. It took diligence to dry meat and fish correctly, and on some occasions, neglect to dry them properly would present itself later when you opened a batch of dried fish or venison to find maggots crawling in it. Lord, they smelled too!

If she ever found a batch or two like this, mommy would give the person responsible a good cussing and a possible lick with the rattan for not paying better attention. I got a whooping or two in those days. I would forget to check on the drying fish and would go out to play with my friends. When I came to check on the fish later, it looked "smoked" on the outside, so I'd assume it was ready and would pack it for storing. Luckily mom was very diligent and would double check our work. If she found something fishy, for lack of a better word, she'd call to you from the pantry. You knew you were in trouble when you saw her in her "Gloria stance." We all knew that posture; she'd put one hand on her hip and point her other hand in the direction of the "problem" with her index finger curled slightly backward. She'd also have a particular look—sharp eyes staring down into your soul as you came close to her. If the situation were severe enough, you'd be told to get the fufu stick, a traditional wooden spoon made for cooking fufu, a dish made from ground fermented cassava. The fufu stick was the perfect paddle for spanking, and when necessary, mommy would use it. After all, this was our long-term food supply; empowering us with responsibility didn't mean turning a blind eye to the results.

Soon, a dusk-to-dawn curfew was put in effect. Staying out after curfew meant arrest or death, and in times like these, the soldiers were looking for a reason to kill anyone. Offices were closed, so mommy stayed home all day. Our house was one of the neighborhood social spots, and her friends would visit and socialize until it was time to make their way back to their homes. I often wondered if they didn't have to prepare for the war as we were, drying food and filling water buckets. But like our house, they too had other people staying with them who did all that work.

They'd sit, laugh and gossip, eat and drink, and we'd play in the neighborhood for as long as possible before curfew hours. For me it was work, then play. I'd do my share of the water barrel filling and whatever other chores, and then have all the free time to read, play, or listen to the gossip between mommy and her friends. I would hear a few things about politicians, cabinet ministers, or people who had left Liberia to save themselves from the war. Someone always had the latest news to share. A common phrase I'd hear during these conversations was, "It shit oh!" This phrase meant that things were going in a very shitty direction as the war came closer to the city.

15

Sourcing food and beer became a bit tough, and some prominent people were fleeing the country.

Mom told a story one day about her flight to Egypt and how she met a prominent leader, the son of our next-door neighbor, on the plane. He recognized her and asked, "Gloria, are you leaving too?" "That ass," mommy laughed, "He thought I was running away to Egypt. How the hell could I have left my whole family here and jump ship to Egypt? But he ran. Most of them ran. They were the same ones who made the mess, now they ran."

With all the news we heard, we'd still be out there playing, walking about, going to the well for water, and carrying on with life. Mom neither stopped us from playing nor did she prevent people from coming to visit. It seemed like nothing would take away the few hours of social freedom we had, and we used it fully. The war situation was the war situation and we never tried to make it "better" than it was. We just continued to live.

Mr. Hard Time

As I saw it, the war was approaching our doorsteps and so was Mr. Hard Times. Mr. Hard Times was one of the many stories mommy would tell us in the evenings of our childhood. When the Thomas Quiwonkpa military coup broke out in 1985, the hydro-electric dam was tampered with, and we got electricity at certain times and none at others. Mommy told us stories to pass the evening when the power went out, and in later years she wrote those stories down for Toye to pass on to his kids. As we prepared and stored rice, beans, canned foods, fish, oil, matches, charcoal bags, and other provisions, I felt thrown into the scene where the thieves come to take all of the stored goods from the man's house while his imbecile wife happily stood by and let them.

The Story, as written down by mommy:

There once was a man named James, who had a wife, Martha, of no formal education. James worked very hard to secure their future. He decided to save a little bit of money each month for the hard days ahead. Each time James brought provisions home, he would tell his wife that Mr. Hard Time was coming and that they needed the money for Hard Time. He brought home gold, silver, dried foods and many other provisions. They lived quite frugally and put a portion of everything away for safekeeping. One day he told his wife

16

that he was going away and would be back soon. James asked her to take good care of the money and remember that it was only to be used for Mr. Hard Time.

As he left the house, James again reminded Martha of the purpose of the valuables, and when to use them. But in the town where they lived were some evil men whose only duty was to rob people of what they had earned. Later that morning, Martha headed to the marketplace to buy food, and while there she began to tell her friends about what her great husband had done. She told them how ready she was for Hard Time to come because she had all these valuables saved for him. Standing within ear distance was one such wicked men, and he keenly listened to what Martha was saying. He alerted a few friends of what he had heard, and that night they made a plan to rob Martha while James was away.

As Martha sat in her hut that night, she heard a knock at the door. "Who's that?" she asked. "It's me, Mr. Hard Time," said the voice. Martha became very excited and quickly answered the door. "Come in. I am so happy to see you. My husband isn't here. He left a lot of money for you, and finally, you are here to get it. I hate keeping money around that I cannot use. Please sit down and wait while I get your money." With a smile, the man took a seat. Martha ran into the room and grabbed every penny they had saved and handed it to him. She even made him dinner with the food they had saved in the pantry. After eating to his satisfaction, and gathering more food for the journey home, he reached into his pocket and handed Martha a silver coin. "Please take this for all the hard work you and your husband have done." He then headed out the door as quickly as he could, met his other friends who were hiding nearby, and disappeared into the night.

Upon his return, James was greeted by a delighted Martha. "I have good news!" She exclaimed. "We don't have to worry about saving all those things for Mr. Hard Time anymore. He came last night, and I gave him everything we had." James became angry and stormed out of the room. He told Martha to follow him so they could go out and find the thief. As they walked, he asked Martha if she had taken care of the door at the house. Martha quickly ran home, and to his astonishment, James noticed her coming, carrying the door on her back. "Why did you bring the door?" He asked. "So nothing can happen to it. I am going to take good care of it as you asked." James held his anger in, didn't say another word, and let Martha bring the door along. They walked all day until dusk, and soon found themselves in the thick of the forest.

James knew that sleeping on the forest floor would be dangerous, so he began to examine different trees until he found limbs that would support the door. He put the door across two branches in a tree and they lay down for the night. The forest got darker and quieter, and soon they were both asleep. James woke up to the sound of voices below, and noticed, from a lantern below, that the persons below were the thieves. They had settled under that tree for the night and were counting their loot.

Martha also woke up and needed to relieve herself. "Why now?" Whispered James. "Because I just have to" whispered Martha. Afraid that something bad might happen to them if they climbed down the tree he told her to relieve herself from where she sat. She pulled up her lappa skirt and began to pee. As the urine fell below the men at the bottom tasted it and shouted, "Wine from heaven! Wine from Heaven!" Soon after peeing, Martha said she needed to poo; once more, James told her to lift her lappa and go. This time the men screamed out "Food from heaven" and ate it all up.

As she wiggled and adjusted her weight, the branch began to move, and within a few minutes, all hell broke loose. The door bounced off limbs and came crashing to the ground. The thieves below were frightened, which give James a good idea. "You dare steal from the poor!" Came a loud voice, from the darkness. "I will send you all to hell tonight." The men quickly began looking around, and with the speed of a hunting cheetah, they ran "helta-skelta" out of the forest as fast as they could, leaving all their ill-gained loot behind. James and Martha came down the tree.

The light from the morning sun soon begin to appear, and James and Martha gathered all the loot and the broken door and headed back to town. They had collected enough to make them the wealthiest people in town. James opened a business of his own and sent Martha to school. As for Mr. Hard Time, real or fake; they never saw him again. The End.

Mr. Hard Time might visit us soon, I thought, and we needed to have a pantry full of provisions to feed ourselves when he arrived. We had rice, beans, canned foods like sardines, luncheon meat, condensed milk (my absolute favorite still), cooking oil, and things necessary to sustain us. We'd eat simply on most days. Most Liberians have their most substantial meal in the afternoon, and mom would try to alternate foods so that eating didn't seem monotonous. On Saturdays or Sundays, she would spice things up a little and cook a bit fancier style foods for us like Split Peas and gravy, or Collard Greens and Black-eyed peas. The local farmer's market still had a few things, mostly cassava roots, cassava leaves, sweet potato roots, and sweet potato greens, or fish caught in the nearby creek or river.

Ungrateful Refugees

The influx of new people coming to town, all seeking refuge from the war zones, meant whoever had an extra room in their home opened it up to refugees. Our house was no exception although we had only two bedrooms. We opened our doors to a family friend, Jo-Ann, and her entourage of three. Add to that number my cousin and stepbrothers, and we had a full house. I noticed that, at certain times of the day, Jo-Ann and her people disappeared into our bedroom for a few minutes, and then emerged later with happy faces. I later found out that they went in there to eat in secret so as not to share anything with us. Apparently, they had some canned fish and dried foods and rationed it to add to whatever meals mom had available. Their actions were a bit disturbing to me because we rationed and shared our food with anyone who was around at lunchtime. For me, this was an introduction to the nature of a selfish person who would come into our house, eat our food, stay in our rooms, and not share a single bit of what they had.

Mom knew what was going on, but from the day I could consciously observe my mother, I noticed that nothing fazed her. She always seemed to take life in stride, and in times of trouble, she remained calm and composed. Months before, my then two-week-old sister Chee-Chee suffered from some high fevers, sometimes leading to convulsions. Mom instructed me to get some cold water and a towel, and I watched as she wiped the baby's face and body to cool her down. Mommy was calm during the whole process. Her practical nature made even the most demanding situations manageable, and as a result, a lot of people looked up to her as a source of guidance.

News surfaced about a break up between the rebel forces, and the INPFL emerged (the Independent National Patriotic Front of Liberia), led by General Prince Johnson, who had taken another route to reach the city form the Bushrod Island area. Johnson also had a vendetta against President Doe; he had accompanied Thomas Quiwonkpa into Exile in 1983 when Quiwonkpa was first suspected of plotting a coup. He later joined Charles Taylor's rebel forces, and now there was an internal power struggle between them. Mommy made an amusing joke that day when we heard about the new rebel force. "The people of this world love acronyms; now he's the INPFL against the NPFL, but I'll call them A.S.S.E.S, with all capital letters."

The rebel forces drew closer, and the citizens grew more anxious. They formed a march on the Executive Mansion and asked President Samuel Doe to step down from office. The marching song was "Today, today, today, Sammy come down," in a melody taken from another folk story about how a lady would call her monkey lover to her by singing. "Tio, tio, tio, monkey come down." The march was important, and many turned up for it. I recall people walking through our yard excitedly telling mommy that they were on their way to the march in the city. "I'm not going to some damn march," she would say, "I will support the march right here with my beer and lunch. War's coming, and I have limited energy to be wasting on marching."

Another rumor that filled the air with the advancing of the rebel forces was that they hid at the top of coconut trees and watched the activities of everyone in the vicinity. We had a coconut tree right over our house, and every morning when I came outside, I looked up at the tree to make sure no one had scaled it, or sat perched atop it. Sometimes I would walk a few feet away to get another angle of the tree, just to be sure. Consequently, some not so smart people in the Liberian military started cutting off the leaves, and sometimes the full trunk of the coconut trees in different areas by the ocean so that rebels would have nowhere to hide. The effect of the mass tree cutting on the coast didn't show until years later when it became evident that the ocean had slowly eroded the land.

Some of the beautiful Liberian beaches looked ugly and bare after the soldiers started cutting the trees down from fear of rebels hiding in them. To the north of us was a mangrove swamp that had crocodiles living there and, apparently, this made it harder for the insurgents to infiltrate our area of town. We heard that a whole group of them had tried to come into Gaye Town through the swamps but had been eaten by the crocodiles. Survivors fled for their lives and took a different route. A few of us used to play by those swamps before the war. We'd throw rocks in the water to see if a crocodile would chase us. Sometimes we'd get into one of the canoes and row over to a nearby mangrove and watch for crocodiles or freshwater crabs.

The news that reached us daily was scary, but the commentaries from mommy were a reason to wait for these strange tidings. One of my favorites was when she heard about the cutting down of the coconut trees by the beaches. "See, illiteracy is not just a sickness, but a crime. These damned fools are cutting down the trees now, but they won't have coconut water to drink when hard time comes. What did the trees do to them? Why not put guards along the coast to see who climbs them? But they're busy killing innocent people and getting drunk, so the trees have to suffer for it." Mom was especially irked by the tree cutting because her agricultural degree was focused mostly on horticulture. She understood the importance of trees, especially their role in preventing erosion.

War, Momma and Me

Jaycee Kesh Akinsanya

Chapter Three

No Requiem

Johnny Nah was a good friend of our family. He was one of mommy's closest friends and had just married the beautiful Famattah Sherman Nah. She was pregnant, and they would both take long walks and visit us from their house down the street. They'd sit on the porch with mom and others and make food, drink beer, and talk about life and news events. Johnny had a very old and loud jeep, and you'd know he was driving in from miles away. But to save on gas, in case they needed to leave the area, they now walked everywhere. I guess the exercise was good for Famattah and the baby, too. I liked them very much; they both made every place a happy place when they entered it. He would call mommy "Gloris," and whether he was walking or driving by, he'd yell "Gloris!" and mommy would answer back "Woohoo!!"

On the afternoon of the thirty-first of July, as we sat on the porch eating beans and rice and drying some meat and fish, two Liberian Armed Forces soldiers walked by and greeted everyone. Johnny jokingly invited them to come and eat and gain some strength: "Y'all come eat something. Y'all gonna need all your strength to fight. The rebels are getting closer, and you don't want them to beat you now." They declined and continued along. These guys were a bit more serious than the Armed Forces soldiers we encountered daily, and their demeanor looked suspicious like they were scouting our house or someone on the porch. Some soldiers even brought us extra food and provisions, and mommy would, of course, share a bottle of beer with them. The visit with Johnny and Famattah ended as usual, and with the curfew upon us, we all went back inside for the night. While inside, we usually played UNO or Scrabble before saying evening prayers and going to bed.

I was asleep on the floor in mom's room, at around one or two in the morning, when I heard a car driving by, followed by "Gloris!" Mommy, startled, woke up and wondered if it was Johnny who had called her name. I told her I had also heard the car and her name being called out. It seemed strange that they would be driving about that late. Johnny wasn't one to break the law, and if he were doing so, he wouldn't just drive by; he'd at least stop and let us know what was going on. Rupert mentioned that maybe Johnny found something out, and was running away from the area. He suggested that we try to get out of the Old Road before things got worse. But we were stuck on the Old Road and couldn't go to Duala where his family had a compound. The other rebel group, INPFL, who had split from Charles Taylor, blocked access to that side of town.

A few hours later when the Curfew lifted, the reason for the drive-by that night unfolded. Johnny's neighbor came over and told us what had happened the night before. Johnny, pregnant Famattah, their daughter Hilaria, and son Johnny Nah Jr, were forcibly taken out of their house, driven a few miles away to the Chugbor area of town, and brutally murdered. It was a somber day around our house, and perhaps the first time since the war started that I saw mommy in a sad mood. In fact, I had never seen her in a sad mood. Mommy's poker face was hard to decode, so we could never tell what mood she was in if she wasn't laughing or reading a book. But today she was sad, and you could see the distress on her face. She was quiet most of the day and would comfort and chat with friends who heard the news and came over to talk about it. We later learned that Johnny's son had somehow escaped, but we didn't see or hear from him after that. We didn't play UNO that night. Everyone sat absorbed in a book or quietly did something else. Mommy's mood set the pace that evening; it seemed as if the grownups were trying to make sense of everything, and were deep in contemplative thought.

That night, I had a dream of Johnny. In the dream, I was playing soccer with my friends when my cousin Vamilar kicked the ball into the street. Johnny, carrying a newborn baby with him, kicked the ball back to us. I ran over to him to say hi and see the baby. Johnny's face looked translucent like he had just shaved, but had not yet washed the hair or shaving cream from his face. He told me to "Tell Gloris that we are safe now. Famattah had a baby boy. Stay happy and keep smiling, we will see you all soon." I woke up, sat next to mom on her bed and tearfully told her of my dream the night before. She quietly comforted me but didn't cry. I said to her while sitting there, "War bad oh, mommy. War bad."

It was the following day that we learned from a witness closer to the Chugbor area of town, how Johnny and his family died. The government soldiers were responsible for this; perhaps the two who had walked by a few days before. I hoped the rebels would arrive quickly and get rid of these useless soldiers. My view of everyone switched—the rebel forces were now the good guys—and the Armed Forces of Liberia, under President Doe, were all scum. It was at this time that the reality of war hit me, and I couldn't understand why people would kill each other, especially innocent people. It also became apparent to my eleven-year-old mind that our house could be targeted as well, especially since mommy was such a social person who welcomed anyone to our porch to sit and take a load off from the stress of war. Because I saw the world through mommy's eyes, it saddened me deeply to see her as sad as she was.

On the morning of the first of August, a few minutes before the dawn curfew lifted we heard a knock on the door. Johnny had just been murdered, it was dark outside, and the knock on the door made me think that our time to die had come. My cousin peeked out the kitchen window and saw a lady at the door. The lady, Margaret, obviously distressed, asked to see mommy. She had just escaped a massacre at the St Peter's Lutheran Church and School, which was the school my siblings and I attended until a few months back when all the schools closed. She told mom that a fortunate few escaped. She climbed over the school fence, hid in the neighbor's mango tree for some time, and crept away under darkness to safety. Others, whose story we heard later, played dead and lay among the bodies until the soldiers left, before escaping to safety. Our house was about four miles from the massacre scene. Apparently, the president wasn't so pleased with people asking him to step down from office.

The night before, the halls we walked through going from class to class; the very yard in which we played many games; the church we sang in once a week at assembly—all those rooms became a killing ground. The Armed Forces Soldiers murdered about eight hundred people taking refuge at the school grounds. People say the president himself was there to see it. Bodies were left to rot in the open for months until after the first ceasefire when a mass grave was dug to bury the bones of the victims. The once sandy spot we played in as kids, is now covered over with cement and a white star marks the grave site. Margaret stayed with us for most of that day. Mommy gave her a fresh change of clothes, some beer, and food, and as was a regular daily affair, neighbors stopped by to visit us and heard her story.

Two days of distressing news took a stress toll on the adults in the house. I could tell that they were coming to grips with how real—how dangerous—this war was. Mom's face looked a little sterner, but she had the responsibility of keeping the house running. In 2009, when I first told mommy about my memoir and asked her about the day Johnny died, she mentioned how distressed she was, and how it angered her inside that she didn't have time to mourn her friend. The lady who showed up the next day had, in a sense, obstructed her mourning for Johnny. She said life had to go on and so she moved about doing things. "What if those damn asses had followed that girl to my house, you know? Luckily, they didn't, or we would have all been as dead as doornails. I know heaven is my home, but I wasn't homesick."

Years later I recalled and laughed with a friend about how as kids, we may have started the civil war or caused the school massacre. The president visited our school earlier, before the war outbreak, and all of us students followed him from class to class. Our school was on Tubman Boulevard, a major road into the city. When Presidents from other countries visited Li-

27

beria, schools on the boulevard would let their students out of class to join the cheering crowd as the presidential motorcade drove past. This time it was just our president visiting us. A few of us walked right behind him as he walked back to the presidential motorcade parked in the churchyard. My friend pointed out to me, "Look, the president is short, he has on high heels." I chuckled at the sight of his shoes but stopped when I looked up just in time to see President Doe turn and look at us with zero emotions on his face. He had heard us, and he didn't look happy. Another friend said to us, after the convoy left, "That man looked vexed at y'all, and he coming kill y'all."

Fearless Gloria

A few nights later, as we played UNO before going to bed, we heard a knock on our door. A soldier told us to turn the lanterns off, as it was curfew hour. It was unusual because no one ever bothered us or any neighbor who obeyed the curfew laws. Mom responded that we were in our houses and not outside, and so could have family time, which was not against the law. The soldier, seemingly drunk from the sound of his slurred voice, said he would break the door down if we didn't turn the lights off. Meanwhile, my cousin got up and started dimming the oil lamps, but mommy wasn't going to be bullied inside her own house. She replied that she had in the house a very big and tall husband, and a few nephews, and sons, and if he came in, either he or we would not make it out alive. My terrified stepfather, Rupert, gestured to mommy to shut up and do as the soldier said, so as not to cause any trouble.

Mom quietly instructed us to go into the room and recite the 23rd Psalm. The house was silent for a while, and then from outside came the soldier's angry voice, saying that he was off to get reinforcements. He never returned. We boarded up the windows with plywood that wouldn't let any light through, closed the curtains, and hung extra blankets over the curtains. We then put many chairs and iron bars behind the door with the hope that no one would break through them. When morning came, we took down all the barricades and opened the doors and windows for fresh air, and then every evening after that, put them all up again. We awaited the reinforcements with a light sleep that night. All of us slept next to something we could quickly grab and use as a weapon in case someone broke in. I think I may have said the 23rd Psalm about a hundred times that night. I couldn't imagine what my stepdad was going through mentally, having a wife who was a lioness; bold enough to fear no evil, yet gentle enough to be approachable by many. She had stood her ground and perhaps put all our lives at risk. It was a risk she was willing to take at a time when people with weapons were utterly ruthless to others.

Mom also had a weapon—her depth of faith. She never talked much about religiosity, but she had an understanding of divinity that I admired. Rupert owned a birthday book in which each day was matched with a Bible verse. For mom, whose birthday was the nineteenth of August, it was the 23rd Psalm, fourth verse: *"Yea though I walk through the valley of the shadow of death, I will fear no evil, for thou art with me."* Her stance, though risky that night, was not out of character for her. We were following the laws by being inside at the given hour. The fault was a drunk soldier trying to intimidate us, and mommy wasn't one to threaten easily. She gave due respects to others but called them out when they overstepped their jurisdiction. She would often state that if you stood for truth, truth would protect you. But you had to know what truth was, and for that, you had to do your due diligence. She also argued that if the government was going to enforce curfew ordinances, they should educate their soldiers as to what that meant.

On the evening of the eighth of August, as we settled in for the night, we heard screams from the neighbors a few doors down. Mommy, having won the battle a few nights before against the soldier by being a brave talker, screamed to the neighbor from our not barricaded kitchen window. She told her not to let anyone in, and to fortify the door as much as possible. My step-father, obviously terrified, tried to get mommy to stop, lest the angry soldiers come to our house. Mommy continued for a bit longer, and then stopped. The screams subsided and the night went on quietly. She was the matriarch of the neighborhood and was bent on saving her friends from uncalled for harassment, especially if they were following the curfew orders.

Her explanation to me, as we talked about that day, years later: "I had reached my tipping point with those soldiers. They weren't doing their jobs anymore, just harassing people. If they wanted to be soldiers, they should have learned the rules of engagement in war. You can't just go humbugging civilians just because you have a gun. That's why you don't give an illiterate person lots of money, or high positions; they will misuse their position and cause havoc for everyone else."

Rustic Living

By now, people hardly left their homes, and some claimed that the rebels were already in the neighborhood disguised as refugees from behind rebel lines. For us, deciphering such a claim was difficult; there were so many new people in the area. People also said that the rebels traveled under cover of darkness and made animal noises so as not to be detected. Again, I looked to

29

mommy to see how she would handle this newfound information of refugee rebels. But, steady as she was, she treated people no differently. She would later tell me that we should never judge a person by his/her situation. A street sweeper could rise to high ranks in the bat of an eye, or a high-ranking person could fall low. She saw many things and knew a lot of information. I heard much about events and people as she talked with her friends on the porch. But in every interaction, even with those people she knew unpalatable things about, she was always kind and personable.

In the city, more murders in numbers were happening, and talk of gruesome incidents filtered in. We heard how some cabinet members and other government officials who hadn't fled to safety had disappeared without a trace. Whether they made it up or not, someone told us that the president had lions at the Executive Mansion and would feed people to his lions. Curfew at this time, went from dawn to three in the afternoon. Being outside meant early morning cooking and gathering water from the well, and that was about it! The time was too short to entertain visitors on the porch. People slowly stopped visiting after Johnny's murder. Others just stayed inside because it seemed too hard to start anything, even cooking, and get it done on time. What to speak of getting other chores done. Although our houses had kitchens inside, there had been no electricity for months now; we used charcoal or wood to cook outside. This war situation was new to us, and sweet Liberia was in a bitter state emotionally.

While conversing with a friend years later, he reminded me of the quiet days when you'd go outside in certain parts of the city and not even see a bird flying. Perhaps they too were afraid of being shot by the numberless stray bullets that flooded the sky. This was Liberia—tropical rainforest Liberia—and not a sign of a bird flying. We can only do our best to speculate the reasons: perhaps the soldiers who hid in the bushes ate them. Maybe they flew to safer forest areas in other parts of the country. Maybe they were fed up with the stupidity of man, and left the country altogether; this would be my guess. Or were they there the whole time but went unnoticed because of the tense situation? Those war days weren't days for going outside to look for birds or smell roses; they were days that pushed you to focus on the bare necessities. It was easy not to notice nature happening right before us. Whatever the reason, the silence in the neighborhood was noticeable.

The busy streets in our neighborhood were empty; no daily market now, just people coming out to do what they needed to do. We even started to draw water for our elderly neighbor, Ma Eya, who couldn't make so many trips to the well. Trips to the well were quicker, with no time to socialize with friends. Weeks earlier we learned to bathe with just one gallon of water, to save well trips. You'd lather the "important funk areas," as mom called them, and then use a wet bath towel to clean the rest of your body. When all was nice and wiped, you poured the rest of your allotted bathwater over yourself to get that "bath feeling" of water pouring over you.

Those who knew mommy, tell about her interesting way of explaining things. She somehow added an element of humor, and for some reason when we laughed, the lessons stuck more easily. Mom laughed a lot. Her pearly whites sparkled, and her eyes lit up when she smiled. She taught us how to enjoy a small piece of fried fish with a big bowl of rice. You'd start eating and break off a tiny bit of fish to go with your first spoon of rice. In this way, you tasted the fish; but from then on with each spoon of rice, you put the fish close to your nose and let the scent mix with the rice you're eating. Finally, with the last three or four spoons of rice, you'd break up your fish accordingly and enjoy the last few bites. Another version, for the more austere, was to eat your dry rice first and then enjoy your piece of fried fish at the end. Now "dry rice" wasn't dry at all; it included a mixture of okra, pepper, bitter-balls (small Thai eggplants), cayenne pepper, and red palm oil. By itself, you had a treat. Even dry rice and fried fish, a Liberian staple, became a luxury for us during the war.

We learned to hang up the clothes we wore the day before to let the air clean out the body odor because there wasn't much time to do laundry outside and wait for it to dry. Simple things like opening the windows and doors for air circulation became very important, especially with twelve people in a two-bedroom house. To give batteries a bit more life to power the radio for the evening news, we boiled them for a few minutes. Specific items had to be used sparingly because there were no shops open to go and purchase them when we ran out. A pea size bit of toothpaste was enough for your toothbrush, or activated charcoal from the wood stove could also be used as toothpaste. The neem tree in our yard became more useful than usual. We usually made neem tea with the leaves, for internal cleansing, or as a treatment for malaria, but now we also used the pencil-sized twigs as toothbrushes. Although seemingly grotesque, we used water to clean our backside, as our Muslim neighbors did before prayers. Mom joked that using water was better, and left no brown stains in our underwear. A can of condensed milk was savored for a few days, instead of eaten like it was going out of style. Instead of a few teaspoons of mayonnaise on your Lebanese bread, one teaspoon was enough.

As for those dried fish and meat in the pantry, they were a rare treat that mom added to weekend meals. Most times we would peel off pieces of venison, monkey meat, or dried fish, and enjoy them the "Gloria way," eating a bit in the beginning, or waiting until the end to relish them. Although under a cloud of war, life was simple and special, having mommy and Rupert at home. Mommy took life easy; we never felt like we had to race against the clock to come outside after curfew, and then hurry back in before. I'd watch Rupert play checkers with the neighbors, or sometimes one of us, and when he was really up for it, we'd kick a soccer ball around the yard.

Mommy and Rupert grew up in the 50s and 60s, a period when technology and convenient amenities were just coming to Liberia, so they knew of simpler and satisfying ways of life. The war brought out the necessity of simple living from them. They'd both tell stories about growing up using chamber pots, going to the well for water, or walking to B.W. Harris, the school where they met. In a sense, the lack of modern amenities brought back simpler times for them.

One thing we had in abundance was music. Mommy and Rupert sang a lot of songs from many genres of music. On any evening you'd hear Anita Baker, Kenny Rogers, Luther Vandross, Pavarotti, or Clarence Carter. Or the Everly Brothers, Tom Jones, Tina Turner or Paul Simon, to name a few. Mom would go into drama mode when she sang Jim Reeve's "I'm Gonna Change Everything." She'd dance around the house demonstrating the things she had to "burn:" the carpet, the pictures on the wall, everything. The Everly Brother's "The Lightning Express" and Dolly Parton's "Coat of Many Colors" were Rupert's favorites to sing. They knew all the songs by heart, and we learned them as well, just by how much they sang. For their wedding day, they both sang, as mommy walked down the aisle, Andy William's rendition of the Hawaiian Wedding Song.

Chapter Four

Jakkass Redemption

On the morning of the ninth of August, a yellow sports car drove by our house; the driver seemed to be in a hurry. Someone said he was the president's medicine man and was headed to the city to give the president some juju protection. A few hours later, news reached us that the car was bombed, and the guy was dead. Apparently, he was on his way to the executive mansion but got ambushed along the way. Rumor had it that the president had a voodoo tattoo of the map of Liberia on his butt, and therefore would not lose the war. He was "sitting on the country," and was confident that he wouldn't lose the war. With the death of said medicine man, his chances of sitting on the country looked bleak; the rebels were closing in. If the rumors were correct, and they were already in our area of town, he only had four or so miles between himself and the danger.

I remember going down to the well for water that morning and peeling some cinnamon bark off the tree that stood next to the well. Fresh cinnamon bark tastes sweet and juicy, with that spicy cinnamon tingle in every chew. We tried to enjoy every bit of time we had before curfew. The well was almost empty with just a few people here and there collecting water. Usually, it was a hub for talking to friends and killing time, of which you had very little. Most friends had left town or were in their respective homes and couldn't come out to play. Walking back home felt longer than usual because of the lack of everyday neighborhood chatter. The weather was cloudy that day too, it was the rainy season but hadn't rained much. Something that my eleven-year-old mind couldn't understand had gripped the area. The atmosphere looked almost apocalyptic with no sunshine, no animals—not even the local stray dogs running around—few people out and about. I knew the neighbors were in their houses but hadn't seen them for days.

Just before dawn on the tenth of August, I woke up to sounds of footsteps and movements. I looked out of mommy's room window and faintly saw groups of people walking and carrying their belongings on their heads. Curfew hour, six o'clock, hadn't been lifted, so the movement got me curious. The sky was cloud free, promising a sunny day. People looked frantic, and men with guns directed them toward the main road. They told everyone to go behind rebel lines and not in the direction of the city, because the city was going to be a war zone in a few days, and people would have nowhere to go.

These men, I thought, were rebel soldiers because they didn't have mil-

35

itary uniforms on. Some had bandanas on their heads or around their arms. Others wore war helmets, with war paint on their faces; they didn't look like a uniformed military force. But they had guns, and that's how I knew they were rebels. Some were kids my age and held weapons as big as they were. They spoke authoritatively to everyone.

Mom got up, opened the door and asked one of the men what was going on. We were told to grab what we could and exit the neighborhood, as it was now a war-zone. Anyone who chose to stay would be in grave danger. They would have no means of getting water from the well or fuel to cook. Furthermore, civilians could get caught in any possible crossfire between the rebel forces and the government soldiers. As far as he knew, the government soldiers had already fled the area, but he told mommy that they could quickly come back with reinforcements.

As fast as we could, we collected a few bundles of clothes and some food and left our house to find safety. I guess all the food we saved for Mr. Hard Times would rot in the pantry. Would we come back home? Where were we even walking? All we knew was that we had to leave and leave now. We joined the line of people and headed for the road. Rupert had a cousin named Emmett in the Paynesville area, and we decided to seek him out and maybe stay at his house if he was there. Paynesville would be almost a day's walk, and no one knew what was happening in that area. Refugee camps had been set up in different places, and rebel forces directed people there.

We took a route that led past my grandparents' house, so mom took the opportunity to ask one of the rebel soldiers about the residents of the house. He informed her that the old people who lived there had already been evacuated and went to Fendell Campus. It was at that moment the rebel soldier recognized mommy, and she, him. He was one of those "refugees" who lived in the neighborhood and who mom had given some food and beer months earlier. You could tell he was very embarrassed to be seen in such a light, with weapons in hand, and threatening the lives of people in line. Mom said to him, "You ass, you're a rebel too?" She said it in a way that she called everyone else "ass," or "jackass." She'd say jackass in a way that made the "c" and "k" merge into one letter. It sounded more like "JaKKass." Anyone who knew Gloria knew that her first greeting to you always involved a foul word. If not the greeting, somewhere in the conversation you'd be introduced to her personality. She was very relaxed in everything, and even now, in what seemed to be the most dangerous situation we'd ever seen, she was herself- one hundred percent. The soldier shyly responded, "Yes mom, I sorry oh."

Mommy was very understanding of the man's situation and spoke to him like one of her neighbors. She told him that he had to do what was necessary, and not to feel embarrassed. It was a war situation, and when things got better, he could settle down and take care of himself. He listened attentively to mom. In that moment, she pulled him away from his rebel persona and reminded him of his humanity. She helped him understand that he was only temporarily duty bound to Charles Taylors cause. Now that we knew my grandparents were not at home, we continued our trek. The soldier escorted us part of the way and was very kind to our family. He gave us water and asked if we needed anything. Mommy hadn't judged his situation. He was proof of why she treated people in the neighborhood kindly, even when we heard that the rebels had come disguised as refugees. To our good fortune, because she was kind to him, he was kind back.

Once we left the Old Road, our area of town, and started to walk on Tubman Boulevard, the reality of war hit us. Our neighborhood was sheltered from the main fighting areas. The swamp served as a dead end, and so we lived in a somewhat protected area. All the fighting had taken place on Tubman Boulevard, the main road, two or three miles away from us. There were long lines of people for as far as the eyes could see. They had bundles on their heads or in backpacks, and from the different directions, it looked like the roots of a tree all coming toward the main trunk. On the road, there was no telling who was rich or who was poor; just a long line of people walking to safety. It was going to be a hot day- the sun came out as I anticipated, but for now, it was still in the morning hours, perhaps eight or nine o'clock.

Rule of the exodus: walk single file; if you step out of the line, you'd be shot. The section of Tubman Boulevard where we walked was covered with bullet shells, and nearby in the tall grasses, we saw body parts. Some bodies were of Armed Forces soldiers, others of rebels; some of children, mothers, fathers, or animals. At times, random people were taken out of the line and shot. Everyone in that vicinity had to watch, and if there were any screaming, or signs of discomfort, whoever showed it was the next to go.

The most unbearable thing during this part of the exodus was the smell of decaying flesh. The stench hit you without mercy and permeated the air. The last thing you wanted to do was be caught holding your nose to stop the smell. How long could a person go anyway, doing that? The stench was in the air for miles on end. Foot movements were the only noise coming from the civilians walking behind rebel lines. Everyone had to walk- the elderly, the young, everyone. Rebel soldiers drove by erratically shouting, some firing their weapons in the air. I walked right in front of mom as she carried little Chee-Chee in her arms. Serenna walked in front of me. All of us- mommy, Rupert, stepbrothers, and cousin, took turns carrying Chee-Chee.

Jaycee Kesh Akinsanya
Shelter Near a Death-Filled River

At the Shell gas station near ELWA junction, after miles of walking, mommy spotted a family friend sitting at the station, having a beer. Velma, we'll call her, lived in our neighborhood and was related to the rebel leader. She used her relationship status to step out of the exodus line and relax for a bit. The road to ELWA was blocked, and the line of people was only going toward Paynesville. Mommy spotted her and said, "Look at that damned Velma girl, let's stop and see her for a minute." Mommy stepped out of the line to greet Velma, but a young soldier yelled at her, "Get back in line or I'll shoot you old ma." He looked about my age with eyes as red as coals and smelled like he hadn't had a bath for months. Aunty Velma beckoned for another soldier who admonished the boy and gave way for mommy to pass. The rest of our family stepped out of line and sat down for a few minutes. As usual, except for the setting, they gossiped about what was happening in the area, whose house was OK to go to, and where not to go. Rupert's cousin was still at home, so he and mommy decided that we would make our way to his house. After finishing her beer, mommy decided it was time to leave, and we all got up and got back in line.

It was while sitting at the gas station that we got the news that Cousin Sam, the old man who lived across the street from our house, had just died in someone's bathroom. He had to pee so badly, and one of the rebels escorted him to the bathroom of an abandoned house. When he didn't come out of the toilet, the rebel soldier broke open the door and found him dead- a possible heart attack. This plight of death came for many old people that day; some died from mere fatigue, others from intense fear.

We bid Aunty Velma goodbye, wanting to reach Rupert's cousin's house before dark. Along the way, a very young soldier, again around my age, approached Rupert, held a gun up to him, and interrogated him. Rupert was a very fit and tall man, compared to the boy's tiny size, and could have crushed him to ashes. I recall a story of a man who insulted mommy one evening long before the war and how Rupert picked him up by the back of his pants and shirt, slid him across the bar and threw him out the door. Rupert also fit the profile of the "government worker enemy" that had been washed into the brains of the young recruited child soldiers. Young soldiers were told that anyone who worked for the government was a supposed enemy, and should be killed. Said government workers were big and fit from stealing all the money from the people and were meant to be punished. The boy was about to shoot Rupert after minutes of questioning, when, for some reason, his gun misfired, and he shot himself in the finger. People screamed in fear at the sound of the fired weapon. Another soldier, who had seen us sit with Velma at the gas station, came to our rescue and we continued to walk on, determined not to stop for any reason. Rupert escaped death that day, and as mommy would say, it wasn't his time to go.

The sun was hotter now as we walked, but that stop at the gas station rejuvenated us to some extent. A few hours later we arrived at Cousin Emmet's house, which was a little further from the main road. He was pleased to receive us, and we felt welcomed and glad to be out of the exodus line. Paynesville was a safe zone, and apparently, Charles Taylor had some relatives and close friends in the area. Some said he even came to the area frequently to see his friends.

Mommy, Rupert and baby "Chee-Chee" stayed in one available room, and the boys stayed in the living room. The living room was sunk into the floor and had an array of books to read on the shelves. I was glad to rediscover the *Iliad* and *Odyssey*, as well as the works of Plato, in Emmet's library. Before the war, when Toye and I watched "*Clash of the Titans*," I asked mommy to buy us the *Iliad* and *Odyssey*. My young mind didn't understand much of Homer's writings, but just the act of reading enhanced my reading skills. She also bought other books which included the stories of Socrates. Another book mom bought, but I didn't get to read was called *Inferno,* by Dante Alighieri. Out in the yard was a big almond tree giving lots of fruit; perhaps the first fresh fruit we'd had in weeks. Emmet also had sugar cane and papaya trees, and when mom made a stew, she would add chopped green papaya to it. Chee-Chee, who was just learning to walk and make some sounds would waddle toward the tree when an almond fell, screaming, "Almonds!"

Rupert didn't come outside of his cousin's house, or its immediate vicinity for days after we arrived. The danger for a man his size could present itself at any time. When things looked a bit quieter, he would venture out to the road and then back to the house. Most days everyone just sat idly on the porch. Within a few months, Rupert had lost so much weight that you could count his ribs. The fear of being seen outside by any of these rebel soldiers caused him to eat very little. Add to that the lack of his regular exercise routine- playing soccer with his friends before the war broke out.

One day he decided to venture a bit further on the road, but came back a little jokingly depressed and complained to my mother about how the soldiers didn't know who to kill or who not to kill. On his walk, he had passed the naked body of a young woman with very plump breasts (called "iron titties"), and he was a bit irked that the soldiers couldn't have had her as a girlfriend and let her live. Who could have brainwashed the soldiers so much as not to recognize youthful beauty? He complained that after the war there would be nothing but saggy old lady titties to look at if the rebels continued killing young girls this way. Mommy joked back and told him not to worry, when the war was over there would be many doctors offering breast implants.

On another walk where I accompanied him, we walked past a child on the verge of death, breathing ever so slowly next to, perhaps, his already deceased mother. They lay about 10 feet away in the grasses. On our way back, a few minutes later, we walked by that same child, this time, a lifeless body. In times like these, there was nothing to say; you just looked at the scene and went deep into thought. Often, after scenes such as this one, I'd hear the grownups quote a Bible verse or a line from a book or poem. Lines such as "Father I stretch my hands to thee," "Lord have mercy," "The evil that men do lives after them," could be heard on a daily basis as realizations of our present situation hit deeper and deeper.

I read many books during the day and would sit in the living room for hours. Things were quiet behind rebel lines. News from the city would come in slowly, sometimes much later than the time it had happened. For now, we knew that the president was in hiding and rebel forces had taken over the city from all sides. For the most current news, when Rupert could spare some battery power, Elizabeth Blunt, our BBC news correspondent was right there with us on the evening radio. I wondered how she hadn't been killed yet, being on the front lines with the soldiers and Rupert explained that journalists and certain other people had access to pass without being harmed in war situations. The best part of it all was the absence of a curfew. Of course, nothing was happening at night, but at least we could all sit out on the porch and chat for hours.

Being so close to the river was also a source of misery. We watched about three to four times a day, a lorry filled with people in the back, drive toward the river. After a few minutes we would hear gunshots, either single shots, or machine gun bursts; then an empty lorry would drive back. Although no one talked about it, as an observing child, I knew what had happened to those people. It almost seemed like you couldn't talk about it anymore, having seen it happen so many times. A sort of ethnic cleansing occurred among the Gio, Mano, and Krahn tribes during the war.

It was in Paynesville that we reconfirmed what Rupert had speculated about, as far as the reason for Taylor's coming into the country through Nimba. The failed 1985 coup and brutal display of the half-eaten body of Quiwonkpa outside the Executive Mansion served as a warning to the Mano and Gio tribes, or any other coup plotters. After this gruesome display, the government forces lead crackdowns on the Gio and Mano, especially in the town of Zuleyee, home of Quiwonkpa and other plotters. The tension started here and increased slowly as the president began a sort of favoritism treatment toward his own Krahn tribal members. We speculated that the people in those trucks going to the river might be Krahn people. As they had suffered before in their villages, the Gio and Mano rebels were now retaliating against the Krahn.

Women played a vital role in nurturing during these exile times. Men like my stepdad were easy targets for killing, so the women were the ones who walked around more, visited each other, gathered food and got the latest news. If sufficiently threatened, a woman was known to angrily show her breast to the soldiers, reminding them that she was their mother, and they dare not treat her that way. Mommy, being the brave spirit she was, walked around and visited friends who stayed nearby. Mom loved a good walk, and I often accompanied her. During the day, we'd sometimes sit on the porch as mom cooked, or the adults drank a glass of ale or two. Someone in the neighborhood sold beer, and, war or not, no one was getting in the way of a Liberian's love for social time.

Mommy also turned forty that year, while in exile at Emmet's house. Her birthday was on the nineteenth, only nine days after we arrived. We didn't have a party, but Emmet brought out some bottles of rum, gin, whiskey, and whatever else he had, to celebrate. Mommy said that she would celebrate when the war was over. She mentioned that now she was officially in her "don't give a fuck years," accept it was in a year when the war fucked with us.

A Wet Lie

My wandering nature as a kid was a bit impeded; sometimes I'd venture out toward the road and then back to the house. I wasn't afraid of being out away from the house, but the smell of dead people was still invasive on the roads, that I preferred to stay at home. I was also mentally removed; distant from the bodies I saw lying in the grasses. I didn't know the people, and could just focus on what was in front of me without having to turn my head left or right. But what could I do about the smell? I had to breathe, and the intake of air brought the funk right to me. It wasn't a smell that could be washed off or incensed away. As long as people were mercilessly killed and left to rot in the fields, we had to bear the smell of their decay.

On days when I could mentally overlook the smell of things, I went a bit

41

further into the abandoned villages and explored. I was born to roam. My spirit feeds itself on the natural surroundings experienced while traveling. Even now, in my more settled life, I must take at least a month off and go out on the open road. Otherwise, I feel starved inside.

During one of my wandering adventures, as I crossed a small river, two men stopped me, just about waist deep in the water. I sensed that they were rebel fighters, and I was very cordial toward them. These people were known to be drugged, and could quickly pull out a gun and send you floating un-willingly down the river. I recognized one of them; he was another one of the "refugees" who had moved into our neighborhood on the Old Road as things were heating up. I didn't say anything about it; he was the one asking all the questions. "Doesn't your ma work for the Commerce Ministry? You live near Gbarbea School, next to Christ the King Catholic Church. You people have all the plum (mango) trees in your yard, and that old lady yells at people who try to pick them. Your pappy works for Freeport, and you go to Lutheran School. Your brother Tweh (Toye), just went to America, right?" The man was spot on!

Some of those rebel refugees had been living among us and observed our every move. Now, I was a very straightforward kid who would say no and mean no, or yes, and mean yes. My brother would say no, or yes, and give a detailed explanation for his answer. If I gave unnecessary information, you knew I was making something up. For example, if I ate the pineapple up-side-down cake mommy made and wanted to lie about it, I would say, "No, I didn't eat it, I was out playing in the fields and then went over to Mesahn's house to eat mangoes. After that, we played his Atari video game, and then we went for a walk to the market—" and the consequence was, "Okay, you're getting a spanking for eating the cake." A spanking I well deserved. If my brother had said all that, mom knew he was telling the truth.

Back at the creek, I told the men a somewhat made up story to counter their inquiries. "My name is Christian (my cousin's name), not Jaycee, and I live near ACS School. My father's name is Christian Bishop (my grandfa-ther's name), and his wife is Fatu (my grandmother). I went to Haywood (the local school, next to my grandfather's house), and mommy doesn't work, she is in a wheelchair (my grandmother was). My father works on his pig farm (grandpa had a few pigs in his yard), and I have no brothers, but just one sister." Angry, the soldier pulled out his gun, pointed it at my head, and said if I didn't tell him the truth he would send me down the river. I insisted that I didn't know what he was talking about, and said that if he wanted to kill me then go ahead, but he will be shooting the wrong person.

I do remember that while in that creek with those two fighters, there was a calm about me; I was unafraid- the Lord was my shepherd, and I felt fearless. If it were my time to die, I would go peacefully. To think I was only eleven with such a calmness gives credit to the woman I looked up to. After what seemed like hours, maybe it was fifteen or twenty minutes, they let me go. I crossed back to shore, wandered a bit as they watched me, and kept walking for some distance in a different direction in case they followed me. I didn't want them to see where I lived, or meet mommy. I'm not sure if I told mommy about what happened, but I lay off on wandering for a few days. When she asked why I wasn't going to walk about the neighborhood, I said something along the lines of, "I'm just tired."

To cure my wanderer fever and also avoid another wet lie incident with soldiers, I took to the library in the living room. I loved to read books and those days without school found me in the living room with the *Iliad, Odyssey, Hardy Boys, Nancy Drew, Calvin and Hobbes,* or *Asterix the Gaul* book. Sometimes I'd even try to read the authors mommy read like Danielle Steel or Grace Livingstone Hill. I'd never finish her books because they were too boring for me. They were of topics I couldn't follow. Then I read *Windmills of the Gods* and was impressed with Sidney Sheldon's writing.

I'd taken up reading because, before the war, I would watch mommy relax and enjoy a good book. She read many books a month and would exchange novels with friends or buy some of those Harlequin romance novels from town. My stepdad read a lot as well; his books were more philosophical or "advanced adventures," as I would call them. He read *The Satanic Verses* by Salman Rushdie, *The Hunt for Red October, A Farewell to Arms* and other books. Looking back, I wonder how they, as well as others, found time to cultivate their minds with literature, socialize, nurture us, and most of all, hold down jobs of great responsibility. We all have 24 hours in each day, yet living today seems like a battle to find balance in one's self-cultivation.

Strays

Some days it seemed like the sunken living room at Emmet's house saved my life. There were hundreds of accounts of deaths by stray bullets going through windows or roofs. No one was targeted. It was usually a few soldiers with guns and alcohol, shooting without care of where the shots landed. Sometimes the bullets came back to bite them in the ass. A stray bullet fell a few feet in front of me as I walked into the living room at a friend's house. We all heard the shot hit the roof and some of us thought the safest place from it would be in the hallway. As I opened the room door and walked out,

I saw a dark dot fall from the ceiling and onto the floor. Incidents like these never registered fearfully though; my adrenaline seemed to want to be the experiencer of all these events. My innocence was shielded like a greenhouse shields tender plants from intense whether like wind rain or snow. Although I let out sighs and "whoas," it seemed more like a shallow experience that didn't hit deep.

Out loud or in my mind, I had continual whoa moments; thanks to the magic of childhood innocence, the war never registered to me as traumatic. Nor did it record traumatically to most of my friends. We did see the effects of stress and uncertainty of war in some adults. I recall people walking around and talking to themselves, screaming, or just plain stoic and bewildered, standing somewhere uncommon like in the middle of the street. Some people walked around haunted. A few days ago, my partner asked if a dear friend of mine had also been in Liberia during the war. Yes, she was, and so were most of my friends from Liberia. I explained how each one of us could write a memoir about that time, and each would have a completely different perspective and view on the same events. We all lived in different houses and had different reactions to certain things. It also depended on who our superiors were and how they handled the stress of war. Maybe the trauma never registered because we held no position of responsibility. We were just kids, and kids played or did homework or house chores.

I walked by a neighbor's house one day and saw a vast mosquito net of a thing set up in front of the house. It was perhaps fifteen feet tall by twenty feet wide, with a table behind it, and grains of rice on the table. I soon found out that it was a sort of bird trap. The bird would see the grains and dive in to catch it, but get entangled in the web, resulting in dinner for the hunter. It was also during this time in "exile" when another side of my mother and many other Liberians revealed themselves. Like the bird trap, people found other ways of procuring food, and most of these "new" ways were "old" ways of living before comfortable living took over. People shared knowledge of edible or useable plants that weren't so mainstream: how to make use of certain roots and plants like hibiscus, catnip, the wild greens that grew by the creek or river's edge. As a man, I now have a deep interest in the lifestyles of indigenous people and what knowledge they carry about nature, plants, and animals. But it was back in 1990 when I learned that certain plants that grew around us were edible or medicinal. Of course, after the war ceased there was no "need" for these "primitive" and "emergency" foods and people went back to convenient foods shipped in from other places. But that knowledge was there in the hearts of our parents and manifested itself in dire need.

Door or Window

Late one evening, there was rejoicing in the neighborhood, as news reached us- via the trusted voice of Elizabeth Blunt- that the president had been captured and killed, and his body was laid out for display. As the news unfolded by word of mouth for the next few days, we learned that the president, who was in hiding, had been invited on to a ship with promises of escape, but Prince Johnson awaited and captured him at the port. He was then made to eat his private parts, fingers, and ears, we heard, and then left on display out in the street to bleed and die. The evil that men did live after them and this man was no exception. He had done the same thing in 1985 to Quiwonkpa, and now the debt was paid.

A few days later there was also a comedic capture of a Liberian actor named Flomoh. Because he was a famous guy, he was quickly recognized, and when captured, he joked his way to freedom: "Aye my people, y'all say y'all came for Door (Doe), now Y'all got the Door, and Y'all want to take the window too?"

We also learned that while in exile, the Economic Community of West African States had deployed a military group called ECOMOG (Economic Community Monitoring Group) to impose a cease-fire, stop the killing of innocent civilians, and make sure the foreign nationals who were still stranded in areas of Monrovia got safe evacuations. Even after my brother left, there were still some American citizens stranded in Monrovia. We heard something about an interim government set up as well. The news unfolded later for us behind rebel lines, but this military group, ECOMOG had already been deployed from Nigeria to Liberia. Apparently, ECOWAS had also convinced President Doe to leave the county and seek exile somewhere; he had nowhere to go and was stuck in the Executive Mansion threatened by rebel soldiers on all sides.

But now, by the time we got all this news, President Doe was already dead, and Charles Taylor's rebel forces were driven out of the city. Nine months had passed, and along with it, thousands of lives lost on account of this president who was now dead, lying in the streets like a dog. We were all displaced. No one knew where their family members were, and there were no telephones to find out. There was hope—only hope—that we would all see each other again now that this president was dead. Things would go back to normal, and I would go to another school since my previous school was now a massive murder scene.

45

Within those nine months, I had many coming of age moments and realizations. I had seen more dead bodies than I ever will at funerals. I walked on roads covered with so many bullet casings and saw more guns than a gun store can carry. In ethnic tension, I saw how holding grudges brought about a war which took victims who had no relations with either tribal group. Blinded by their anger, and manipulated by angrier men of power with dangerous allies, these tribes fought without seeing their connection as Liberians. Like a fire in an apartment building which starts in one unit, but subsequently burns every other unit around it, the civil war made its way throughout the country, leaving destruction everywhere. I saw mommy, the brightest spirit I knew, in a sad mood. For two days, her light was visibly dimmed, as she came to grips with the loss of her dearest Johnny.

But I had also been sheltered under the guidance of mom's bravery. Her calmness kept me calm, and her jovial spirit kept me jovial. Mommy's humorous commentaries taught me how to understand life. As she told me many times, in later years, "The biggest problem in the world was that people took themselves too seriously. They walk about tight as virgins and stiff as pricks." I saw how much she cared for the people who lived around her, and how she would risk her own life to protect them. I was only eleven, reaping the fruits of an offense I did not sow. Many of us had no involvement in the politics of war, but because we were there, we felt the effects and bore the burden as though we played a role in the war's beginning.

I often wonder why people who instigate wars don't find a specific place to meet and fight it out; like a designated wrestling arena where matters could be dealt with, and no loss of civilian lives. When the fighting is over, the victorious ones can come marching through the city with no need for the bloody aftermath and broken infrastructures. Instead, in every corner of the earth that has been touched by war, it's the civilians who are left to wail among the rubbles or wander displaced in another's country trying to pick themselves up from the wreckage. But the perpetrators sit in their comfortable homes or offices, counting valuable human lives as statistics; I wonder if they would ever send their children or relatives to war, to be counted among such figures. I highly doubt it.

War, Momma and Me

Jaycee Kesh Akinsanya

Chapter Five

Strewn Miracles

The fighting ceased after the capture of president Doe, and talk of his brutal arrest spread like wildfire. Those who could move around the port area flocked in to see his body laid out for display. My parents decided it was time to go home since there was no more fighting in our neighborhood. We figured there would be a pantry full of food, and we would have something to live on until life became more stable. Mommy talked about the possible reality that we had no home left. Buildings had been bombed or destroyed in some way, and so we would go back to whatever was there to call home. In most cases, we were among the lucky ones who didn't experience the actual crossfire between the rebel forces and the national army. The direct gruesome experience we had so far was that tenth of August day during our evacuation. We had to be ready for anything. Worst case, we could go to my grandfather's house and stay there until they returned from wherever they were.

We packed our belongings, and cousin Emmet gave us a ride back home in his pickup truck. As we drove home, I looked around and observed everything around me with thoughtful examination. The road was covered with more bullet shells than we had seen on our way to Paynesville. There had been more fighting in the area as the rebels advanced toward the Executive mansion. The many bullet casings on the streets looked like crushed rocks, and of course among the shells were the shells of once animated beings-humans, animals. Some skeletons were intact, lying where they had fallen. Some were bare bones, and others had underwear, or whatever clothing the person wore. Some bones were scattered, perhaps pulled away by animals looking for food. The smell of decay was still in the air, but not as prominent as before. Luckily, we were driving through this time, so we passed the stench quickly.

The ride home was tranquil; we sat in the back of the pickup, while mommy, Serena and baby Chee-Chee sat in front. Every one of us had lost some weight, but it showed more prominently on Rupert. All, and then some of the weapons we only hoped to see in movies were seen right before our eyes in the last few months. RPGs, AK47s, and others were easily recognizable. We recognized guns like American kids know cars. Kids my age had carried these weapons. They were drugged and made a part of a war they did not understand. The saddest part, mommy would say, was that these kids weren't considered human beings with a possible future. The kids were pawns, omit-

51

ted numbers in the pages of history. "The leaders have so much blood on their hands. And once you have blood on your hands, no matter how much power and money you have, you'll never have a peaceful night's sleep."

Our town was deserted. The neighborhood we left a few months before was tainted with the ravages of war. Some of the commanders in the rebel army had settled in various houses, ours being one of them, and had spray-painted their names on the walls inside and out. CO Deadbody lived in our home, so our furniture and clothes remained intact. Walking into our house had an eerie feeling to it; a different energy had occupied it while we were away. Of course, without letting a moment for commentary pass her by, mom made her first one, since arriving back home. "Those damn country asses, writing their name on my house. What, they thought they were going to stay here forever while we stayed behind the lines in refugee camps or their shanty houses? I beg them yah."

Our neighborhood didn't see much of the fighting. It looked more like a settlement area for the rebels. There weren't as many bullet casings lying around; no smell of dead things and buildings were still intact, except for some minor broken doors or windows. I think it was because of the swampy area north of Gaye Town. And the main road, Tubman Boulevard, was a few miles away. It seemed to me that by the time the rebels had evacuated our area, most of the soldiers had retreated toward the Executive mansion; there wasn't much time to fight in our neighborhood.

Our furniture was rearranged; no plywood on the windows like we left it last August. We didn't lock the doors when we left either; there was no use in doing so, mommy thought; especially if someone would possibly break in. She was right. Mr. Hard times had left a few things in the Pantry for us too — mostly canned stuff — but the dried fish and meat had been eaten by CO and crew perhaps. Mommy was happy they ate the dried fish and meat so that they didn't rot. There were still a few bags of beans, bags of bulgur, buckwheat, and one or two fifty-pound bags of rice. My parents had stocked the pantry to last us at least two years, and those guys ate all the food in a matter of three months. They must have had regular feasts! But they left some, and for that, we thanked them.

Nature had her part to play in all this too. Out in the yard, there were beans, peppers and other greens growing wild everywhere! I guess whatever pods of beans or pepper seeds that were strewn out in the yard with the washing water sprouted over time. Food was needed, and nature gave us a gift of fresh stock. The pepper bushes were laden with peppers; green beans climbed up the trees, and jute plants, called palava sauce, grew abundantly. Green papaya hung from the trees, and in a few months, green mangoes would be ripening. The banana orchard in the backyard by Aunty Kolubah's house had a few bunches of bananas on them, and soursop hung on Ma Eya's tree. A few pineapple plants that Ma Eya had for a fence, had fruit, and so we were thankful to be back with some food provisions.

A neighbor later taught mommy how to steam green soursop, and add oil and spices. She said it tasted like potatoes. Not to me, it didn't. I did like green papaya though. Mom said we could eat green papaya like we did green mango, with salt and cayenne. She said in some countries people made green papaya salad. I knew we could eat cooked green papaya because mom used it when making papaya pie. The coconuts in the tree had aged sufficiently, and my cousin would climb up and pick a few. We'd pound the coconut shell against a large rock until all the coir peeled off the shell. Then we'd break open the core, drink the juice, and eat the thick coconut meat. It was during times of wonder like coming back home to fresh produce in the garden that mommy would say, "Some way or the other the Lord will provide." Her favorite Bible verses of assurance were Matthew 6: 25-34, and Psalm 90, and we would recite them regularly. When reciting the passage from Matthew, mommy would say, with deeper emphasis, the last verse: "*Therefore do not worry about tomorrow, for tomorrow will worry about itself. Each day has enough trouble of its own.*" For Psalm 90, her emphasis verse was verse 12: "*So teach us to number our days, that we may apply our hearts unto wisdom.*"

The absence of noisy human activity in the neighborhood made it feel as though we were in an echo bubble. Every sound we made carried an echo, which became play to us; yell, then listen to your voice shout back in the distance. The new silence wasn't accompanied by the fear we felt months earlier when the curfew was enforced, and the anticipation of war crippled us. There was a sense of peace in the air; the kind you'd feel if you were out on a hike in the woods. There, you could relish the experience but remain alert to sounds around you in case you came across a predator. Slight movements, perhaps a lizard ruffling the leaves, would stiffen your body a bit, making you think it was possibly a snake. The serenity of our neighborhood was assuring, yet the caution of possible danger remained in our minds.

Nature was alive, and the birds flew about and sang again. The smell of nag champa flower and plumerias filled the air. Mommy's gardenias were blooming, and the ivy on our porch had grown wild. The wind blowing in the trees made sounds of different melodies, depending on the tree, or intensity of the wind. I was happy to experience all these sensual explosions again. When I first learned to use my senses, I would get lost in sounds, smells, and touch sensations. Everything was unique, and I wanted to have a full experience of it. Before the war, I wandered around our neighborhood in my little world, chasing after sounds, or something I saw or smelled. One smell that always called to me was the scent of ripe, exploded sweet balsam apple. In the bitter melon family, but sweet tasting, these small fruits grew on vines and turned bright red or yellow before popping open and releasing their fragrance. My nose was very keen to that scent, and I would follow the smell like a hound. Now that we were back home, all I wanted to do was resume my wandering.

People were slowly returning home to pick up pieces of their lives and make sense of the new world to which they had arrived. Down the street, our neighbors, the Telewodas, were also home. "Aunty Sue," Mrs. Telewoda, started a donut-making operation and boy, could you smell the donuts from miles away! We'd wait for the smell, and then like zombies, float over to their house and wait on the bench for hot donuts covered in sugar. Her son Joe and I were classmates, and we all played together as kids. Our neighbors, the Jacksons and the Dee families had also returned home. "Champ," Solomon Jackson, and E.D were friends I used to play and wrestle with, and I was glad to see them and hear their story of where they had been. Cousin Sam's house was deserted and remained so for years. After he had passed away in the bathroom, we never saw or heard from any of his family members again. Each neighbor greeted the other with joy mixed with happy tears, sad tears shed for those lost to the war, and gratitude for being back home.

We all had a story to tell, and the next few weeks and months slowly crept on as people returned, reunited and rebuilt. Some neighbors were traumatized by the events we had all experienced and had some psychological meltdowns. Some could be seen pacing up and down the neighborhood and talking to themselves, and others erratically screamed in terror. People resumed their regular visit us and hung out on the porch, asking questions, and speculating about the cause of the war.

Because of the lack of food transported from areas still caught up in some tension, the marketplace became filled with furniture of all sorts. People were selling their belongings for a few cups of rice or beans. Televisions, coffee tables, stereo sets, and books were on display in exchange for little food. Stores belonging to foreign merchants who had fled the war were looted, and the products were up for sale at the market.

Desperate times did call for desperate measures, and another activity which followed the return home was rampant looting. Under cover of darkness, you could hear people move about and break into homes. In our now quieter than usual neighborhood, the echoes of doors being broken down by looters was another addition to the "what will people do now" mentality happening in the area. I recall a funny incident of a guy trying to break into our house early one morning. Mom heard the noise and slowly crept up and stood behind the kitchen door. When the thief stuck his head through the window bars, mom gave him a good whack on the head with a big fufu stick. She recognized his face, and a few days later when we saw him walk past our house, mom jokingly asked him where he got the bump on his head.

When the ECOMOG peacekeeping force arrived in our part of the city, one way they kept the peace was by apprehending looters. One guy who was caught breaking a neighbor's door down was made to carry the door on his back while the soldier stood on top of the door. The rule was not to drop the door or the soldier. He was due for some good whipping because the door could never stay steady. Mom watched the scene unfold, chuckled, and then told a story about how a country she visited would treat thieves. If a person were caught stealing they would sit them down and cook them a feast, feed it to them, then bend them over and stick a few limes up their rear end. After that, the person's hands were behind their back, mouth gagged, and then set free. Mom said the thief would die a slow death because he couldn't breathe, evacuate or relax. What a gruesome way to go, just because of stealing. Then again, the humor came with a lesson in the consequences of stealing. Looters were apprehended continuously and flogged, yet somehow more looters would try their luck and meet with the same fate.

Looters ransacked my aunt's beach house beyond recognition. I vacationed with her many times before the war and knew her furniture very well. Their home was one of the posh ones in town with a beautiful fenced yard, a tennis court, swimming pool, two very large French-German Shepherds, servant's quarters, and many other amenities. She had missed the whole war due to work circumstances, so her house was empty after our return home. The caretakers she left there evacuated at the same time as we did. I walked through the marketplace and saw her coffee table —the one so expertly carved with elephant legs— her televisions, kitchenware, leopard print chairs, all sold in exchange for food. By the time we could visit her house to see what was left, even the roof, wood beams, electrical sockets, and everything that could be ripped out of the walls, had been taken. If they could have repurposed the concrete, I'm sure they would have looted that as well.

The Lord Gave/Took

My grandfather's household also returned from Fendell Campus, but sadly without Fatu, my grandmother. For years she had rheumatoid arthritis and was confined to a wheelchair. The evacuation to Fendelll Campus proved difficult for her, and a few weeks after they arrived she passed away. My grandfather told us that right before she died, she stood up from her wheelchair and stretched out her hands. It was the first time I cried unabashedly, mourning the loss of a sweet soul. She was my mother's stepmother. Mommy was born as the only child of Isabel, her mother, and first of ten children of Christian, her father. But this made no difference to the relationship she had with her stepmother, who we all called "mommy" or "Godma Fatu." Mommy and Godma Fatu had a unique relationship and treated each other almost like sisters. Same for my grandfather; his relationship with mommy reflects how my siblings and our relationship with her unfolded. We also learned that my uncle Gbarcon and cousin "Small G," Aunty Somo's son, had passed away as well.

Formality had its place in our family but seemed to be left hanging in the closet most of the time. "Mr. Bishop," as we called my grandpa, loved coming over to our house to hang with mommy. They called each other "Bishop," and would sit on the porch every Saturday morning around nine in the morning, drinking coffee and smoking their Benson and Hedges cigarettes. My sister Cheryl nicknamed him R.O.T because every Saturday he would show up *right on time*. We'd look out the window and see his blue pickup truck pull into the driveway, and Cheryl would yell, "Mommy, R.O.T is here!" He was a very fancy dresser. At home, he'd wear his jeans and deep V-neck T-shirt with his famous Pith hat, also known as safari helmets, used back in the day by explorers on safari; but when he left the house to go elsewhere, he was almost always in a suit. He wore dark glasses, and had a very cocky stance and walk. Our maid Mary, who used to tease mommy about her walk, would say she knew from where Gloria got her walk.

Reuniting with my Aunt Zoe, mommy's younger sister is one of my favorite memories. She had been on the other side of the city during the whole war, and knowing she was alive was such a blessing. I ran up and jumped into her arms when I saw her walk toward our house. She later moved in next door to us, where Steve used to live. Aunty Zoe also loved to sing, and so our compound was again filled with music. I learned the songs of Skeeter Davis and Don Williams when she moved next door. But the song she'd burst out singing at any given time was *Telephone to Glory*. She knew it in two different melodies, a mellow one and an upbeat rock and roll one. Aunty Zoe and my sister Cheryl were about the same age, so she was more like a sister than an aunt. My grandfather would joke that he could have gone on having more kids, but mommy got in his way and had Cheryl. Mommy would jab back at him and say, "You didn't stop! You went and had Muneh too!"

In the evenings, we continued listening to the radio with my stepfather, but this time, to a guy who told jokes. A few minutes later he would follow up with a series of lost and found messages from people looking for lost relatives or alerting their families that they were OK in some other part of the country. Many people had taken political refuge in neighboring countries as well, and they sent radio messages describing how their families could find them.

At night, we listened to "*Unshackled*," a dramatized Christian radio show put on by Pacific Garden Mission in Chicago, via ELWA radio. These stories told of people who were living life in one way or the other- mostly in contradiction to the "word of God"- and then something miraculous happened, and left them "unshackled." We even memorized the zip code and address of Pacific Garden Mission; that's how much we listened to the shows. After listening to *Unshackled*, we'd slowly wind down for the evening. Winding down meant mommy and Rupert sang old songs or told stories about their childhood and what Liberia used to be. Mommy would tell stories about how naughty she used to be as a schoolgirl, and how much trouble she got into, or which countries she went to for boarding school.

A game life played with us was called "adjustments," and we got quite expert at adjusting to things. The well closest to our home was deemed unfit for drinking; someone thought the bodies that had rotted away from the 1990 war might have contaminated the water. Diseases like cholera and dysentery were everyday occurrences from eating contaminated foods or drinking contaminated water, and so there was a lot of caution when it came to food and water. In fact, a few months after the first war outbreak, after we returned home, I got the runs beyond compare. It was just for a few hours one evening, but it took everything out of me. I must have lost about ten pounds that night. I felt like if I would stand up and the wind blew, it would carry me off with it. Mom said to let the effect run its course and then she made me some rehydration salts with salt, sugar, lime and distilled water. After drinking the tonic she made for me, I fell asleep and woke up the next morning feeling better.

At that time, we had to walk about two miles away to get drinking water from a U.N. dug well. We also got a bit smarter in this process. Since the well was on a flat surface, we would put a few five-gallon container with lids in a wheelbarrow and wheel it to the well. Another way we lessened each other's burden was by agreeing to help each person fill his household's water gallons. A few of us would bring one load of water to one house, and when that house had enough water, we'd do the next house.

Jaycee Kesh Akinsanya
"Good Afternoon, LIBA."

As roads opened up and some stability returned, some business owners, along with mommy, started the Liberian Business Association, LIBA. LIBA was formed as a support network for Liberian business owners, offering mentorship, legal advice, and other requirements for successful business ownership. I resumed visiting mom's new office after school, like my brother and I did before the war. I loved hearing her voice as she answered the phone in her office: "Good afternoon, LIBA," and then the laughter in it as she chatted with a friend or the formal tone as she enrolled a new member of the association.

Businesses were reopening in Liberia or business owners who had left before the civil war, or evacuated, were returning to help rebuild the country. Mommy had dealt with many of these people before when she worked at the Ministry of Commerce, so the relationships rekindled and many of them, Indian, Jordanian, or Lebanese nationals, were happy to be interacting with "Gloria" again. The smaller airport, Spriggs Payne Airfield, reopened, and some traveling began again. Direct flights in and out of Liberia to or from places like the US, Europe, or Asia, had to be broken up; you'd fly to a neighbor country's international airport, Abidjan, Ivory Coast, for example, and then to your destination.

For lunch, we'd eat at CHAMS Lounge, a restaurant owned by mommy's close friend, Aunty Harriette. Her restaurant was classy with white tablecloths and plates, spoons, knives, and forks set out in proper arrangements. When guests sat down, they would be given a hot towel to wipe their hands. It was one of the happening places in town, and I would spend my afternoons bugging the staff for a taste of all the dishes made that day. Aunty Harriette had built her restaurant from the bottom up, starting with a small venture and then moving to this new location. Aunty Harriette attributes the brains behind her restaurant to mommy.

Many different faces and ranks of people came into CHAMS Lounge. Aunty Harriette recalls a story of some foreign dignitaries arriving at the restaurant to eat, and mommy speaking with them in their language. She was shocked to know that mommy spoke other languages. Mommy had gone to school at different periods of her life in Nigeria, England, and other places, but never publicized her achievements. In fact, mommy's attendance at Lincoln University in Jefferson City Missouri and the University of Missouri in Columbia Missouri, where Toye was born, were scholarships granted to her by President William V.S. Tubman. Something I learned from her high school best friend, Esther, my godmother.

To me, and to a lot of people, she was just Gloria. We knew she had traveled much and learned much, but her relationship with everyone hid her achievements quite well until incidents like that at CHAMS lounge arose. At home, people from the U.S embassy would visit Gloria, like her friend Barbara, who taught me that in America, dogs were trained to guide blind people, or open doors, and do other tasks. Barbara would bring me many books to read because she sensed my interest in literature. Before leaving for America, Barbara gave me all her Reader's Digest magazines. She apologized for doing most of the puzzles but said that there were jokes I could learn in there. I may never know many things my mother did; who she knew or helped. People just seemed to like her as much as we did, and everyone wanted to hang out with her.

Chapter Six

Jaycee Kesh Akinsanya

Mini Adults

After the war, I became an altar boy at the neighborhood Catholic Church, sang in the choir, and played in the drama club. I met new friends, and some of us who were altar boys at the church, would go home and imitate the gestures and personalities of the priests. A few of us would sit in my room and turn it into a chapel and say mass. We turned a chest of drawers into the altar and covered it with a tablecloth. For chalices, we used mommy's crystal wine glasses and good china saucers. For priestly vestments, we used bedsheets and other fabrics I took from the linen closet. Priestly imitation cost me some spankings from mommy when she found out that I had been using her fabrics as my holy tunics. We weren't just wrapping the cloth around ourselves; we cut holes in them! These were fabrics mommy brought back from Lebanon and India and other places. They were embroidered—the main attraction for our priestly garments— and some had been handmade as gifts for her.

Another activity that reconvened after the war was our love for late night cooking. As we did before the war, when mommy thought we were all in bed, we'd sneak into the pantry and gather some goods for our night outing. Everyone would bring something from their house, and we'd make a fire under the mango tree, cook a big pot of food, and then go into the room to eat. As boys would do, whoever was asleep would not be woken up, but we'd sit as close to his bed as possible and eat. Sometimes someone put a spoon next to the sleeping person's nose to smell the aroma of what they were missing out on. They'd usually wake up, only to find scraps of food left. If I were the one who woke up to this scene, I'd threaten to tell mommy about the cookout, and the boys would let me have the rest of the food. Years later, in a conversation, mom gave me her commentary on our activities: "My room was next door, y'all thought I didn't hear the movements? I could smell the food too, but I would laugh. I figured it was OK, and you guys were hungry. Plus, if you woke up tired for school, you got to learn the consequences of staying up late."

We were twelve going on thirteen, "mini-adults" hanging out with each other, and in a sense, imitating the ways and gestures of our parents or older siblings. We wore tailored, bright-colored African designed attires, especially for "Color Day," a one Friday a month event, when we'd go to school without our usual uniforms. We talked about topics we didn't understand but had heard about while eavesdropping on the adult conversations.

To bring some entertainment to the neighborhood, someone decided to open a "cinema," made of plywood, or corrugated metal walls. We'd pay a small fee to go in and watch the latest movies. These cinemas played videos mostly from Bollywood, or Chinese karate movies. On weekends when mommy had friends over for longer periods, we'd sneak out and go to the cinema. Usually, they played adult movies at night, and with thin plywood walls or corrugated metal walls, we heard everything, minus the visual. If you were caught, you'd be chased away. We ran faster, and a cinema man leaving his door post meant someone else could sneak in.

We had independence unlike any other. We'd wander the town for hours, exploring various parts. But a responsibility came with it; people knew our families, and so as rowdy or carefree as we tried to be, we respected an etiquette, and there were limits we didn't cross. Grown-up eyes were always watching, and we didn't want news reaching our parents' ears of us acting the fool. Spankings were frequent for the misbehaved, and if we ever deserved one, we prayed our spankings happened inside and not outside where other parents would see us, ask what the matter was, and request an extra lash or two for our misbehavior.

After wandering around a bit, we'd all head home to get our schoolwork done. No one wanted to be left behind as core friends went up a grade. We were all in this together—work, play, church—everything. There was still no electricity unless you had a generator, and with a generator running, especially at night, you practically got no sleep. I preferred the candlelight. Mommy would say the "early to bed, early to rise" quote and make a point that electricity gave you the illusion of thinking you had more time in a day. But then you'd get to sleep late and feel unrested when you woke up. Mom woke up early.

Even before the war, she was up at four in the morning and would wake us up to get ready for school. Back then, we could stand right in front of our house and hail a taxi to St. Peter's Lutheran School. Yes, it was common to see eight and nine-year-old kids like us, hailing a cab to school. We had our older brothers and sisters with us and learned to do things like they were doing. After school, we would take another taxi back home, or take one to the city and hang out at the Commerce Ministry where mommy and her colleagues worked. We'd run up and down the stairs into people's offices. They all knew us, and we'd get candy money from lots of them, especially on report card days.

I'd always complain to mommy how lazy Toye was. He'd bribe me with his portion of lunch to wash his school uniform because, the moment we got home, he was off to the soccer field to play. He figured that mommy wouldn't eat all her portion, and when he came back, he could ask her for what was left. When the maid cooked, the food was portioned out into bowls and set on a warmer. Mommy instituted the food-warming system because she loathed eating cold food. Toye also irked me because we had to share white T-shirts, and his soccer escapades or WrestleMania imitations would get the T-shirts dirty and stained. We had many sibling rivalry fights and would end up punching and claw at each other. He'd say he was the best son because mom had him in America, and my dad was a country African Nigerian man. I'd reply that mom loved me more because she left his dad in America and came to be with my wealthy African dad who drove a Peugeot. Mommy would watch us fight and ask us whose womb we came out of since we fought like ragamuffins.

Now that we were back in school, mom's early morning waking up resumed; this time, for my stepbrothers and me. She hired another maid, Massa; as Mary, our previous maid was still somewhere unknown. Taking a taxi to school required us to now walk to the main road, at Joe Bar Market, or further to Tubman Boulevard, by the Catholic Hospital junction. For me, this meant I had to prepare my uniform and do school work the day before. It was an early bird catches the worm situation because everyone was trying to make his or her way to school or work. School started at eight o'clock, but you had to be out the door as early as six, or sis-thirty to make sure you got a cab to be at school before eight. A regular cab that would technically fit a driver plus four would usually seat the driver, two in the front passenger seat, and five or six in the back, some of us sitting on each other's laps. Busses filled up even more than usual and the designated "bus stops" were ignored. If you wanted to get down at a stop, you yelled "Bus Stop," and the driver would stop.

After school, a similar scene unfolded. If by chance you saw a family friend with a private car, you'd wave down for a ride. When the person stopped, a few of us would run and jump into their car, grateful for the ride. A free trip like this was nice because we got to save our money for other stuff. The city had with more people than usual; people who once lived in other towns and cities, but were now displaced by war.

My cousins and I enrolled at St Patrick's, a Catholic Boys School a few miles from home; our old Lutheran school was too much of a ghastly scene to shelter students. The bullet holes in the concrete walls of the St Patrick's school building indicated that there must have been substantial fighting in the area; the school was close to the Executive Mansion. Workers were later hired to patch the bullet holes and give the school a fresh coat of paint. We had to share whatever schoolbooks were available until the archdiocese pro-

65

vided more books from abroad.

Our school principal was sister Shirley Kolmer, of the Adorers of the Blood of Christ order. She had spent nine years in Liberia as a University professor and was now our school principal. Her assistant was Sister Kathleen, of the same order. They and other missionaries had come back to Liberia to help with reopening schools and rehabilitating young kids who had been mentally scarred by the war. The school grounds included a library, cafeteria, a church, and housing for the Don Bosco brothers. From the gate, you could see the Atlantic Ocean at the bottom of the hill, and some students would go there to hang out after school. I spent a lot of time in the Library reading about the world, the Saints, and the history of the Catholic Church. I was impressed with their standard of education and discipline of students; us kids needed both after the war. Of course, other religious organizations had their schools and structure, it wasn't just the Catholic Church, but Catholic schools were popular.

One thing we treasured back then was the perfection of our penmanship. It was a "thing." Whether cursive or regular, you made your handwriting your own and gave it your unique style. It also served as a way for friends to copy notes if they weren't in school that day. My cousin Vamilar had the neatest handwriting, and he was the go-to guy for copying missed notes. His writing looked as close to something typed up on a typewriter as can be.

At St Patrick's we had to wear a uniform: khaki colored pants and a button-down white short-sleeved shirt for boys, seventh to eleventh grade. Seniors wore long-sleeved shirts with a black necktie. It was imperative that we ironed our uniforms properly. Some of us drifted away from the regular "khaki" style of pant fabric and went to the waterside market to buy a silkier flowing style pant material, khaki in color, for school. There was one amusing problem with the fabric—it wasn't preshrunk. You'd go to school with your freshly tailored pants, and then by nature's arrangement it would rain. In Liberia, a tropical rainforest, it doesn't just rain cats and dogs; it rains hippos and rhinos as well. For some reason or another, it always rained in the midday, about the time when school was about to be let out. Your teenage self would be walking around like George Jefferson from The Jeffersons, when—splash, splash, patter, patter—would fall the rains. Minutes later your nice khaki pants would shrink up to four or five inches! Back then to be styling, your pants had to be long enough to reach the heels of your shoes, but not touch the floor, and baggy enough, but not too baggy to look like a hoodlum. The shrinkage in the pants gave them that Michael Jackson, "Billie Jean" look, and we weren't going for that. Needless to say, after a few of those incidences, we found a better fabric for our uniforms.

When Brothers Greet

It was at this school where I saw, for the first time in my life, two guys kiss each other. It wasn't hidden or anything. They were with a group of other friends by the water fountain during lunchtime, and I had gone for a drink when I heard one boy from the senior class say to his friend, "The Bible says to greet every brother with a holy kiss." One boy sat on the balcony ledge as the other stood between his legs. They kissed each other, and their friends laughed. I was intrigued by what I saw, but they weren't my friends. I just got some water and went about my business. Those boys had been to America also, so I thought it was something cool people did in America. I knew that in some Middle Eastern countries, men kissed each other as a greeting, but this kiss looked a bit different to me.

Our St. Patrick's schoolboys were also the envy of the town. Every girl wanted to date a St. Patrick's boy, and every boy wanted to date a girl from our all-girl sister school, St. Theresa's Convent. We were all hitting puberty, and each boy was on the lookout for his St. Theresa's Convent girlfriend. Something I had heard a few years before the war, came up again in a few conversations. Boys were encouraging each other to lose their virginity, because, as I had heard at age nine, if you hadn't by the time puberty hit, you'd be the guy in the crowd with premature cum spots on your pants, or oozing out of some other body part. I have no idea who started this "sex education," but the picture the young boys in school painted was horrifying. They claimed that if you had not lost your virginity by puberty, which happened anytime between eleven and thirteen years of age, you could find yourself in a situation where you coughed, or sneezed, or even sweated, and semen would ooze out of your body.

Out of fear of being "that guy," I figured out a way to lose my virginity. Before the war, mommy used to bring home a few movies from the video rental store, and we'd invite friends over to watch a movie. I invited a local girl to watch a movie and asked her about what I heard my friends say. She was a few years older and had already lost her virginity, so she said she would teach me how to lose mine. But we couldn't do it in our room because anyone could show up. So, we left the house and went to an abandoned unfinished building. After a few minutes behind in the building, I became a man, immune to premature ejaculation.

But my puberty age, when it arrived, had very little to do with a sexual blossoming. Instead, I wanted to be grown up already, filled with the knowledge of the world like mommy and stepdad were. I had a lust for learning about the world. Any book or movie that depicted somewhere special became dear to me. I re-read Heidi, and mentally studied her grandfather's cabin in the Alps; learned more about Morocco and the Sahara Desert, and looked up books in the library about Asia. Asia fascinated me; the floating markets in Thailand, boathouses in Kerala, India, and the rice fields in China, from where some of our rice came. I'd mentally mark these places so that I could visit them one day as a grown man.

A good friend, we'll call her Kate, lived close to the American Embassy and we'd walk up the hill to Mamba Point to visit her. Kate and I were going to be boyfriend and girlfriend one day; she was even set on marrying me. I wasn't as reciprocal with her as expected and had my mind on other things besides relationships. Something about the war opened my eyes to human nature, and I wanted to learn all about it. Why had the war started? What did Johnny do to those soldiers who murdered him and his family? I tried to understand the cause of things that had happened. Also, along the way to visit Kate, I'd always notice the Indian school and memorized their motto, "*Sa vidya ya vimuktaye—knowledge is that which liberates.*" I figured my key to helping humanity and living like the saints would be through knowledge. I became more thoughtful and philosophical than connected to what my friends were doing.

I started spending more time in the Library. When we read about philosophers like Plato and Socrates, I'd go to the library and do more research about them and whatever books they wrote, or what more they said. I didn't understand much, but I read anyway. Apart from the library for reading books, I had mommy to talk to about philosophical and mystical topics. Whatever she knew, she shared with me. We would discuss things I had heard in passing or read in a book, and I looked to her for more explanation. For example, I asked her about Galileo and astronomy. I had read in one of the library books that the Church had admonished him for his teaching of a heliocentric solar system, to the point of labeling him a heretic and sentencing him to life imprisonment. Why would he be persecuted for an excellent achievement? My mind couldn't comprehend how long of a time 1633 was, in relation to 1993. I wasn't the best student at arithmetic, so subtracting the years to know the exact time wasn't as easy for me. I wondered about astronomy and astrology. Why did people say that I was a Capricorn, but then some Indian people at the Indian store said that in their country I was a Sagittarius? I tried my best to connect the dots by asking questions. Mommy said that she too had some questions like mine, because if God made everything, but one church was saying one thing, and another was saying something else, then how do we know what was right. She said that she was raised Christian, and would fol-

68

low her Bible and let God answer the questions when she met him. She quoted a song we usually sang together: "*Blind unbelief is sure to err and scan His works in vain. God is His own interpreter, and He will make it plain.*"

1992-1995 went like that for me; so many questions, and lots of time in the Library during recess. I wanted to understand why people fought each other. I wanted to go back into history and see where the problem started and then try to help fix it. I read books and learned, instead of looking for a girlfriend. After all, I had already lost my virginity and thought I was in the clear of losing semen accidentally. That was until I had my first nocturnal emission (wet dream), and felt utterly lost. Had I not recently lost my virginity? Why was there semen in my pajamas? The agony the experience caused me. It happened frequently, and I hid the knowledge for years. I was a teenager now, and although I asked and talked to mommy about anything, wet dreams never came up as a question. I felt like I hadn't entirely lost my virginity, and felt even more embarrassed to go back to that girl for a retrial.

Interrupted

Things seemed to be getting back to normal until the fifteenth of October 1992, when Charles Taylor launched another assault on the capital. This time it had an op name, "*Operation Octopus.*" An interim government was in place, and he had some issues with the setup, so for two months another battle ensued, and the ECOMOG soldiers pushed the rebel forces out of the city for the second time. People said that Charles Taylor wasn't stopping until he, and no one else, was the president of Liberia. Schools closed—again—and we had to stay home. We'd hear rocket launchers go through the air making a whistling sound, and then landing somewhere with a loud "boom." If it landed close enough, you could feel the earth shake. One such rocket fell under one of our mango trees one Saturday morning and shook the whole house like an earthquake.

During this short-lived insurgency I saw, perhaps, the ghastliest scene. While leaving the Fulah store to go home, we heard one of those whistling rocket sounds, and some of us took cover not knowing where it was going to hit. In the distance, I saw a mother with her child on her back running to get out of harm's way. Instead, she ran right into harm's way next to the Mandingo graveyard, and the missile hit her directly. All that we saw was a splash. Again, for whatever reason, my mind registered this like I was watching a movie, and filed it in my atrocities of war folder; I felt no distress or fear, just the adrenaline rush to get back home. Our area of town was affected this time, and in conversation, I would hear the elder folk say that this two-month outbreak took more lives than the 1990 war.

To this day I can withstand gruesome scenes, and sometimes consider that maybe I should have been a surgeon, using my desire to heal others right there in a hospital room. What I cannot tolerate is the day-to-day petty treatment from one human to another. When my friend Luke asked me the other day about how I handle problems, I answered, "philosophically." I can easily forgive people when I understand the motive behind their actions. When someone does me wrong, I feel obliged to forgive, but am left with unanswered questions. The unanswered question is the burden I carry. Saying "That's human nature," or something similar never fixes things for me. I never once saw my mother in a fight, and so I never learned to fight with anyone. By this, I am not talking about growing pains like sibling rivalry or such; I'm talking about human envy, which causes people to harm each other physically or emotionally.

Within a few weeks, this war was over, and we were allowed to go back to school. At school, we all talked about what we had experienced; now it was just us boys talking about it, and some details from friends were quite gruesome. Some of us "mini-adults" imitated our parents and their friends in conversations, repeating what we had heard them say and giving arguments as they would. Whether we understood what was going on or not, we were little big men—not just reading the newspapers and hearing about a distant war event—we had been a part of the experience.

Most of us kids would joke around about the war, and when school reopened, we joked in class by starting a long whistle that imitated a launched rocket. The noise would start from the back of the class and make its way to the front, and then we'd all stump our feet as hard as we could on the ground to imitate the rocket hitting the earth. Boy, did our teachers hate us for doing that! We especially carried out this rocket launching tomfoolery in our French class. Ms. Renee, our French teacher, was gorgeous, and of course was the talk of the all-boys' school. Somehow her class was the one where the most trouble happened. Mom said it's because we were young boys in heat, and when men were in heat, they did the dumbest things to attract attention.

Adored.

It was during that random 1992 outbreak that our principal, Sister Shirley, and four other nuns of the Adorers of the Blood of Christ, along with four

Liberian Novices for the priesthood, were murdered. A few days later their bodies were discovered, and the story appeared in the local newspaper. Two nuns, Sisters Barbara Ann Muttra and Mary Joel Kolmer, had driven their convent's security guard home but never returned. The rest of the Sisters, Shirley Kolmer, our principal, Kathleen McGuire, Assistant Principal, and Agnes Mueller died three days later. When school reopened, there was lots of sadness due to the loss of the sisters, and Mr. Goodwin, the dean of students, became the acting principal. When mommy heard the news, she extended her condolences to my school and me and told me that when things cleared up, she would try to get me out of the country and off to the US to stay with my dad. At least there I would get to finish my schooling without having to stop and start constantly.

The sisters were very kind people and had dedicated years of service in Liberia, even before the war. Their fate was quite unsettling. I could never understand why humans would behave so brutally to each other, especially toward peaceful nuns. Each action like this by warring factions went into my caution box. I wanted to understand what made people act so dangerously. I saw the cause of these killings as the lust for position and power. Part of my desire to live peacefully stems from incidences like these. I figured out that the more you wanted, the more you had to do unpalatable things to get it. If I could live without encroaching on someone else, what was wrong with that? The nuns' death showed me that even people living faultlessly were not exempt from malicious acts.

Last December 2017, while doing some research work for this memoir, I came across an article about the nuns which lead me to discover that their convent was only an hour away from where I now live in Missouri. I immediately sent them an email, asking if I could visit with them. I wanted to personally thank them for their selfless work in Liberia, done under extreme circumstances. I was overjoyed to get a reply back, agreeing to let me visit them. The following Tuesday I drove to their convent. Twenty-five years later, the nuns were older and now retired, but their spirits were still youthful as they sat with me reminiscing about their time in Liberia. Sister Elizabeth, the sister of my school principal, Sister Shirley, was there, along with other nuns who were relatives of some of the other murdered nuns. They joked around with each other, calling each other names. I could tell a "Liberian-ness" had rubbed off on them. It was also enjoyable to hear white women from Illinois talking about the good time they had in Liberia.

We had lunch, and one nun made me stand up and introduce myself to the whole cafeteria. They all cheered and clapped for me and thanked me for visiting them. Almost half of them had spent some time in Liberia, living in rural areas to which I had never been. After lunch, we walked over to the cemetery where the five sisters who died in Liberia were laid to rest. It was a very overwhelming experience for me, but it was something I needed to do. Tears welled up in my eyes as I stood in front of the sisters' graves, looking at their names. I remembered Sister Shirley's bright smile that showed the gap between her teeth. She would always pat me on the shoulder whenever I walked by her standing by her office. The five of them, Sisters Shirley Kolmer, Kathleen McGuire, Agnes Mueller, Barbara Ann Muttra and Mary Joel Kolmer, are now known as the Martyrs of Charity. I felt a relief come over me after I left their convent that day. The importance of gratitude hit me.

I had only interacted with Sister Shirley and Kathleen at school, and just for a very short period. But they were a significant part of my life. They had left their own home to come to mine and help us out of a mess we made. Those women had sacrificed themselves because they believed in treating people kindly and educating them. As I sat with them, they praised the resilience of the people, especially the women of Liberia.

Chapter Seven

Jaycee Kesh Akinsanya

Uprooted

By the middle of 1992, mommy and Rupert decided to move to Duala, the part of the city previously controlled by Prince Johnson, the leader of the INPFL. Rupert's family had a compound there, and they decided to turn the duplex into a house by breaking down one of the walls. I was dead set against it; everything I knew was on the Old Road. The church I attended was next door, my friends were in the neighborhood, most of our family lived there, and school was much closer. I feared the task of relearning a new area; the transportation route alone would involve making two connections to get to school. The idea of not being able to see my friends regularly angered me. I pleaded with mommy not to take me with her; maybe I could stay with Aunty Zoe next door. Aunty Lois was back in the country and had renovated a part of her beach house; perhaps I could stay with them. I wrote a long letter to Aunty Lois asking her to speak with mommy and not let me go to Duala. Aunty Lois invited me to visit their house for the day and have lunch with her but spoke nothing of my letter. We just hung out and had a sweet reunion.

Finally, the convincing argument came from mommy herself. She told me that I was her right-hand man, and she needed me to watch over my little sisters, Serenna, and Chee-Chee. Mom was expecting another baby soon and said the house would be a bit bigger and all of us kids won't have to sleep in the same room. The girls could have their room, and the boys—Rupert's three sons and I—could have ours. I reluctantly agreed to move, feeling a sense of responsibility for my little sisters. But I also felt sad, and that sadness grew a bit more each day because I wasn't hanging with my usual group of friends.

As a welcome to the neighborhood, one night, under the noise of heavy rainfall, armed robbers broke into our new home. They held pregnant mommy at gunpoint and took her purse. A few days later someone miraculously found the bag close to our house and delivered it to mommy, minus the money that had been in it. I was livid about the whole situation and blamed my stepfather for putting mommy in such a dangerous position.

Sensing that this could happen again, mommy proposed to start building our house on a beachfront plot of land she had bought in the early eighties when she was with my father. My dad worked for the Ministry of Public Works at the time and built some roads in various parts of the country. When he found out that the beachfront plot of land was for sale, he alerted mommy, and she bought it. For ten years the property sat there, and now something would be done to it. Every weekend in '92 and '93 were good weekends for me; we spent the day at the house site with the builders, and I could wander the area and explore the new environment.

Things eased up a little in Duala; I got used to my new school transportation routine and resumed my inquisitive wandering around the neighborhood again. I didn't wander as far as I used to on the Old Road; the armed robbery event made me uncomfortable to go too far into the town. I was fascinated by our Muslim neighbors; their daily prayers and chants played on a PA system, and the Arabic language intrigued me. Ramadan, their one-month period of fasting during the day, had just begun, so I would go over late in the afternoon and help them prepare their Ramadan rice dish for breaking their fast. Earlier in the day, the women soaked some rice for about an hour, then washed and drained it. The rice was then put onto a large bamboo tray, called a fanner, and set in the sun to dry. When it dried thoroughly, I helped pound the rice in a large wooden mortar until it became powder. The powder was sifted and rolled into balls and then cooked in sugar water to form a porridge.

In Duala, Runette Calvina, my youngest sister was born. Her name was a play on Rupert's and mommy's name: Runette for Rupert and Antoinette, and the "a" added to Calvin, Rupert's middle name. She was a joy for Rupert because she was the first girl for his all-boys' fatherhood. Mommy showered Calvina with love, like she did all of us, and took a maternity leave for a few months to take care of the new baby.

Mommy and Rupert were kind to the kids in the neighborhood. He had a connection with the YMCA and would bring home some sports equipment like soccer balls, badminton sets, and volleyballs, all to give us kids some exercise and fun activity to do. On New Year's Eve, the end of '92, mommy decided she would give out gifts to us kids, and when she tried to separate the boys on one end and the girls on another, Chee-Chee, then age three, went to the side of the boys. Mommy noticed this and burst into laughter for a few minutes, "She thinks she a boy! She thinks she's a boy!"

Chee-Chee Don't Care

Chee-Chee did think she was a boy; I was her alpha and would play rough with her. I'd have her climb up to the top of the bunk bed in the girls' room and then jump down to the queen size bed. At school, girls had to tuck their uniform blouses into their skirts, but Chee-Chee refused to do such a thing. The boys in her class didn't have to, and she thought she was a boy. She refused to get into fights with girls but welcomed a fight with any boy. Her three, going on four tough girl self, challenged a six-year-old boy one time, and gave him a good whooping. She then told the boy, "my name is Chee-Chee don't care, and I just beat you."

As I sat on the porch doing my homework, the boy's mother barged into our yard with him in tow, sobbing. She spoke to me in Bassa, mommy's native tongue, asking where this "Chee-Chee don't care" woman, who beat up her son, was. I held in my laughter, as I assessed the situation, looking at the boy who looked obviously older than my sister. "Chee-Chee," I called to her, "Come here for a minute." My baby sister walked out to the balcony to the bewilderment of the mother. Turning to her son, she asked in Bassa, "uh mon Chee-Chee don't care (is this Chee-Chee don't care)?" The boy, still sobbing, nodded yes, to his mom. She then turned to me and said apologetically, "I sorry yah, I instigated you." She grabbed her son's hand and walked away.

Instigated me? The poor woman knew very little English, and she had tried her best at it. Perhaps she meant to say interrupted because I was doing schoolwork when she came over. First, mommy told me to stop playing rough with Chee-Chee, so that she can learn to be a girl. Then she nicknamed Chee-Chee, "Chee-Chee don't care," and that name stuck with her. Finally, she laughed about the lady's try at English and misuse of the word. We all did such a thing when someone misused a word or used a word we didn't know. It was a kind of innocent fun. The person we laughed at the most was mommy, because she had an extensive vocabulary, and she'd say words like ubiquitous, meddlesome, and lackadaisical; words we had never heard before. We called it "chopping," meaning the speaker was chopping up the language.

Mommy laughed at the "instigated" incident, and made a joke at her tribal people's expense:

"These damn Bassa people, we like book business (we like education). One Bassa man went to "S'America" (it's America), and one day while he was cooking his fufu and palm butter, his kitchen caught fire. He dialed the fire brigade, and when the receptionist answered, the Bassa man decided to practice all the book (knowledge) he knew. 'Uh, my domicile is being consumed by a massive inflammation.' The receptionist, unclear as to what was going on, asked the man, 'Pardon me?' 'My domicile is being consumed by a massive inflammation.' All the while his fire was spreading through the house and into the living room. After his third 'domicile inflammation' rant, he finally screamed into the phone, 'Help! My house is burning down.' By the time the fire brigade got there, his domicile had turned to ashes." She concluded her story by telling us that it's better to speak in simple English so that people can understand you than to try and use big words and burn your own house down.

Jaycee Kesh Akinsanya

Priceless Lessons

My first lesson in the adverse effects of selfishness/hoarding, or whatever it's called, was learned around this time at CHAMS Lounge, Aunty Harriette's restaurant. My dad used to send me some "pocket change" through a friend who was coming back to Liberia from a visit to the US. Western Union and other money transfer places cost a fee, so he'd tell me, "Uncle/Aunty so and so is bringing you some pocket change," but I wouldn't see the money until a few weeks later. In most cases, the person ran into my dad weeks before but didn't return to Liberia for a while longer. I'd have to wait until the person returned to Liberia, and then mommy would contact them in town, and bring home the money from my dad.

Once upon such a time, I had to buy some cloth—the better kind this time—for my school uniform pants. It would cost about twenty-five U.S dollars for three pairs of tailored pants, and I knew my dad had sent me a hundred dollars. Mom had taught me to use my own money wisely, buying things that were necessary, and so I felt like an adult when I would buy my uniform and other necessities. At CHAMS lounge I asked mommy, while Aunty Harriette sat close by, if she would give me the twenty-five dollars in advance, and then deduct it from my hundred when Uncle Willis returned from the US. Aunty Harriette chimed in and said she would love to pay for my pants, provided I pay her back when the money came. I agreed, got my twenty-five bucks and had three pants made.

The money arrived, and mommy gave me my hundred bucks. Now, Aunty Harriette knew that uncle Willis had come, because he would regularly, if not daily, eat at her restaurant, so she knew I had my cash. But then I stopped showing up as frequently as I used to; I was trying to avoid paying what I owed. Mommy watched all this go down and said nothing. When I would show up at the restaurant, Aunty Harriette would ask for her money, and I would give some excuse, or promise to bring it by soon. In my mind, she was mommy's best friend, and so she should just let me have the money. She was working and making money, and I was thirteen, and her lovable nephew.

"Soon" dragged on for three weeks until one Saturday morning when Aunty Harriette showed up at our house; she had not come to visit mommy, but to see me specifically. She demanded her money, and I begrudgingly handed it over. "Jaycee," she said, "let me tell you something. If you had given me those twenty-five dollars when I had asked you for it the first time, I would have taken it, and given it right back to you. But since you kept it and avoided my restaurant, I came to collect it, and I won't give it to you. But I want

78

to see you back at the restaurant next week after school." If I didn't know what shame was, that day, I felt ashamed. Deeply. I felt like fool number one.

This incident involving Aunty Harriette and how much of a fool I made of myself, weighed heavily on my mind. I would go to CHAMS Lounge again but was a bit more cautious and quiet around people. Aunty Harriette and mommy noticed my mood, and took jabs at me, "Look at Mr. Attitude over there, pouting his mouth like a duck's butt." The shame was weighing heavily on me. I had made a fool of myself and felt like everyone in the restaurant knew about it, and were just being kind to me out of pity. But it would have been worse to not go to the restaurant after Aunty Harriette requested me to do so. For a few days, every time I entered the restaurant, I felt a heightened sensation on my skin; like every eye in there was focused on me, as a prison camera focuses on the cell of the inmate who tried to escape.

One day, I came straight home from school without going to CHAMS Lounge. I felt unfocused and lost, like I had done something wrong, but couldn't point to what the wrong was. I didn't know what depression was, and I can say this was my first taste of it. There were times I would pout and cut-up for no reason, and mommy named me, "Mr. Attitude," because of my mood swings. This day, however, was different. I was unhappy in our new neighborhood and found it especially hard to make friends as I figured we'd be moving to our new house soon, so there would be no need to build lasting friendships. I did make a few friends in the neighborhood, but we didn't hang out as I did with my friends on the Old Road. I felt completely out of place, and all my emotions seemed to want to manifest at once. I couldn't cry, although I wished to, and I couldn't get angry because I didn't know what to be mad at.

This new sad feeling was something I had not felt before. I felt a sense of loss and grief when I heard about my grandmother's death at Fendell Campus. Losing our school nuns brought tears and sadness too, but I don't think my mind was equipped with the maturity to grasp what had happened. Most of these incidents made me thoughtful. I internalized them, not just blanking out the trauma, but exploring the reality of what was happening. I handled most experiences philosophically, wanting to go deep into the heart of things. That afternoon, I was experiencing something very new. I was uncomfortable with the feeling; I wanted it to go away. But it weighed heavily on me, and I had no understanding of its source. I felt truly helpless. I felt overtaken by a force I couldn't sing my way out of, write off, walk off, or cook off. I was stuck in a weird time warp feeling of which I had no way out. The only thing I could do was just sit there and watch the world go by. Neighbors walked by, and I didn't lift my head to greet them; I was in a sound-proof mental bubble, and no one could reach me.

Mommy sensed the feeling too when she came home from work and saw me sitting on the porch looking down at the ground. Usually, I would say hi, or run and help her with the market bag she was carrying. More realistically, I would be buying those goods with her at the marketplace, and walking home with her. Without writing it of as one of my mood swings, she walked over to me. She sat next to me and asked what was wrong, and said that she didn't see me at the restaurant that day. I told her I had come straight home from school and wasn't feeling too good. I was not sick, but just felt sad, and I didn't know why. She said it was called feeling depressed, and that it was something everyone experienced. She was sitting right there with me; I had all of her attention, and this somewhat brought me out of my funk. Then she said she knew a song that she liked, and maybe it would help. We went inside, and she put on Regina Belle's "*If I could.*" She sang along and handed me the CD booklet to read the lyrics. Tears finally flowed as I read the lyrics, and mom sat there and held me, all the while still singing. Coincidentally, someone lent us a VHS of the 1992 Essence Awards where Regina Belle sings "*Sista/ If I Could*" as a tribute to Nancy Wilson. That song has been a favorite of mine since that day.

I felt better. I had made it through my first recognizable feeling of depression. As I try to analyze it now, I get the feeling that mommy too was trying to adjust to the new neighborhood. She had also been uprooted from her familiar space and was trying to make the new adjustment work, keeping a steady attitude as she always had. Perhaps her stopping to focus and give me some loving care, instead of leaving me to my own devices, also helped her. I do know that the moment the music started, and Gloria sang along, and the moment I read those lyrics, I was happy again.

Lie Man

On another occasion, as we walked from the Road to the house, I told her that I would love to have a kid soon. She chuckled, and in her straightforward Gloria way, said, "Well, just keep in mind that the same "s" that spells "sweet" and "sex," is that same "s" that spells "shitty" and "sour" when you're unprepared for a baby." I understood her purport without wanting more elaboration from her. What I didn't understand was why she had five children, and also loved adopting, or having random people stay with her. Her answer was simple: "When you start working for the Commerce Ministry, or wherever you'll work, you can have as many children as you want.

War, Momma and Me

But you knuckleheads and refugees in my house still make it shitty and sour."

I wasn't an ordinary thirteen-year-old; at least not mentally. When the civil war started, I had graduated, in my mind, to adult status. I had put away the child. Mommy taught me adult skills like managing the needs of the house and taking care of my little sisters. She delegated and empowered me in such a way that I felt grown up and matured, although in real time I wasn't. Not only was I her right-hand man, but Aunty Harriette also called me her handbag. She took me everywhere, and I wanted to be with her and her friends and hear about great adult topics. And because she treated me with such familiarity, a common theme in our family, I would often wish for "big people things," like having a kid, without knowing the prerequisites. I was a child playing house in the playground; building houses in the sand and pretending to be a real husband coming home to a real wife and kids. But I didn't know what it took to play house in the real world, with real cars and real wives and real kids. Mommy's humorous breakdown of "s" was her way of saying, "Don't do anything you're not prepared for; here are some of the consequences that could happen."

She said things in her own way. Later in life, I would hear other anecdotes and be reminded of something similar mommy would say. For example, to describe a stingy person, she would say he or she was "tight like a virgin." When I watched Ferris Buller and heard Ferris say, "Cameron is to tight, if you stuck a lump of coal up his ass, in two weeks you'd get a diamond," I laughed double- once for his saying, and again for connecting it to my mother's. She'd describe two people who were close to each other as "shirt tail and butt hole," always in proximity. I later learned the phrase, "like two peas in a pod," and remembered her saying. I'd often ask her where she got these sayings from, and she'd say that the old people used to say them, but I never heard anyone else say them.

She would describe someone who she thought was full of shit as "lie man." You had to see it to believe it when it came to lie man. She'd say, "If lie man says it's raining, you should go outside, in the middle of the street to make sure he's not just pouring water from a hose over your roof." If she felt, during a conversation that someone was hyping themselves without credentials, she would say, "Lie man says, 'my wife on the farm.'" The farm was too far of a drive to get proof of his wife, so you just took his word for it without challenge even though you knew he was bullshitting you.

7-9-7, 7-9-7

When telecommunications were finally up and running again, I would call my dad almost every weekend, even if it were just to say hello. Rupert's sister and her family lived next door to us, so I would use their phone to call my dad. The AT&T operator became familiar with me; I seemed to call at a specific time, which was also her work shift. I'd dial the 797-797 number and on the other end would come the response, "AT&T operator, how may I direct your call?" I'd give her my dad's number, and she would ask, "Is this Jaycee?" I would acknowledge, and she would say, "Hold on sweetie, let's get your dad on the line." I would then hear dad answer the phone, and she would say, "I have Jaycee on the line from Liberia, would you accept the call?" He'd agree, and she'd connect us. It felt very cool to be recognized by someone I didn't even know; she had the kindest phone voice, and I never got her name, but it was always a pleasure to hear her voice on the other line before talking with my dad.

As far as his occupation, I learned that daddy had been invited to Liberia in 1962 to work as an Assistant Project Manager in the construction of the Executive Mansion Grounds. He also had a law degree and would do pro bono legal work for people. In America, daddy worked mostly on the east coast helping with projects like the Philadelphia Airport expansion, New York Public Schools in Brooklyn, Southwark Plaza Modernization Project, and the Amtrak and Long Island Railroad Westside Yard Construction. Like mommy, he was humble, never talked about any of the work he did. I knew nothing of his accomplishments until after his passing.

Talks began to surface between mommy and dad about making arrangements for me to go to America; mom was making her promise to me come through. After a few trips to the US Embassy, my case was granted for passage to America. My dad, now a U.S citizen, filed for me to come live with him. My visa status was called, IR-2, which is a visa granted to children, under the age of twenty-one, born to U.S parents, or adopted children under the age of twenty-one. I understood the rationale behind my leaving for America. Our country was unstable, and My dad was in a stable place with regular school progression. Random outbreaks of war and recruitment of child soldiers were also deciding points in my going to America. Dates for my departure were still being discussed, but for now, my friends and I enjoyed roaming the neighborhoods, hanging out with each other, and living in post-war Liberia.

Tailed Creatures

After a year and a few months in Duala, we finally moved to the house on the beach in ELWA. I was 14 now. I learned from mommy that ELWA stood for Eternal Love Winning Africa. The area was known as such because the Pacific Garden Mission, the group who put on the "Unshackled" radio show, had a large compound there for their missionaries.

Our new house was finished as far as structure, doors, and windows, and mommy had the workers on duty, fixing the ceiling and finishing the electricals. The house was plastered and whitewashed (most homes in Liberia are built with cement blocks). Mommy said she wanted to take her time deciding on the color scheme. We moved in at this stage because she was afraid that if we left the house alone, looters would ransack everything. We lived in Duala, about an hour in the opposite direction, so her reasoning made sense. I was captivated by our new area. There were a few houses around us, some still under construction. About a quarter mile away was a lagoon, and one neighbor's son and I, Chris, we'll call him, would go swimming in the lagoon. We would try to hold our breaths for as long as we could while feeling the floor of the lagoon, looking for bubbling hot springs. Unlike Duala, making friends on this side of town came smoothly, although there weren't many neighbors around.

Someone replanted some coconut trees that those "heathens" cut down in fear of rebels hiding in them. I helped mom shop for, and plant two cashew trees, an almond tree, four coconut trees, and a variety of shrubs and flowers. We had no fence around the yard, so we could see the Atlantic Ocean, about eight hundred feet away from our house. We were close to where the fishermen pulled their boats in, and as they passed through our yard, taking the fish to market, mommy would make some of them stop so she could have the first pick of the fish they had caught. She told them it was the tax they had to pay for making a shortcut through our yard to get to market. Because she was a loyal customer, soon the fishermen learned to just stop on their way to market. If she weren't at home, they would leave the fish with me and tell me a price.

Although she loved freshly caught fish, it was the sea crab mommy waited for, especially when she was home on the weekends. Sometimes she wouldn't even wait for the fishermen to walk through the yard; she took a stroll to the beach when she saw the boats row to shore. She would invite her friends over for crab, cooked in beer. She also loved crab that we cleaned and added her special blended spices to, then let sit and marinade, before getting steamed. Mom would make funny faces at us as she enjoyed her lunch by the ocean. It didn't matter where we lived; her friends found a way to come and visit us. Some of them liked the area and bought available plots of land there. A few years earlier Nadia, Uncle Frank, and Kamal had all taught me how to make traditional Lebanese foods like hummus, babaganoush, etc. Mom had helped them establish their business through the Liberian Business Association, and over the years we became family to them, as well as to other members of the Lebanese community. They would even pay me to cook for them, and so I saved my money to spend when I got to America. I collected a total of $390 US Dollars.

To add to my fascination with this new neighborhood, there was a large black rock on the beach where we believed mammy watas (mermaids) sat and basked in the sun. It was thought that these beautiful mermaids would sit on that rock and comb their golden strands of hair, and if you startled one of them, they would drop their comb on the rock and rush back into the water. When you took the comb, the mermaid would come back up and beg you to give it back. She would also offer you anything you wanted in exchange for her comb, but you had to make sure she saw to her side of the bargain first, before giving back her comb. As kids, we believed that some wealthy people in our neighborhood had encountered mammy watas and were being provided riches through them. We thought that they kept the mermaids' combs long-term, continually asking for favors, but not giving back the combs.

You also had to be kind to the mermaids, or they would take you away when you went swimming. When angry, they took on a hideous form that the locals called "neejee," and drowned whoever it was that angered them. To validate our story, those wealthy people around the neighborhood never went swimming, and we thought that it was because they were afraid to drown. Probably why I learned to swim later in life; I was scared to swim in our ocean, and be taken. People said that the mermaids would come to shore and sit on that rock when no one else was around; usually between 3-5 pm when we were supposed to be doing our homework, and the fishermen had taken their fish to market. There were days I would hide in the bushes and watch that rock. I wanted to find a mermaid's comb. I would ask her to buy me an airplane with unlimited fuel, so I could travel all over the world and see the places mommy had seen and more.

My hiding in the bushes came to a halt one day as I walked towards the beach from a different direction than usual. As I came closer I heard a ruffle in the tall grass, about twenty feet away, then a big lizard-like creature darted across the path. It could have been a crocodile, it could have been an iguana, but I ran without double checking. I ran fast. To make matters worse, a few days later, while sitting under a tree, a rainbow agama, or red-headed lizard, as we called them, jumped from a tree branch, into my shirt. Startled, I jumped away and took off my shirt, and the agama fell to the ground and ran away. For days, I could still feel the slithering sensation on my back, and could hardly sleep at night. I have since had a fear of lizards.

Non-negotiable Friday

1995 was pretty low key as far as political tension. A conference sponsored by ECOWAS (Economic Community of West African States), the United Nations, and the OAU (Organization of African Unity) brought about a proposed ceasefire agreement between Charles Taylor and other rebel leaders. In August, there was talk about Charles Taylor coming to the city, this time in a peaceful manner. In September 1995, I went back to the Old Road area to visit some friends, and we all gathered along the main road, Tubman Boulevard, as a convoy of leaders, including Charles Taylor, drove to the Capital. Emotions were mixed on the road that day. Some of us got to see the face of this Charles Taylor who had started the war. Some people were angry, or silently watched; some waved and cheered as the convoy rode past. A ruling six-man council was set up to oversee the presidential elections scheduled for the next year. Some people were skeptical of this new council involving Taylor. An older man who lived on the beach next to us commented that leopards never changed their spots. He was right. Six months after I departed Liberia, the peace agreement broken and another war took place.

When mommy bought my ticket, the date was set for thirteenth of October 1995. I convinced her to let me skip the first few months of the 11th grade since I would be starting 11th grade all over again in the US. She agreed and let me stay home. I spent a bit more time with my three little sisters, Serena, 10, Chee-Chee, now 6, and Calvina, 3. I would wake them up and get them ready for school, make them breakfast, and then walk them to the main road and take them to school. Then I would go to the marketplace and buy fresh vegetables for the day's meal. I enjoyed this responsibility of being "house manager." As her right-hand man, mommy gave me charge of the money she would withdraw from the bank in the city. She paid the house workers in cash, and we used cash to go to market, so she would give me a bunch of Liberian dollars and tell me to hide it and keep it safe, so that no one else knew where it was, or saw me go to retrieve it. I'd make my rounds through the house, making sure there was enough dish soap in the kitchen, detergent and bleach for laundry, and oils and spices for cooking. I'd do the same in the bedrooms and bathroom, making sure each bathroom had bath soap, shampoo for mommy, skin lotion or shea butter, which we called donut grease, and sometimes palm kernel oil for dry skin. If we were missing any of these items, I'd tell mommy, and she'd buy them in the city, or have me buy them.

As the day of my departure for America drew nearer, my excitement for traveling faded. It became a reality that I would be leaving home for an uncertain world. I'd be leaving my three little sisters, CHAMS Lounge, my friends, cousins, and neighbors; I'd be leaving Liberia. Maybe things were getting better, so I could stay. I had conflicting thoughts after so much work was done on both sides—my dad and mom—to get me to the U.S. I could work and pay mommy back for the ticket money. I wanted to stay and help paint the new house and design the garden. It was a strange feeling, but the die was cast.

Since I hadn't been to school for a few months, I decided to enjoy the freedom it gave me to wander and visit everyone. I took cabs into town at any time to see mommy, or hang with my friends after school. Mommy took me shopping and bought me some dashiki shirts and African style leather slippers, as well as some necklaces, bracelets and other trinkets. Then one by one, family and friends started visiting our house to wish me farewell and a safe journey. Their visits made things harder for me. I wished I could just close my eyes and be in America already without having to say goodbye to all these people.

On the morning of the thirteenth, a Friday, with my packed suitcase, full of clothes and favorite African snacks, mommy, Aunty Zoe, my siblings, grandpa R.O.T, and cousins took me to the Airport for my flight to the Ivory Coast. I would then take Air Ivoire to Dakar Senegal, and then Dakar to New York. It used to be a direct eight-hour flight to JFK from Roberts International Airport, but now that airport was closed, and we had many stops before New York. Mom was calm, but I could feel her heart tear up inside. Externally she smiled, which caused me to smile back. I was the last one to board; mommy said there was no hurry, and I had an assigned seat. Since I was flying as an unaccompanied minor, she said the flight attendants would take excellent care of me. She was putting me in their care now, and that moment is forever marked in my heart. Who would be her right-hand man now? My feet felt wobbly like I could collapse as I climbed the staircase and into the aircraft. Standard notions of airport security didn't apply at this time; a person could get on and off a plane as many times as they wished before the flight. It was common for family members to greet each other, or bid farewell right on the tarmac. I just sat in my seat and watched my family through the window. As the plane taxied down the runway and took off, I could see them waving goodbye. I glanced over the Liberian landscape as the plane rose higher and higher. I was America bound.

.

Me

Jaycee Kesh Akinsanya

Chapter Eight

No Man's Jaycee

I was fifteen and traveling without an accompanying adult, so the flight attendants were very friendly to me. I had a very short layover in the Ivory Coast but had about eight hours in Dakar, Senegal. I was fascinated with the people of Senegal and how they dressed. My eyes wandered everywhere. I walked around the Duty-free shops and other stores, admiring the arts and crafts of Senegal. In a sense, the books I had read in the library about all these places were opening before me. I didn't see much of the culture from the airport, but watching the people and walking around was fulfilling. It was dark when my plane boarded for New York. There was a video monitor in front of my seat on the flight from Dakar to New York, and the flight attendant told me that I could watch the flight progress. He spoke French to me, assuming I was French, and I responded in French. Most schools in Liberia taught French from fifth grade onward, and mom had friends who were French and would chat with her in French. In addition to French class, when we attended St. Peter's Lutheran School, we learned Kpelle, one of the thirty dialects of Liberia. My great aunt Kolubah and her family spoke Kpelle, and I would practice chatting with them. In our home, mom spoke Bassa, and so did our maid Mary. Mary taught me to speak a bit of Bassa, and at one point even taught me to read Bassa, a skill I have long forgotten.

My heart was up in the air. I was sorely missing the world I just left, and uncertain of where I was going. I had been somewhere between Liberia and Ivory Coast; somewhere in Abidjan and Dakar, and finally, I was somewhere in between the continent of Africa and the continent of North America. I was no man's Jaycee; recently released from my mother's navel strings, and sitting in a capsule, not yet connected to the shelter of my father. These flight attendants were taking good care of me, as my mom had promised, bringing me a constant supply of snacks and juices. My backpack had a few books to read, and I relaxed with very little sleep throughout the flight. Mom told me to walk up, and down the aisle, if I felt tired of sitting down, so out of curiosity, I walked about a few times, looking to see who was on the plane with me.

Hearing about America from people who had been there was very interesting for me. It wasn't enough to know that America was "cool," I wanted to understand what made it cool. I learned from my stepdad Rupert, that America "moves at night;" that was when all the Trucks carrying merchandise for stores traveled long distances, or the roads were fixed. I heard of places like JC Penny and Walmart from him as well. From mom's friend Barbara, who gave me all the *Reader's Digests*, I learned about her home state Utah. She said that there were lots of places for camping and outdoor activities in Utah. She also gave me a tank top that said Utah Jazz on it. Rupert told me it was the name of the Utah basketball team. Barbara was Mormon and gave me a Book of Mormon as a gift. Mommy had lived in America, and my brother was born there, so it made him automatically cool for being born in a foreign country. She would talk about her sorority from Lincoln University, and all the fun she had while attending there. My grandad, R.O.T, had also attended Lincoln University, so I heard much about Missouri, which mommy pronounced, "*Missourah*." My dad left for America when I was about five or six years old, and so I felt like I had an ally in America who would send me some cool things from this America place.

America was heaven, and in heaven, you could have anything. McDonald's pumped out food very fast, clothes were ready-made, which meant no tailor had to do your measurements anymore; a machine figured you were a small, medium, or large. There were tall buildings everywhere, and you could live in a "deluxe apartment in the sky," as the theme song form *The Jeffersons* put it. Friends would have cereal brought back from America, or new sneakers. The grocery stores in town carried some American products that came at a higher price tag. Any connection with America made you automatically cool.

But although the cool things America had to offer glittered in my mind, I wanted Morocco and Portugal; I wanted India and Papua New Guinea. I wanted Las Palmas and the Canary Islands. I wanted Brussels. Mommy had traveled extensively, and although she talked to some extent about America and her time at college, it was when she spoke of places like India, Papua New Guinea, Egypt, or Israel, that I would observe her eyes light up. The excitement in her eyes captured my childhood imagination, and I wanted to see these places. Her eyes displayed the fun she had in those places. I wanted to meet her friend Jacinta in Papua New Guinea. I wanted to meet all the women she met on her trip to Egypt for that Women's meeting. I wanted to know why her eyes lit up when she talked about these places.

Because of mom's descriptions of the places she traveled, I got so lost in daydreams that before the war, at school in Liberia, during recess, I spent some time in the library looking for books on other countries and the people who lived there. I was in the fourth grade when all the travel craze started for me. The houses in the books, the food, the dress, all created in me a lust for these places. I almost failed the fifth grade because most of the time I sat writing about countries I had read about earlier during lunch break. I even wrote a book called "*Exilia*," about a family who were exiled from their homeland and then settled somewhere else to start life all over. Their houses reflected one of the houses I had read about, their faces in my mind's eye were Asian or South American. I would get so caught up in my book and would torture my friend Saidu with every detail. He couldn't help it; every instance I got, I told him about the adventures in Exilia. That book also cost me a lot of school notebooks, because I would sit in class writing my book, instead of what was on the blackboard. It was never a published book, just something I wrote to pass the time. My Geography teacher was especially puzzled when he saw how low my grades were. I was always taking notes, he thought, so why was I promoted to the sixth grade on probationary status? Little did he know that all my "geography notes" were of me, with some made up family, in some made up part of the world.

The most beautiful thing in my life was the understanding that the world wasn't just America, Liberia, and England; through mom, and the library books, I learned that there was Morocco, Burma, Iceland, and Canada. There were seven continents, and people lived everywhere. People lived in igloos, houses on stilts, wood houses, stone houses- the world was a diverse place, and I knew people who had visited some of these places. I couldn't wait to travel and see all these places.

Mom was my one-stop-shop for many travel experiences, and from a very tender age I soaked it all in as she spoke about places she'd been. I longed to see Israel and swim in the Dead Sea. She brought back mud from there on her last trip in 1990. She said the Dead Sea was the only water she would ever swim in because she wouldn't drown. She raved about the food and the ancient architecture and going to the Jordan River and other holy sites like the birthplace of Jesus. She said being in Israel was like walking through the Bible.

Lebanon intrigued me since I could read about it; the Bible talked about the cedars of Lebanon. Mom had a jar of olive oil from Lebanon which she used very sparingly on her skin. Uncle Frank told me they had the best olives and olive oil and since I had learned from him how to cook Lebanese food, I dreamed of the day when I would sit in a Lebanese home, say, in Beirut, and have a beautiful dinner with the people. As far as India, it seemed to be mom's favorite place although she didn't spend a long time there. We had kurtas, slippers, and comics called *Amar Chitra Katha* that mom brought back with her. She had pictures in our family album with some Indian dignitaries in Delhi. My favorite thing mommy brought back from India was a metal fridge magnet of Vishnu. For me, Vishnu was good luck and would protect our house. As a child, I would look at our family album and get absorbed in the pictures of mom in India at a meeting, or Geneva, and the more

I looked at these pictures, the more I became a fan of my mother. She was the coolest person to me; she had traveled and stood in photographs with influential people, and seemed to relish the fact that the world was full of diverse people. On the bucket list of my daydreams, I wrote the names of places I'd visit one day and make friends of my own.

The only place on my list that I wanted to visit which had no connection to mommy, was Budapest. I had read a biography of Elizabeth Taylor and had also seen an interview with her in which she talked about Budapest. The way she said the word *Budapest* made it sound like in this place, there was no suffering, no life problems, no work—just pure joy. I envisioned myself sitting by a pool one day in Budapest, being served Budapest style foods and wandering the streets as an explorer. One of my fantasies on the flight to New York was to one day meet Elizabeth Taylor and get her autograph. I started reading her biography because while she was reading it, mommy showed me a picture of Elizabeth Taylor's violet eyes and I thought one day I'd stand before her and look into those eyes myself.

No man's Jaycee was soon awoken from his daydreaming as the captain and flight attendants announced the proximity of JFK. The flight attendant instructed everyone to put their trays back up and fasten their seatbelts. They then went around the aircraft collecting cups and other trash items. I put away the books I brought with me and gazed down at the now slightly visible New York landscape.

E Kaaro

My Dad met me right outside the gate. It had been about ten years since I last saw him. He looked a little older, grayer hair and less hair, as his hairline had receded. His face wore a bit more stress than I remembered from his days back in Liberia, where he was a mover and shaker. But his signature parted hair on the right, and Santa Clause belly was still visible. After a happy hug and collection of my luggage, we went to an immigration room where they took my fingerprints and photograph. We then left the airport and drove in his Toyota Camry to Willingboro, New Jersey, via a quick tour of New York City.

The adrenaline rush and conversation with daddy kept me awake on my first ride out of JFK and through some parts of New York City. It was a quick "let me show you the area," drive. We drove through Manhattan for a while; I saw the Empire State Building, the Chrysler building, and the World Trade Center, where dad's train stop for work was. After a long drive through parts of New York City, we made our way to the Lincoln Tunnel headed for New

Jersey where he lived. Dad told me that the Lincoln Tunnel was a mile and a half long, and laughed at the thought that some people attempted to hold their breath through the whole tunnel. He was certain no one could ever hold their breath that long because every time he was ever in the tunnel, traffic was slow moving. Dad joked that perhaps traffic was delayed because some fool may have tried to hold their breath and fainted, thus causing a traffic jam. It felt reassuring to hear my dad's voice again; he had a kind of light, but authoritative voice. He too, like mommy, smiled and laughed often.

At the other side of the Lincoln Tunnel, on our way to Willingboro, I was mesmerized by the fact that America had different colored trees—yellow, red, orange—whereas, in Liberia, our trees only had green leaves. Of course, we had learned about the different climates, and season changes around the world, but I hadn't been around the world, or even to most parts of Africa, to experience what the textbooks were teaching. Hands-on learning always worked for me; most of what I learned in the school books, I forgot after taking the quiz, test, or final exam. Education, for me, implied some sort of direct experience by me, the learner, in the process. What I had learned in my Geography class didn't stick with me, as far as climates and terrains in other countries, until I began to travel to those places and experience them. These brightly colored trees caught my attention; no one in Liberia who visited America ever talked about the trees. They talked about the buildings, like the Pentagon in Virginia, World Trade Center in New York, malls, and places to eat like IHOP, McDonald's, and KFC. In Geography class, we learned about Mt. Rushmore and the Appalachian Trail, or the Rio Grande and Death Valley, but no one ever talked about them outside of class, so they were of no major significance in my mind. These different colored trees now sparked a new interest for exploration in my mind.

It was Saturday, October 14th and marveling at the October leaves filled me with amazement and awe for a part of the world where the leaves had different colors. Seeing these leaves made America cool to me. I paid very little attention to the buildings unless dad pointed a significant one out to me. I was enjoying the changing colors around me. Most of the flora of Liberia were evergreen, and although we had theoretically learned about coniferous and deciduous trees, I, again, had no experience of these types of trees. I did not connect the dots from what I learned in school about the four seasons— Winter, Spring, Summer, and Autumn—to what I was experiencing as we drove to dad's home.

Somewhere along the way, dad stopped at a fast food place, and the lady gave us some French fries through the window. It was called a Drive-thru, where you spoke your order to a digital box that had picture menus one it, and then pulled forward to get what you ordered. I have no recollection of which chain of fast foods it was. I wasn't used to the notion of fast food, and I never ate fast foods again until years later when my friend Ty dragged me to White Castle in Minneapolis for his slider burger.

"Doba'le"

From day one my dad meant business for me in America; as we drove to New Jersey, he delineated the glories of all the opportunities the country had to offer, but close to his heart was civil engineering. If anyone else had been in that car, they would have thought my dad was a recruiter for the Civil Engineers Association of the world, if there is such a group. But it wasn't just recruiting; it was a must-do scenario. Dad was known as a disciplinarian; he grew up in Nigeria where the father was the breadwinner, and when you saw your father walk into a room, you greeted him by falling flat in a prostrated pose called "doba'le." My elder brothers, Sheena, Sunde, and Deji, who grew up in Nigeria, knew this form of greeting. Biodun, our sister Yabo and I were born in Liberia and raised with different customs. Dad adjusted to our Liberian customs to some extent, but carrying on the tradition of the father being the authority was natural for him. Mom taught me the doba'le, as well as some simple Yoruba phrases when I was growing up, but it was sentimental, not an expectation since my dad was already in America.

Unfortunately, my fifteen-year-old mind wasn't like other fifteen-year-old minds looking for career dreams with a future of a big house and cars and all the toppings. In fact, I was looking for a different world, one that I had previously seen before the war with friendly faces and much less competition for powerful posts. My fifteen-year-old mind didn't grasp at the time, that, competitive or not, one needed a career just to earn a livelihood. Just like my thirteen-year-old mind didn't understand the prerequisites to have a child when I told my mom I wanted one. It seemed that day that my dad was prepping me for a busy, competitive world that I knew nothing of. I wasn't in the mindset to understand what he was saying, and after all I had seen happen in Liberia, my heart wasn't open to the idea of going to get it, and making it to the top. I had become disillusioned with the world of competition, and the conversation in the car triggered some negative feelings in me.

During the war, I would listen to an album made by a childhood friend of mommy. He is the renowned pastor Momolue A. Diggs, and his nephew Joma and I went to St Patrick's together. His album had a few amazing songs, and

War, Momma and Me

most of which I learned by heart. The song I loved the most was *"Go build a World,"* sung to the tune of *"O Holy Night."* Part of the lyrics read:

> *Come see a world filled with malnutrition*
> *Where children starve just because they can't find bread*
> *Come see a world stocked with ammunition*
> *Where man must kill if they want to get ahead*
> *Where children laugh and play as kids together*
> *Then grow as men and fight and kill their pals*

> *A world filled with pain, broken hearts and sad faces*
> *A world where hate reigns and strife seems not to cease*
> *Where friends betray each other*
> *Then they say, "soul rest in peace."*

This had been a reality for us in Liberia, a tiny country; and scenes of betrayal, starvation, grief and whatever else war leaves in its trail were all we could see at one point. Through it all, people like mommy remained steady in their kindness and virtues. I attributed everything in that song to man's greed and what a person would do to get ahead of another.

As dad spoke, I listened intently for opportunities for me. How could I help rebuild the world, not just be another person starving for bread and having to compete, betray or worse, just to "survive." My survival didn't need to be because of someone else's demise. At one point, as he spoke, I asked my dad exactly what I was thinking: "Dad, would these opportunities involve me selling myself, or killing someone just to live?" These were my fears. Something had pushed me to ask that question, and for some reason, my dad internalized it so much, that for the rest of the ride home he said nothing.

Later, in a future conversation, he told me that he went quiet because he realized that what I said was a reality from what I had experienced, and therefore did not argue. My question was loaded with the lyrics of that song, and dad caught the deeper subtleties of the issue. I was bent on taking my time to absorb and understand things in this new environment before getting involved with them. My dad had reunited with a son he left in Liberia only a few years before; but now instead of just a son, he was sitting next to a boy who had been exposed to darker parts of humanity. I had learned to navigate life with mommy's guidance, and I needed to know how I could use those skills in this new atmosphere and counteract the evil I had seen people do. If America was a land of opportunity, I wanted to know what opportunities I had, as far as community development and interpersonal work.

Chapter Nine

Jaycee Kesh Akinsanya

Clogged Channels

It was in my first few months in America that I learned about racism, religious segregation, and sexual discrimination. In Liberia, I attended a Catholic church, and mostly because it was a few hundred feet from our house on the Old Road. As Christmas Eve approached, I asked if we could go to Midnight mass at the local Catholic church like I used to do back in Liberia. Dad said no, we were Episcopalians. I had no idea what he meant and only heard the no, more prominently. Mom never told me we were Episcopalians. How was I supposed to know these things? I felt my first barrier to exploring America in that one sentence. I was awakened to the fact that mom and dad were different people and approached life in different ways.

Back in Liberia mommy was Methodist, my stepdad was Baptist, and I went to a Catholic church, and no one had ever stopped me from worshipping where I chose. Sometimes Mary, the maid, took me to her Pentecostal church. Mom often said that behind all the religious doors was the same God, and people just wanted to worship him differently. We had Seventh Day Adventist friends, Mormon friends, Muslim friends, Hindu friends, Jewish friends, and all other kinds of friends who were of various religious beliefs. But a "no" that evening felt like a dismissal. I had no say in it. I later teased my dad that if it were up to him, not every Christian would go to heaven, only Episcopalians would.

I would move into a Vedic monastery at one point in my life because I couldn't understand how all these faiths claiming to worship the same deity would fight amongst themselves for exclusive rights to the kingdom of heaven. Was it about love for God, or desire for exclusive rights to God's kingdom? Of course, dad couldn't understand why I would go all the way to India to find God. I could write a whole other book on the philosophical fights with my dear father.

I even went as far as accusing my dad of being hypocritical when it came to religion. He argued that our ancestors were Christians, and therefore we had to stick to tradition. I claimed that if we were to hold to tradition, then we had to follow our traditional Yoruba culture. I said that dad had to live out the tradition that was found even in his name, Olu, derived from Oluwa, meaning "god, or deity" in Yoruba. The Yoruba culture existed in Nigeria and had an intricate religious culture long before Christianity arrived there.

My point of hypocrisy accusation was that names, especially traditional

given names carried meaning, and we couldn't just keep the name on the surface, and then take on an entirely foreign religious culture. Dad liked a good
argument that wasn't disrespectful and invoked thought. When I brought up
the meaning of Oluwa, dad was pleased and asked where I learned Yoruba.
Mom taught me a few phrases, like daily greetings— e kaaro (good morning),
nibo ni iwon lo (where are you going), and other short conversation pieces.

Derogatory Words

As for my awakening to racial tension, it happened after the Christmas
break. We had to stand and say something in class; the memory is a bit vague
now as to what the specific project was. As I spoke, I mentioned the word,
"nigger," followed by some stares from students in the class. I continued
speaking, but after class, my teacher called me to his desk, and the conversation went something like this:

"You know, Jaycee, that word is a very derogatory word, and we don't
use it around here."

I, clueless as to what word he was talking about, asked: "What word?"

He: "The 'N' word."

I: "N-word?"

He: "Yes, it's a very derogatory word, and we don't use it here.

I: "Sorry, sir, I don't know what word you're talking about..."

He (very uncomfortably), "The "N" word, as in "Nigger."

I: "Oooh, mommy calls us her little niggers. Is it a bad word?"

He then went on to tell me how people use that word here and what it
implied; he explained everything in depth, and that was my first education
on the racial tension in America. Later in the year, he told me that when he
called me over, and I questioned him about the "word," he thought I was
trying to frame him to say "Nigger," so I could take him to court. But he said
that, while observing me during his class, he realized I honestly did not know
about the racial tension.

I was no stranger to the history of slavery; the very country I was born in
was set up to accommodate freed slaves who wanted to go back to Africa.
The word Liberia comes from the Latin word "liber," meaning, free + "ia,"
meaning, place. I had read about the KKK, Jim Crow, Dr. Martin Luther King

Jr., Rosa Parks, and some of the racial tension in America; but I thought these were things of the past and not something of present contention. Like most Americans who had not experienced the impact of war, but had watched war movies or heard about war—and perhaps even experienced emotions related to their experience— I had also heard of the racial tensions in America. I had also possibly shrugged at the way people behaved toward each other. But I hadn't experienced it first-hand; therefore I had an air of naiveté about the subject.

Liberia had such a mixture of cultures and races, and people, in my teenage experience, treated each other kindly. The white people I interacted with in my life in Liberia were treated honorably. Some of mommy's friends were white, and again, it never crossed my mind that these people were different from me, except in their skin color. In a sense, meeting people of varying skin color was a good thing for us; it meant we made friends from different parts of the world and could brag about it, or one day visit them in their country. I had a friend who would name all the babies she wanted to have one day; she wanted seven kids, one from a race on each continent.

It is not to say that there is no history of racism in Liberia or Africa; I was the one who had no exposure to it. My mother's interaction with people showed me how to interact with others. She never showed signs of negativity in her treatment of foreigners, so I learned to treat foreigners as I treated locals. I was ignorant about the persistence of racism in American society because I had only been in America a mere three months. In those three months, I had minimal personal interactions with people except my dad's friends. My use of the "N" word flowed innocently because mommy used it without reference to its history.

I began to see that there was more to America than buildings and food places. America had a dark historical past that I would have to learn. It wasn't a utopia like people who had visited made it sound. In a sense, I felt unprepared. No one ever described how people interacted with each other, nor did they have to. In my inexperienced mind, I figured people everywhere lived like the people who visited our house; visiting each other, laughing and drinking on their balconies. I had both my parents' example to follow; mom was kind and accommodating to everyone, regardless of race, and dad, as I had seen him so far, was similarly respectful to others.

Leather-chapped Kevin

My exposure to sexual discrimination was also an eye opener to how much

105

I had to learn in this new world. At school in New Jersey there was a very handsome guy in one of my classes, and for some reason, I wanted to make friends with him. I made friends with a few girls, so far, but had no guy friends. This guy, Kevin, we'll call him, was very quiet, walked intently, and would chew a lot of gum. He was on the school football team and wore studded earrings, which I thought was cool. Some guys in Liberia had earrings, so it wasn't new to me. When we occasionally talked, he'd smile, and his dimples showed. Kevin seemed, to me, very grounded and uninterested in showing himself off, and because of that "depth" he carried, I wanted to be his friend. He sat right in front of me, and at times we did group projects together.

I asked one of my friends, Betty, we'll call her, about Kevin. I wanted to know more about him and how to be friends with him. I was easing my way into American life and needed to make friends so that maybe my dad would let me go hang out with them now and then. For my dad, hanging out with young American girls outside of school was out of the question. He talked about the alarming increase in teen pregnancy in America. He also cautioned me about young boys becoming gang members and doing drugs, but to me, Kevin didn't fit the profile of someone who wanted to be in a gang. If I got to know him, perhaps dad would let me hang out with him.

Betty cautioned me about Kevin and told me not to hang out with him unless I wanted to turn gay. She talked about how gay people were sick and did sick things, and how all gay people ended up dying from AIDS, so I should do well to stay away from them. Betty described in detail their sex life and how they wore leather chaps and carried handcuffs in their backpacks. Not sure how she knew all the detail, but for all she knew, gays were freaks to be avoided. By the end of her anti-gay speech, I lost the desire to want to get to know Kevin, although what I observed about him, didn't make sense with what she was describing. Did Kevin have handcuffs and leather pants in his backpack? Did his friends on the football team know about this? Was the football team gay? My brain rattled with questions.

My mind flashed back to the two guys I saw kissing by the water fountain at St Patrick's in Liberia. Were they gay? They couldn't have been; they quoted the Bible about greeting each brother with holy kisses. It was just a holy kiss. I had read the quote in a few different places in the Bible. We knew a gay man back in Liberia, who walked around the neighborhood. He was always well dressed, wore a lot of white linen pants, and walked very much like a lady. People teased him now and then, but no one physically harmed him, as far as I can remember. Kevin didn't fit the same profile as the guy from Liberia. Kevin was athletic. I now had another new example of what a gay person in America looked like.

Another experience with Betty and my ignorance of gay culture was when I came to school one day and told her that I had seen the most beautiful woman on TV a few nights ago on VH1. She was a tall black woman and hosted a TV show called *RuPaul's Party Machine*. My dad watched the show for a minute but switched the channel to something else. Betty laughed hysterically at me. "Your dad was right to switch the channel man," Betty said, looking at me as if I was the biggest idiot on the planet. "That pretty lady you saw was no lady at all. RuPaul is a man." A man? I didn't know what to think. How could a man look that beautiful as a woman? Betty told me it was called "drag" and many gay men dressed as drag queens. Did Kevin dress like a drag queen? I was intrigued, bewildered and partially understood why my dad switched the TV channel. Since Kevin was the first gay person I learned about in the U.S, every question I had about gay life, was cross-referenced to him. To Betty, gays were sinister.

In later years when I told mommy the story about my RuPaul revelation, she laughed heartily and joked that the problem in society was that people took themselves too seriously, and this RuPaul man was having a good time, getting paid, and the rest of them were jealous. Mom acknowledged that some of the overt exposures of gay men, like the assless leather chaps during parades, were perhaps a bit over the top for some observers. She could understand why a parent would be homophobic, thinking that their child who was once a wrestler or football player, could now be dressing like a girl or showing his private areas in public. But she also knew gay people who weren't part of the external exhibition culture; gay lifestyles also had a grayscale, not just black or white.

I eavesdropped on a conversation back in Liberia, before my departure, where someone told mommy that I walked a little "care-freely" and that she should make sure to tell me not to turn gay when I came to America. Because I had a very limited picture of what gay was, I knew the "care-free" walk of mine that person talked about was way off the mark, so I didn't even entertain the thought. I recall mom saying she didn't think gay was something people "turned," and that "Jaycee will be whoever he will be." I had very little interest in gay or straight life back in Liberia; I was too intrigued with reading books and discovering what worlds lay in them. If there were romantic interests in me, the persons would have probably found me awkward, because my radar for romance was off. To be honest, I was thirteen. Or fourteen. And although sex wasn't foreign to me, having a girlfriend was way off my radar.

If today I were to meet and talk with that person who cautioned mommy about my carefree walk, and its indication of my being gay, I would hope to educate them on the fact that gay is not a walk, or a look, or even an attitude. I'd tell them that gay wasn't something one "turned." You turned a page or turned a corner. I would caution that person about the fears and prejudices others project onto a young person, which sometimes leads to bullying and suicide. I would let them know that it is common, and natural for young boys and girls to experiment sexually and that usually, a first sexual experience happened between members of the same sex. I have many heterosexual friends who have admitted that to me. I would finally ask them to look at what contributions a person made to their community, and not who slept in their bed. Finally, since that person was a staunch Christian, I would advise them to leave the gay person and their activities to God for judgment. After all, nothing is outside of God's creation; He created everything.

One good friend, gay, with no trace of femininity or a so-called care-free walk, in response to the "gay look," would say being gay was not a choice, but in most cases, acting overly feminine was. I've known many gay men who go completely undetected because they don't fit the perceived "look" of a gay person. And to this day, I still have a good friend, happily married with two beautiful children, who everyone thinks is secretly gay, because he dresses and dances too well.

In my first few months of American life, I was drawing some very negative conclusions: avoid gay people, some people did not like me just because of my skin color, and God seemingly only loved Episcopalians. My introduction to America was off to a bad start. I neither loved the knowledge that was coming to me nor did I like how it made me feel; like I was being forced to hate people because society hated them.

As I said before, these issues do exist in Liberia as well, and one just needs to look for stories on the internet to see how absurd humankind can be when making policies. The information coming to me pushed me to want to do my own research and not trust what someone like Betty was telling me. But I had only been living with my dad for a few months in America and had no independence to venture into explorer mode. I locked away my desires to learn more about an America no one told me about.

Not Mom's Way

In life thus far, my frame of reference was mommy and how she did things, or how she treated others. Suddenly I felt like I had no more access to her wit, her humanity, her love—nothing. I began to notice the world from a very fearful place, and the fear started to validate itself. Neighborhood watch signs had me thinking that people were watching my every move, but I couldn't see or interact with those people. We lived in a neighborhood with rows of townhouses, each with a small backyard. I never saw my neighbors on either side of us. The furthest my dad let me go out of the house alone was to the "Wawa" convenience store across the street, and playing in the backyard was about as much social time as I got. In his defense, he had never raised a sixteen-year-old, at his age, in a foreign country where his lifestyle was completely different. He had valid concerns and fears for his young son in a new world.

I came from a war-torn country where I was free to wander anywhere at any time. I could walk into any of my friends' homes and hang out with them. We mostly weren't even home; we were out flying kites, playing in the swamps, messing around in quicksand, being boys. Now here I was in a free country, unable to play or wander freely out of fear that I might join a gang or get a girl pregnant. Furthermore, I had come to the U.S at a time when most teen-agers were looking for where they fit in and forming friendship bonds. I left my whole gang of friends in Liberia and came to a new environment. I realized it would take time to settle, get checked out by local cliques, and then be accepted. Or not. Some kids in school were cordial but too shy to make friends with me quickly.

As a result, I began to harbor a type of anger toward mommy. Why did she send me to this place? I had never been cautioned so much and had no one to talk to and just blow off some steam. I didn't even want to take up the topic of sexuality or racism with daddy. I feared he'd just bring down the 'No!" gavel without explanation, or he'd bring down the gavel with way too many negative explanations. Daddy didn't know that I learned life the "Gloria way," with anecdotes and examples. There was no laughter in his voice to help the lesson stick, so all my frustrations became mommy's fault. That sad feeling I had experienced in Duala crept up again in me, but I didn't know the words to "*If I could*" to make me feel better about my situation. I felt alone with no ally.

On weekdays, dad was at work, and when he came home he ate dinner and watched TV, or the TV watched him as he snored and sometimes woke himself up. He'd then go upstairs to sleep and do it all over again the next day. His waking up due to his loud snoring was an amusing topic for both of us, and he blamed it on how much commuting he did daily just to get to and from work. Dad was out the door by four in the morning to commute from Willingboro to New York. We talked on weekends in between chores, or as he prepared meals for the both of us for the week.

Flowing

Dad and I had some fun moments, like when the Blizzard of '96 happened in New Jersey, and we had to climb out of my room window to shovel the snow away. What a "welcome to American weather" that was. Snow covered almost the entire front door, and all I could see when I looked out the window was the second floor of every house in the neighborhood, and half or less than that, of the first floor. I enjoyed jumping out of the window into the snow and making a dent, while dad handed me the shovel to start clearing the snow away from the door. When I finished, I shoveled a maze from the front door to where our car was parked. When I went back to my room and looked out the window, I could see that the rest of the neighborhood had also been shoveling snow from their doors to the street. My shovel route just took a few turns before reaching the road. I was having a blast being out in the snow, and dad let me do my thing. He didn't go to work for those few days, and I didn't go to school, so we had a few days of father and son bonding.

One conversation with him that made him laugh hysterically was when I told him about my linguistic class. I guess to help foreign students speak English better, the school set up a class. And since I was foreign, I had to take it. The whole class was comical to me; I stare at the teacher in bewilderment as she would teach. The phrase I recall so well to this day— and the way she moved her mouth while saying it— was, "When you speak English, you have to use your lips, your teeth, and your tongue." She'd emphasize the words lips, teeth, and tongue, and at the same time move her mouth to match each word. When she said lips, her lips would move dramatically. She'd show her teeth prominently when she said teeth, and she'd stick her tongue far out like a lizard when she said tongue."

People probably thought I was crazy because I always left that class laughing to myself. When I told dad about the class, and demonstrated the facial movements, he laughed so much and asked if the teachers expected foreign students to walk around trying to speak English in such a manner, with the matching face movements. He thought such a student would make no friends. He also chuckled at the fact that people would think that because a person was from a foreign country, he/she was automatically bad at speaking English.

Twice, in later years, I would be asked about my coming from the "jungles of Africa," and how hard it must have been to learn to speak English and adjust to civilized life. I had to be respectful to the persons who asked those questions, but there were times I wanted to start speaking with click sounds and dramatically gesturing with my body to indicate what jungle life looked like for me, back in the "country of Africa." Instead, I took the time to educate such persons, telling them that English was my first of the few languages I spoke then— languages I've lost most of because of lack of practice. I also educated them on the fact that I lived in the city, and that Africa had many thriving and beautiful cities like those found in the Ivory Coast, Morocco, South Africa, and many other places.

Another memorable time was when we drove up to Rutgers University to visit my sister, Yabo, who was up there attending medical school. We were driving safely on the highway when another driver zoomed past us, only to get stuck in traffic right next to us. My dad was furious! Why was that guy driving so fast only to get stuck in traffic? Dad complained that people in this country just want to kill each other with their reckless driving. He went on and on. And as we pulled up next to the guy my dad lifted his index finger in a vicious up and down movement to give the guy the "middle finger." I looked over and said "Dad, you're using the wrong finger," and we both burst out laughing for the rest of the way. More time together was the medicine we both needed, but he had to work to continue earning a living, and I had to continue my schooling.

Life was different for sure, and my dad was different. He was stressed, and I had no idea how to live with him. Although I was a child when he left Liberia, I remember how much he smiled and was very light-hearted to be around. He was also a disciplinarian when need called for it, but the person my dad had become made me sad to be around. I couldn't understand his struggles. As a parent, he never discussed his life with me, and I didn't want to impose the many interests and questions piling up in my head. We found some shelter from this tension through movies and whenever I played the CDs in his extensive collection. For some reason, he would lighten up whenever I did this, and that would make me very happy. On one such occasion, as I played Luther Vandross and he made our weekly meals, he stopped for a moment and joined in the singing with me. Then he said, "my brother, you know your music, man. Your mom knows her music too."

Clogging

But the stress continued despite our best efforts, and my new inhibiting lifestyle caused me also to resent my dad. I began to spend more time in my room and only talk to him when I needed something for school. The straw that broke the camel's back was one night when I asked him for money for the school yearbook pictures. He seemed more stressed than usual and spoke harshly, asking if mommy had sent me to the U.S. to strip him of his money. Struck in the heart by that statement, I replied that I needed no more of his money, and would make my way in life without a cent from him. Furious, dad told me to go to my room, and as I walked up the stairs, he followed and pulled me back down toward him. I turned and balanced myself on the stairs, and right in his face, told him that if he ever laid his hands on me again, either he or I would end up in the hospital or jail.

The whole scenario made no sense to me; he was my dad, the man whose lap I used to sit on as a kid as he rocked me up and down, back and forth. And now, living with him in America was utterly unsettling, and there was no one to talk to about it. The tension increased, and I internalized everything. After that disturbing staircase incident, in the mornings before he left for work, he'd open my door and put some lunch money on my dresser. For a week, the money piled up without my touching it. I'd stayed up in my room and came outside when I heard dad leave the house. After school, I took a jug of water to my bedroom for drinking and didn't use the bathroom when he was home.

Deep inside I was hurt for a few reasons; I couldn't relate and jive with my dad as I did with mommy. I was just getting to know him, and he, me. Under the circumstance of time constraints, it was difficult for either of us to connect with the other. Next, I felt put off by the question from him about mommy sending me to take his money. I was afraid of money and only needed it for what was necessary. Money was something I had internally decided use with caution. The old folk would say, "Money is the root of all evil; there's no telling what a person would do for the sake of money." I had seen a whole country torn apart by those with big money. Such leaders claimed to want to "better" Liberia, but their bettering efforts only left destruction and broken lives. If I were to get money, I promised myself I'd use it to educate people on how to use it for good. For now, all I wanted was to go back home. I prayed mommy would call and tell me the war was over and I could go back home.

Finally, one weekend, my sister—mommy's eldest daughter Cheryl—drove up from Virginia to New Jersey and, after a sit-down chat with my dad, agreed to take me back with her. Dad had reached out to Cheryl for help with me as tensions between us escalated. I hadn't seen Cheryl since she visited Liberia briefly in '94, and when she arrived, I was in a state of trepidation. I blamed the time distance between my dad and me for the tension and feared that such tension could also arise between Cheryl and me. I still hadn't seen Toye or any of my other family members. We were all scattered in a different part of the U.S, and each person was absorbed in managing their own life. It wasn't as easy as driving after work, from Virginia to New Jersey, or Staten Island where Toye lived, to Jersey to see me. At the end of her visit, I got into Cheryl's car without even hugging my dad goodbye. Something had taken over me, and I had no way of understanding it.

Advanced Placement

In Virginia, I started my last year of high school at J.W. Robinson High School. Cheryl was busy with her university work, and I had a little more freedom living with her. I would use her boyfriend Curtis' bike to explore the neighborhood. They told me there were many trails in the area, and I took advantage of them, just to be outside. When I learned the route the school bus made, I started to walk home more after school, taking my time to explore the places around me.

Most of the classes I took were AP (Advanced Placement), or an elective. My AP English teacher, Dr. Hudgins, was an engaging teacher. She made literature like Chaucer's Canterbury Tales and Shakespeare's Macbeth come alive. Her class felt like a discussion room where she'd call upon us to give our thoughts on the book we read. Dr. Hudgins cautioned our class about becoming "mini-mes," only reiterating what we heard from her, and not processing the lessons and seeing where they fit into our own lives. She also introduced us to an author whose work I had seen in Liberia but had not read, Dante Alighieri. We read Dante's "*Inferno*," followed by the book called *Linden Hills* by Gloria Naylor. Linden Hills was a modern version of Inferno, and we had very lively discussions of both books in class.

Mr. Hemmingway, our AP Government teacher, educated us on the American system of government and loved to bring up many fun facts that we could use in daily life. For example, he talked about the Interstate Highway System and how to navigate them. Even numbers on the interstate map usually ran from west to east, and odd numbers ran north to south. He said it was essential to know the directions and connections, so one didn't lose one's way and end up somewhere other than the desired destination. Some highways, like I- 5, were major highways going through a few States like California, Oregon, and Washington; I-405 acted as an auxiliary Highway system. Auxiliary Highway systems, Mr. Hemmingway explained, were only found in one of the states – California – in this case. I was fascinated by the interstate system and studied a map book I bought because I envisioned myself on adventures using these routes. He went into more depth about places I learned about in Geography class in Liberia, like the Pacific Crest Trail, Yellowstone Park,

113

and other U.S landmarks. For a field trip, Mr. Hemmingway took us on a trip to Washington DC, where we got to sit in on the 105th Congress. It was during this Congress —not while we were there—that the impeachment of President Bill Clinton Happened.

I didn't learn much about the Congress that day because I previously made friends with the class clown, a guy who was an expert at creating distractions in Mr. Hemmingway's class. Some students in the class were set on becoming one-day U.S Senators and Representatives, and so were quite serious about learning the subject. I was in that class because my guidance counselor thought that I learned a bit more about U.S History while in Liberia. But this class clown, Marc, we'll call him, was set on lightening the tone of the class. We found it comical when he'd raise his hands and ask to go to the bathroom and "powder his nose," or ask unrelated questions in class. One time someone—we all though it was Marc—brought in, and spilled, a few bottles of Brut cologne in the room before class started. The scent was so overpowering that we had to have class outside on the lawn which meant, in a sense, no class, because of all of the outside distractions.

My Fashion Marketing teacher, Mrs. McDowell, was a fascinating lady who discussed the fashion world with us. There were only two boys in the whole class, but no one minded that, and we seemed to get a lot of attention. We were encouraged to do extra credit by watching TV shows like VH1's *Fashion Television* and giving a report on the episode. We learned about all it took to make and sell an article of clothing. We even did a personal fashion analysis where we would put all of our body specifics, like neck size, shoulder size, length from shoulder to navel, length of legs, and other information into a computer database. Analyzing the data one put in, the computer would then print out a long spreadsheet telling you what type of clothes looked good on your body, or what kind of clothes to avoid.

Mrs. McDowell also had a friend who owned a modeling agency and suggested that I become a model, saying that I had a unique look, being from Africa and all. A few weeks later she invited her friend, Kathy, to speak to our class about the modeling world. I met Kathy that day, and after her presentation, she gave me my very first modeling job, a runway show in collaboration with Seventeen Magazine, at a nearby mall called Tyson's Corner.

I got a job at the local Boston Market fast-casual restaurant, and we were allowed to take some chicken home if there was any left at the end of the day. Not wanting to get fat from eating so much chicken, I decided to become vegetarian. I had dabbled a bit with vegetarianism back in Liberia, although it wasn't a typical thing there. I would just pick out the meat from my food when I ate. I had heard a conversation between mommy and one of her friends that if you wanted to be healthy, you had to cut meat out of your diet and do more exercise. Back in Liberia, I cut meat out and started going for runs and walk on the weekends. My diet didn't last very long, especially when I learned to make Lebanese food. Plus, mommy told me that fish was a healthier choice than meat, and since we lived by the ocean, we were getting the best of the catch.

My vegetarian diet also didn't last long at my dad's house because he told me that meat was necessary for health. He preferred goat meat, since, he said, it had little fat content. I didn't even attempt to not eat meat at the table with him since we ate dinner together. Now, at my sister's house I ate more roots like sweet potatoes and plantains, and Curtis, her boyfriend, liked to cook, and I enjoyed his food. Plus, I could use his bike to get my exercise.

Damn, Jaycee!

One day, while at work I asked a coworker if I could sit in his car and listen to some music he had introduced me to earlier. He agreed, and I went into the parking lot with his keys, turned the car on, listened to the cassette tape. I had skipped Driver's Ed in New Jersey because I had no interest in it, but a curiosity arose in me as I studied the letters on the gear shift. I wasn't a complete fool when it came to driving; I had heard that to start a car, you had to press on the brakes and then shift gears to do what you wanted. So I stepped on the brakes and put the car in "D." I didn't know what "R" or "N" meant. I knew "P" meant "Park" and "D" meant "Drive." I wanted to drive, so I shift the gear to "D," and the car started to roll forward. Excited, and afraid I wouldn't know what else to do, I tried to press the brakes quickly so that the car would stop. Instead, I pushed down hard on the accelerator, and the car went crashing into the tree in front of me.

I had to pay for the damage: $350 for a dent made in the front of the car. I had to use my paycheck for it. My sister was angry at me, but the worse news came from my dad, who wrote me a letter saying that I was a disappointment to his family for doing such a thing. Nothing cut as deep as those words, and I decided that I would look for a better job, and after high school, move out on my own and stop getting in everyone's way and being a disappointment to them.

My breakaway came when I got kicked out of my sister's house a month before graduation. I tried to download America Online, one of the pioneers of the internet, to explore the world around me. In my Computer Graphics class, Fashion Class, or at the school library, we could access the internet under the guidance of a teacher, to research stuff for our homework. What I didn't know was that to use America Online you needed to pay for the services. I wasn't making that much money working two days a week at Boston Market. With some research, I managed to download the AOL folder onto my sister's computer, but never got access to the internet because I didn't have a credit card. When my sister saw the icon on her desktop, it upset her very much, and a verbal fight ensued, which ended in me leaving the house in the car of a friend of mine, Rebekah, who was already on her way to pick me up to hang out. As we took off, something I had never done before happened. I took Rebekah's cigarette from her, took a puff, and blew the smoke out toward my sister's townhouse. I then told Rebekah of my situation, and she talked with her parents to see if I could stay with them for a few days.

I stayed with Rebekah and her family for a few nights and then in a play-ground for three or four more nights, all the while attending school, finishing my schoolwork in the Library and going to my new job at a local music store. The playground wasn't frequently used, so I slept in the playhouse part at the top of the stairs and hid my clothes in a tree. To shower, I used a hand towel with water from the playground's bathroom sink.

Staying with Rebekah's family was the first time I had hung out with a white family in the U.S. Earlier, while at my sister's house and telling others of my interest in modeling, someone, name withheld, had cautioned me, to never forget that I was a black man in America. I snapped back at them and said, "No, I am Jaycee in America." I had taken enough of the racial tension when my teacher told me about it back in Jersey and had no desire to en-tertain it. Furthermore, I saw no connection between being a black man in America and a model. Wasn't Tyson Beckford and black male model?

Soon, other parents heard of my situation and another family, the Graneys, took me in for some time. Their daughter Marin and I were seniors together, and they treated me like a member of their family. The friends at whose hous-es I stayed were mostly girls, but none of us were ever romantically involved. It also wasn't lost on me that staying with girls was a direct rebellion to my dad who didn't want me hanging with young girls outside of school. But as fate had it, I was on my own now. I was a disappointment, and the taste of rebellion had touched my lips, so I blocked out any feeling of guilt for stay-ing with girls.

One day a lady approached me and introduced herself as Mrs. Weedah, a mother of one of the boys at school. She heard that I was staying with dif-ferent families, and asked me to follow her to the school office. She asked if I had a cap and gown for graduation or a class yearbook. Yearbooks had come out, and because I couldn't afford one, I didn't think much about them.

War, Momma and Me

Graduation would be in a few days as well, and I resolved just to pick up my diploma, instead of going to the ceremony. I told Mrs. Weedah I had neither cap and gown, nor yearbook. She then bought me a school yearbook, cap and gown, and gave me some money to attend prom. I never saw that lady again and wish I could thank her one day if she's still alive. A few friends and some teachers wrote in my yearbook, but the line I cherished, and always will, was what my dear friend Marin wrote. It was about me taking life in stride, and how she admired that. She encouraged me to always do so, despite whatever circumstances life might bring.

Prom was a beautiful experience for me. We had dinner at a restaurant in Washington DC called Sequoia. The theme for prom that night was "A Night in Hollywood," and coincidentally, Shaquille O'Neil, as well as Robert Stack, the host of the TV show Unsolved Mysteries, were also at the restaurant having dinner. Their presence made our prom theme more meaningful. My prom date was a girl named Rachelle, whom I had helped to do some research work for our senior prom. I attended graduation, and after the ceremony, I took a bus to Tyson's Corner to stay at a motel my brother Biodun had arranged for me. I had contacted him a few days before, was going to stay with him in Minneapolis. Mentally I prayed not to have to keep dealing with negative incidences with family members.

During the two days at the motel, I decided to go shopping for some fresh clothes with the money I had received from some well-wishers at graduation. I had also won some money from a money-blowing machine at our senior party. It was a cube that you'd step into blindfolded, and then the air was turned on from below, blowing real, as well as fake money around. Time in the cube was limited, and you had to reach around and grab as much as you could. I won about $150 that night after a few tries in the machine. I also had some money left from the $390 I saved up in Liberia. I had nowhere to spend it, so it stayed in my suitcase. I went to Neiman Marcus and headed up to the Men's section. With what I had learned in my fashion class, I figured I could get some key pieces of clothing to have something useful to wear in Minneapolis. High school was over, and I would be looking for a job now.

At Neiman Marcus, I was helped by a young man who gave me all the time and attention in the world, and during our interaction, I felt some weird desires rise in my stomach. It was uncomfortable, but also intriguing. I bought some chinos, a few shirts, as well as some leather pants and a Jean-Paul Gaultier leopard print shirt and Le male cologne. I decided to invite my salesman friend to my hotel after work. I knew the feeling was sexual, and I wanted to explore and experience it. I was, after all, a free man now, wanting to show my dad and sister that I could, in fact, be myself without their per-

117

mission or intervention.

I went to the hotel, showered, and dressed up in my newly bought Jean Paul Gaultier shirt and leather pants, sprayed on some cologne, and waited for my guest to show up. I had no idea what I was doing, but the feeling felt exciting. Looking back, I don't know what possessed me to think leather pants and a Gaultier shirt would be something one wore to a job interview. To my dismay, the guy didn't show up, and I felt jaded and never told a soul about it. I just laid in bed watching TV in my fashionable outfit, wondering what it was that I had done wrong that caused him not to show up. I also felt a bit awkward that I was attracted to a man that way, especially after not making friends with Kevin, the boy from my school in New Jersey for fear of "turning" gay. The feeling didn't scare me; it was just another new feeling for me, and I couldn't experience it because there was no reciprocation from the salesman. I didn't leave the room either because I felt self-conscious in my leather pants and leopard print shirt.

I chuckled to myself thinking what she would say to me if Betty, the girl from school in New Jersey, walked into my hotel room that evening. My leather pants weren't assless, but would she think I had handcuffs? Would Kevin, the guy from school, be pleased to see me in this outfit? Was I even gay now?

Chapter Ten

Jaycee Kesh Akinsanya

Minneapolis Unleashed

My brother Biodun lived in a suburb of Minneapolis, and before getting to his condo, we drove around uptown where he showed me all the happening places in that area. I noticed a spot called Café Wyrd and tried to pronounce the name in my head for the rest of the ride home. We also drove past Lake Calhoun, and he told me that it was a favorite place for running or kayaking. At home, I got to meet his wife, Sharon, their two-year-old daughter, Rae, and his mother-in-law, Amanda. Sharon had a very self-assured presence, was very kind to me, and briefed me on all the fun things to do in Minneapolis, as well as possible job availabilities at the Mall of America, or around town. She seemed to know every little detail about what was happening around town.

I was given free rein to explore Minneapolis and learned of a few clubs I could go to that allowed age sixteen and over on certain days. They would put a wristband on you, which meant that you couldn't drink alcohol. It was at one of those clubs one night that I danced with a guy who ended up kissing me on the lips. It was just a smooch—nothing profound—but the act itself felt liberating. I thought about the "holy kiss" biblical reference, but this guy wasn't my "brother." I had never met him before, and our holy kiss also involved our body pressed tight against each other on the dance floor with no six-inch room in between us for the Holy Spirit. I was in a club where I could do such a thing without reprimand. The next morning at breakfast my brother asked how my night was, and I told him all about it—about the kiss. "Did you like it?' He asked, and I said yes, I did. He told me maybe I was bi, and his wife recommended I meet their gay friend Johannes. Johannes came for 4th of July lunch, and I met him, but we had no connection. They weren't trying to hook us up but just wanted me to have a link to the LGB community.

Minneapolis was very good to me. My brother and his wife knew Prince; she had worked with him in some capacity, and I learned that Prince would invite people to his house every Friday night during his studio jam sessions. I met a friend named Andy, who also knew of these Prince parties, and later in the year I got to attend a handful of those night jam sessions and had such a memorable time. I remember one time in particular when Prince played about six of his songs in a row. He began with more upbeat songs like *Little Red Corvette*, and *Raspberry Beret* and then mellower ones like *Purple Rain*. For number seven, he played "7." The table I was sitting at, a group of young kids who didn't know each other, screamed very loudly at the sound of, *"All seven and we'll watch them fall—ching ching!"* We were hysterical and screamed over everyone else in the studio. After the session, as he walked back into his house area, he stopped at our table and commended us for the enthusiastic cheering. I was high for the rest of my existence; Prince had talked to us, at our table—his table—and asked how we liked the performance. He said he noticed we were obviously having a great time, and so he wouldn't ask if we were. I mean, he was right there! He was small in stature but larger than life in personality and gentleness. He heard us scream and wanted to reciprocate with us. He made us feel like we mattered and he was glad you were on planet earth, as well. I didn't want to shower or wash those clothes ever again. Those clothes were less than three feet from Prince.

I got a job at the GAP at the Mall of America, and there I met some co-workers who invited me to hang with them after work at this place called Café "Weird." When we got to the café, I noticed that it was the same place with the name I had tried to pronounce earlier, Wyrd. We would go there after work, hang out, drink coffee or tea, and it became a regular hang out for me. One day this very beautiful beam-of-light of a guy walked in. He had on a turtleneck and some County Seat Overalls, and he sat next to us with his coffee and took out his books to study. He introduced himself to our table; his name was Tom, and he and I instantly became friends and have been since. Some members of our group went to every 18-and-over club, beginning on Thursdays – Sundays. Because their condo was too small, I moved into Biodun's mom's house which was closer to the mall, and the hangout spots. Biodun's mom, Louise, was very kind to me and gave me the same free rein I needed to blossom. She also had a humorous side to her and we would sit and have many conversations about life. Those times were exciting for me; I was letting life happen with people my age, who were also exploring and enjoying their time with each other.

It was at the Gay 90s Bar that I met another lifelong friend, Ty. We both had a liking for Janet Jackson. Ty was a few years older and had a "real job," working at a local hospital. The rest of us worked retail. On certain days, before going out to the clubs, we would go to Ty's house and get ready for the evening. Ty lived with his parents, who I thought were the coolest parents on earth. They had a gay son and loved him nonetheless. What scared me the most was Ty's driving, especially when he would pull up behind another car at a stoplight. He would pull so close to the next car before braking, and I always felt like we were going to hit the car in front of us. I think he did that just to see the squirming reaction on my face. Ty loved White Castle, and we would drive there almost every evening after clubbing. It was either White

Castle for his burger, or a place called Embers, which we nicknamed "Fembers," because of the gay crowd that went there after the clubs closed.

Later I was recruited from the Gap by the store manager of Victoria's Secret, and then a few weeks later, hired from there by the District Manager of Nine West Shoe stores, only to find out that Tom also worked for Nine West, as well as another guy, Nate. Nate loved theater, wore a trench coat at any time of the day or year, and we would harmonize to many songs, our favorite, "*Tell Him*," by Celine Dion and Barbara Streisand.

At Café Wyrd I also met Brendan, a beautiful soul. Brendan was perhaps the only one of my friends who hung out with me outside of the clubs. We'd go to the parks and sit down and write in our journals, or just walk around town aimlessly. He was very thoughtful and every chance we had, we'd find time to write. Brendan, I observed had an introspective personality about him; like he was happy being around the coffee house crowd, but internally, he was somewhere else. There was something about Brendan's eyes which I admired. They made me feel like if I looked into his eyes long enough, I could see all the worlds and adventures he was thinking about. When the rest of us were loud and rowdy, Brendan was shy and composed.

Minneapolis gave me an array of friends: Brendan, Crysil, Ty, Thomas, Cameron, Boonepon, Andy, Andrew, Jeff, Davers, Jason, Curtis, Nate, Brent, and Togba, another Liberian. We were all one big gang, and we aimed to have fun and stick it to the man, especially the man who hated LGB people. T, Q, and the rest of the letters came way later. We were as cool as we wanted to be; we shopped at any store we wanted to: Contempo Casuals, Gap, Levi's, Abercrombie—anywhere we could mix and match our clothes. Prince's fashion intrigued us, and some of us even tried to wear some women's boots that looked a bit more androgynous.

I hadn't talked to mommy since before leaving high school, but here in Minneapolis I felt more connected to her; I was finally free to express myself again. I had friends, and my brother gave me wings to be myself. It wasn't exactly as I had known it in Liberia, just showing up at someone's house, or sharing foods from the same plates. We had meeting places like Café Wyrd, Ember's restaurant, the malls, and parks where we would associate with each other. Music and dancing was our common stage, and we did a lot of dancing. I found a group of people who I could hang out with, explore life, learn about myself and have some good clean fun.

Ethereal Love

As far as romance, I was still jaded by that Neiman Marcus experience, and I never saw that stud who kissed me at the club again, but I had friends, and that was OK. Later I learned about internet chat rooms and discovered a few, one was for pen pals, and another was called Gaychat. I made a profile on Gaychat and was soon talking to this faceless figure on the other side of the ether world. We got to know each other quite intimately—I got to share my life story with someone quite intimately. And to make our so-called relationship more relevant to the times, Janet Jackson's *The Velvet Rope* album had just débuted, and her song *"Empty,"* was a song I could relate to while chatting with this guy.

"...Your phrases, descriptive and through the textured words with beauty, you post it and use such colored verbs. We've never met..."

My friends and I would go out all night, and work all day, and in the interim, I would chat with my Internet lover. One day this lover and I decided that it would be nice to meet, so I told him he could stop in and visit me at the Gap. I described myself again and told him I'd be the guy greeting customers at the door, so it'd be easy to recognize me. I said that I would be wearing my green gap sweater and some jeans, and I'd talk with him as though I was helping a customer. He said he'd come in at around one in the afternoon. I made a mistake of not asking him what he looked like. The anticipation of actually meeting someone excited me all through the night, and although I hung out with my friends at Café Wyrd, I was on cloud nine waiting for one o'clock the next day to show up.

So, there I was working away, and at one o'clock as planned, I waited with anticipation for my friend to show up. I scrutinized every young guy who came into the store; their height, build, did they pay much attention to me. Was he there, but shy to approach me? Then two, three, and four o'clock showed up, with no sign of him. I thought maybe something had happened to him, and I'd find out later online. I took the bus and headed home after my shift, eager to turn on the computer and ask what the matter was. I skipped the early part of the coffee house and waited online to chat with him. He never replied to my chats ever again. My new favorite Janet song on *The Velvet Rope* became, *"Every time." "I'm scared to fall in love, afraid to love so fast, cuz every time I fall in love it seems to never last...."*

I was hurt. Again. Many questions flowed through my mind, not just from this stand-up, but from the Neiman Marcus experience after high school. I felt unqualified for love and resolved that if I were indeed unqualified to be in a relationship, I would just learn to be satisfied with my friends. From that day on I pulled all energy away from romance and focused on work and friends. My life with my friends went on as usual, and I met more young and adventurous people like myself. One friend Jeffrey and I would walk around Lake Calhoun holding hands, and sometimes people would walk by and say something like, "faggots." We didn't mind; we were doing our best to piss off the radical rights. Another time at the Mall of America a family of 5 entered the elevator with us. We were dressed quite "Prince-ly," and the dad turned to us and muttered, "to the rear of the bus."

Restless

After a while, the fun seemed to hit a plateau, and no matter how many hours we stayed out at night or hung out at the coffee shop, I felt bored and wanted more. A need for adventure welled up in me. We had a summer of beautiful concerts lined up. Janet Jackson was on tour, and we bought tickets to see her in Minneapolis. We sat stage left, balcony second row. What a night that was. It was my first ever concert, other than the jam sessions at Prince's studio. Janet's show was very theatrical, and at one point she sat on a stool and sang a few slow songs. When she sang "*Again*," and came to the lines, "*...don't you stand there and then tell me you love me then leave again...,*" she prolonged the again in a beautiful crescendo. The room was silent, everyone mesmerized by her voice. A few faint whistles sounded in the arena. I screamed, "I love you, Dunk!" She looked in the direction of the voice and nodded approval. I lost it and gave Ty a huge hug. "She heard me, Ty! She heard me!" Dunk was her nickname given to her by Michael, her older brother.

A few days later, another good friend, Dave, invited me to see Shania Twain in concert, which was also a fun time. We knew every song and screamed to our heart's content that evening. Those July nights in Minneapolis were magical for me, although I was feeling a bit antsy. As we left the Arena, I told Dave about my desire to go and explore the world more. I confided in him my desire for a genuine relationship as well, and just needed to "*water my spiritual garden,*" a line from "*Special,*" a song from *The Velvet Rope.*

Dave chuckled at the addition of a line from a song to my desire to explore and said that I lived my life with a theme song playing in the background. Music helped life make a little more sense to me; growing up around mommy was all about music. There was never a day when we didn't have music playing if she was at home. Mom and Rupert sat for hours on the porch after work and sang old songs to each other.

As we walked back to the car after the Shania concert, Dave tried to convince me to stay. He told me he knew someone who may be interested in me. Internally I thought he was just trying to get me to stay and would say anything to make that happen. I later found out that *he* was the person, but at the time I was clueless and couldn't see a friend turn into a lover. I had also closed shop on potential relationships, although I desired one. I had developed my own poker face, playing off romance like I was above it, yet scrutinizing every beautiful or handsome face in the room, hoping for that reciprocating glance. A stare that could un jade me and make me feel sexy, or wanted. I wasn't going to make an effort, so I probably passed up some good relationship prospects.

I wanted to see more of the world. I had the utmost appreciation for my brother and the atmosphere to which he had introduced me. But something was missing deep in me, and I felt pulled to go and find it. One night while sitting at Café Wyrd, I told my friends that I was feeling unhappy in Minneapolis and wanted to leave for somewhere else. I expressed to them that I had reached a plateau with all the fun, and wanted something more. I said, "Just say the name of a place, and I'll go there tomorrow." Brendan, my journaling partner, blurted out, "Seattle; and if you go, I'll come with you." He too had been expressing desires to get out, and the rest of our friends sitting there at the table commended us for our wishful thinking. But the moment Brendan said Seattle was the moment I had already left to go there in my mind. My interests in Minneapolis dried up just like that. I knew nothing of Seattle and had only heard the name from the movie *Sleepless in Seattle*; I had not even seen the movie.

The next day, which happened to be payday, I collected my check from work, bought two Greyhound Bus tickets to Seattle; one for myself, and one for Brendan. I left a detailed note for my brother, explaining to him why I was unhappy and needed to go and find myself. I left the note on the coffee table and yelled up to his mom who was in bed in her room, that I was going to the coffee house. She said goodnight and that was the last time she heard from me. That night our friends stood in disbelief as we boarded the bus, Togba balling his eyes out. Togba cried easily—even a puppy walking by would make him cry. We settled into our seats, and a feeling of the mysterious unknown made me feel focused and calm. I was happy to have Brendan as a traveling companion. I knew we'd find places to sit and write, a new coffee shop, make new sets of friends, and grow into men in Seattle.

The bus drove away, taking us through North Dakota at night, and then

Montana for most of the day. My eyes were glued to the passing world out-side. Montana stretched out for miles in the distance, and I promised myself that I'd come back to see all these places. As I looked on, I wondered what was happening in those towns; who lived there, and what was their lifestyle. The curiosity I had in me as a boy was reawakening, and I could feel my spirit take in as much as it could. We had been listening to our CD players; Brendan listening to Madonna's Ray of Light, and I, of course, to the Velvet Rope, when we pulled into the Billing's Montana Greyhound station. We got out for a minute, and Brendan took his cigarette break. After that we looked around us and simultaneously turned to each other, arms opened wide for a hug. "We're stooooopid, dude," said Brendan, and I chimed in, "Heck yeah, dude."

We were definitely in a different setting; although not yet in Seattle, we could feel and see the beauty of the mountains around us. Brendan didn't talk much during the bus ride. At times, we'd both write in our journals, or put our headphones in each other's ears when a favorite song played. We had about one more day on the bus and then we'd be in Seattle.

Broke Fast

We arrived in Seattle during Seafair, a Summer festival in Seattle involving boat races, U.S Navy flight areal displays, and a series of citywide festivals. All the hotels and hostels were completely booked—all but the penthouse suite at a prestigious hotel. The price was two hundred and something dol-lars, and so I decided we would stay the weekend. We would have to find jobs immediately because the hotel bill ran us broke.

The next morning Brendan suggested that we both split and check out the city and then meet later and write in our journals in a park. I headed for the waterfront area where the Seafair festivities had taken place and walked in and out of the shopping areas on a discovery mission. I met up with Brendan later that day, but he was in a hurry; his dad had found him some work of sorts in Vancouver. I forgot to ask him if it was Canada or Vancouver, Wash-ington. We only had pagers at the time, and so we promised to page each oth-er and keep in touch. I was a bit disappointed that he had to go, but if he was in Vancouver, then it meant we could see each other around and share stories.

As the years went on, and as my life's adventures unfolded, I longed for the day that I would meet up with Brendan, and we'd sit again like we used to at the café and wrote in our journals, or read a book. We would talk about what happened after he left for Vancouver, and I would tell him my adventures in India, Malaysia, Japan, Kenya, and wherever else. We'd talk about the hiking places in America, the Hot Springs, the open road—we'd reconnect and talk about life. A few years ago, Togba told me that Brendan had passed away and that pain struck so deep that I couldn't get out of bed for days. All the adventures I had been on turned to dust that day and blew away. I was encouraged to write a memoir and include them, as I am doing now, but at the time, writing for a different audience seemed like cheating on my journal buddy. All these adventures of mine were meant to be shared with him. We were meant to be sitting in a park somewhere enjoying a beautiful reunion.

Grandpa Christain M Bishop, dressed to a T, at our beach house during construction.

Teenage Gloria in Nigeria.

Handsome Dad,
opposite page
.
My sister Yabo,
cousin Christine,
and me in my
cowboy hat.

Mommy and Toye (left)
in Missouri.

Mommy sitting in a friend's office at Commerce Ministry

St. Peter's Lutheran School, place of the July 31st massacre.
The whole yard is now a mass grave.
Opposite page: The graves of the five murdered nuns. They are now
known as Martyrs of Charity.

Front of my
composite card

This is the photo form a local Seattle magazine brought to Re-Bar that night by my so-called fan.

My favorite picture from my
portfolio.
Opposite page: a photo from my
portfolio I gave to mommy for
Mother's Day.

Chapter Eleven

Jaycee Kesh Akinsanya

Namaste

I had about ninety-two dollars left and found out that there was a hostel, The Green Tortoise, where I could stay for twenty dollars a night. I booked myself in for four nights and went around the area job hunting at local shops. With only twelve bucks to my name, I budgeted to make sure I ate twice a day- two bean and cheese burritos from Taco Bell, ninety-nine cents each. In a week, I should have a job, and then would be able to feed myself.

At the hostel, I stayed in a room with Fred, a guy from Australia, and Leanna and Liz, two girls from Vancouver, Canada. Fred was very peaceful and always had a smile on his face; he had come to visit Seattle for a month and had a few more days to go. He spoke softly and carried on his day very conscientiously. The girls were in town for a week and were heading down the coast. They had come to town for the Seafair weekend and decided to stay a while longer.

After talking for a bit and getting to know each other, Fred mentioned that he was staying at the hostel on a work-trade basis. For two or three hours a day, one could help the hostel like hotel staff, cleaning out vacated rooms. They offered this position to certain travelers who were in town long-term, and he suggested I see if there was an opening while I looked for work and my own place. He also told us that there was a vegetarian communal meal in the kitchen every evening. Some farmers gave away vegetables at the farmer's market in the evenings. There was also a dairy shop where you could get discounted or free products that were expiring that day or the next.

I took advantage of dinner that evening. I was vegetarian; I had finally made my switch to a vegetarian diet toward the end of my stay in Minneapolis. My body and mind felt lighter on a vegetarian diet, and the people I started to associate with in Seattle were all coincidentally vegetarian. As people mingled that evening, I decided to go for a walk by the waterfront and explore a bit more of the city. Since it had been a festive weekend, the town was busy with people so I walked as far as I could away from the crowd. The waterfront looked very beautiful at night; the city lights glistened on the dark liquid and gave it a mysterious feel. Across the water, I could see lights in the distance. I added the site of the distant lights, Bainbridge Island, to my to-visit list and headed back uphill to the hostel.

The next morning Fred woke up very early and invited us to do yoga on the lawn at the waterfront. The girls had some exploring to do, and I decided to

145

join the yoga session. We took our yoga mats to a grassy area next to a Native American totem pole by Pike's Place Market. He taught me how to do sun salutations – yoga poses done to show respects to the sun. We did ten sets of them, and then we headed back to the hostel. Checkout was any time before eleven, so we had time to eat breakfast and relax for a bit before heading to the front desk for our daily tasks. I had already paid for four nights, so my work-stay would begin on Thursday night. I also found out that there was an extended hostel stay connected to the Green Tortoise, where you rented the space on a monthly basis as you settled into the city. This hostel was in the Queen Anne area; I planned to work my way to get a place there. There was a waiting list, and I added my name.

Each day new travelers would arrive, and the meeting of like minds seemed never-ending. Some were young students taking a year off before school; others were on a personal vacation with a budget, others missed their flights and decided to stay the night—so many stories. The locals knew of job availabilities around Seattle, or some distant fishing job in Alaska, which gave me options to consider. But now, during the days, I wandered about Seattle, taking in as much as the city could offer.

One day, having nothing to do, Leanna asked me if I had ever done a past life meditation, which helped a person see from where they reincarnated. She explained that when doing the meditation, it wasn't always one's immediate past life. I heard of such a belief from my mother after her visit to India. Mommy talked about the Indians' belief in reincarnation and practice of non-violence. Leanna suggested I try the meditation with her, and so I obliged, and we sat in a corner. She closed the window to block out the city noise, and her friend Liz left the room. Fred had departed earlier that day. I was very open to this experience; after all, I had come to Seattle to "find myself," and perhaps this could help.

Leanna guided me through a meditative process during which time I found myself in a different space. I glanced at my feet and saw that I was wearing some Arabian style pants, walking through a desert toward a canyon. I seemed to me that I was walking as close as possible to the earth, without actually touching the ground. I couldn't see my face, but it seemed that I was an authority figure who people were delighted to see. At one point an enemy figure came up to me and stabbed me on the shoulder, but I rubbed my hand over the wound, and it disappeared. I was walking toward the canyon's edge on my way to the opposite side, and as I walked, I floated over to that side with no effort. There seemed to be a party going on, and I was dancing with a blue-skinned child who floated around with me in circles.

As Leanna guided the meditation experience, she asked if I had any specif-

146

ic questions, and so I asked to see how I died. I then saw a scene where I was playing a type of soccer game with my friends. I had a green emerald toe ring on, and when I kicked the ball, the ring flew off and fell into the nearby body of water. I went in after it and drowned. We then stopped the meditation, and Leanna guided me back to "Seattle time," and for the next few minutes, we talked about past lives, karma, and reincarnation. I was intrigued by all this but also took it with a grain of salt. It was Leanna who told me I was an old soul, which was why she felt the need to do a past life meditation with me. I had no idea what old soul meant but was ready to experience everything put before me. Leanna and her friend Liz left a few days later.

Four years later during an astrology and tarot card-like reading, by the workings of some supernatural force, I picked a series of cards that my reader explained represented how I previously died. One card had an emerald, and another had a raven with a pail of water. Without my mentioning the meditation with Leanna, the tarot reader told me that I had drowned because of a jewel. I was again told, a third time, by another random person, that she sensed a fear of water in me like I had drowned in a previous life.

Next, at the hostel, I roomed with Natasha from Austria, Nancy, a girl from Pennsylvania, and a guy from London whom we'll name "Abe." We had a room that overlooked a parking lot and could see most of Pike Place Market. Our room was a bit bigger, and the staff liked to hang out with us in there. In a sense, we were temporary "staff," working a few hours a day for our stay. During the day, I'd expand my exploration of Seattle; the Space Needle area, Queen Anne, and Bainbridge Island.

Fortunate Glow

One afternoon as I walked to the Barnes and Nobles bookstore I encountered some unique people. I was close to Westlake Mall, and the street seemed overcrowded that day. In the midst of the hustle and bustle stood a young lady in an Indian Sari, with two bright yellow lines on her forehead, which ended down on her nose in a leaf-like stamp. She had a glow about her that I had not yet seen in the U.S. I've always had a flair for the exotic and here, amongst jeans and t-shirts, suits and dresses, stood this person, apparently not part of some cultural presentation at the square that day. I approached her and saw that she had a few books in her hand. I was beaming with a smile and so was she as we greeted each other warmly. I asked what she was doing, and she told me she lived in a temple and was distributing books on eastern knowledge.

I had about three dollars left to my name, and so I couldn't take a book, but promised her that I would in good time. While talking to her, I looked across the street and another lady, similarly dressed, and equally beaming, waved at me; who were these women? Were there any men? My thought was answered as I looked in another corner and saw a male, dressed as a monk. In total, I saw four of them that day; two men and two women, and their appearance stuck in my memory. I walked on to Barnes and Noble, and then to Taco Bell for my bean and cheese burrito.

On the way back, with the $1.92 I had in my pocket, I stopped and chatted with one of the monks; the ladies had left, it seemed. His name was Alex, and I told him I wanted to donate to his cause. I only had $1.92 and thought to give it all. I would eat, like I had been doing for a few nights, with the crew at the hostel. We had ample vegetables in the fridge from the farmers market to feed me for a few days. He gave me a small book called *Sri Isopanisad* with the face of Vishnu on it. I recognized Vishnu because of the magnet mommy had brought from India.

I saw that Alex had the *Bhagavad-Gita* as well. Mommy had told me about this "Bible" of India and said how different cultures have different conceptions of God, and each had their specific literature. More interestingly, on the Old Road, we lived in a neighborhood of a variety of religious faiths: Muslims, Catholics, Seventh-Day Adventists, Jehovah Witnesses, Mormons, other Christian denominations, Hindus and many others. As far as I know, no one ever persecuted a neighbor for their religious practice. As kids, we'd even mock each other's religious cultures, joking about how the Muslims had to do gymnastics while praying three times a day; and my Muslim friends would in turn joke that our Catholic priest drank all the wine from us and gave us dry bread. We'd tell our Seventh-Day Adventist friends who went to church on Saturdays that they didn't know how to count the days right because the Lord's day was on Sunday.

Where I come from, the people I knew would joke about everything, and when I arrived in America, it seemed odd that some people I met took things very sensitively and personally. I began to speculate that perhaps joking was hard because of some of the tensions in people's lives; maybe regarding race, sexuality, or economics. I find that to this day, twenty-three years later, I am still learning how to safely navigate my way in getting to know people on a personal level. I have come to see, though, that when a barrier or boundary is let down, the tensions those boundaries caused also drop. Joking and cussing were just a regular part of life around the people I knew in Liberia; if there was ever a physical fight between people, moments later peace was remade. If people had grudges or bones to pick, you hardly ever saw it manifest. Except for the wars.

Anyway, when Alex gave me that book, I felt like I had given him very little for the book and promised to give him more when I got paid. The next day I landed a job at the Pike's Place Bar and Grill as a host, and I was happy to be employed again. But paychecks wouldn't be for two weeks, and I also wouldn't get tips from the waiters until Friday, so I was a bit broke for a few days.

When I got home that day, I laid in bed and read *Sri Isopanisad*, and from the start, I found myself in philosophical agreement with all that I read on the first few pages. Paraphrased, it said: *God is a perfect being, and everything emanates from him, including the phenomenal world, and no matter how many worlds and creatures emanated from "him," "he" remained the perfect balance. Furthermore, everything belonged to God, and we each are given assets as our quota; to stay balanced and happy meant that one should be satisfied with his quota, and not encroach on that of others.*

I had heard mommy speak like this many times when she would say, "Everything comes from God; people just worship God differently." Or "I have my charge to keep and my God to glorify, and you have yours." In fact, it wasn't just something she said. It was something practical; she encouraged godliness, regardless of where you resonated with divinity. Mom was a Methodist, my stepdad a Baptist, and I went to the local Catholic Church. During Ramadan or Eid, we'd celebrate with our Muslim neighbors, as well as Passover or whatever other festivals our neighbors celebrated. I had no idea of the religious tensions that occur until I left Liberia and came to the more "developed" world.

I remember a conversation which took place because I was being lazy and hadn't cleaned our room for perhaps two weeks. Mom looked in and asked how we could live in such filth; hadn't we ever heard the phrase, "cleanliness is next to Godliness?" I said to her that I didn't believe in God that week, so the room can wait a bit. She retorted, "So you will sell your soul to the Devil just to not clean your room? Lord, look at this heathen, can you "emmajine?" I promised her that when I felt the Holy Spirit and became a believer again, I'd clean up. She suggested another method; she could voluntarily spank the Holy Spirit into me much faster than me waiting for the spirit to come upon me. I replied that I had converted to Islam, but Gloria—the ever-witty Gloria—said, "Well good, you just raised the cleanliness bar higher; your new people bathe three times a day. For them, cleanliness *is* Godliness." I cleaned the room, pronto.

So there, in my hostel bed, as I read, I too began to beam with excitement about the knowledge I had come across. It resonated with home, with what I

149

had heard and seen. I felt again like there was a bigger connectedness in the world than I had experienced in my last few years as a high schooler in the US. I hadn't recognized the connectivity as a child; it was just a part of life, undisputed and undiscussed. I read as much as I could, shared a paragraph or two with my roommates, and went on about my day. The book was going to be a quick read since I enjoyed it so much, and I knew I would want more, but I had no money and would have to wait a few days for tips. However, that very night a series of fortunate events unfolded.

Riches, Abe, and Me

My English roommate Abe and I sat by the front desk chatting with the girl on duty; he was down to one dollar, and I had just given my last $1.92 to the monk earlier in the day, so we were talking about finding some odd jobs. The phone rang, and the girl answered, chatted for a minute, and put the caller on hold. On the line was a guy looking for someone to do some quick painting work. He had hurt his back and needed a few hours' worth of help. One small problem—the job would be on Capitol Hill— the designated "LGB" area of town.

Although I was "bi," I felt the need to keep it under wraps since I lived with a variety of people. My friends at the hostel didn't care, nor did I give a damn, but something just stopped me from being open. Brendan had left me by myself; he was the closest thing I had near me to family and had come with me on this journey. Now it was just me in a city meeting new people. I was confident and open, but cautious since the hostel had an influx of guests. I felt it was better just to be me without advertising of my sexuality. In Minneapolis, we were young punks "sticking it to the man"; we had power in numbers. In Seattle, I was on my own.

My English friend was a bit leery of the late-night house-painting proposal in the "dodgy" section of town, but we were broke, and we thought up a plan to defend ourselves should we be sexually assaulted. If anything happened, one of us—or both—would scream as loudly as possible to get help. We bragged to each other about being from London and Africa and knowing some fighting maneuvers. We were also nineteen. We agreed to the painting proposal, and the girl at the desk told the guy we would do the work. Pay was decided upon to be $350 split between Abe and me. We'd have a few more bucks, and I would save up for my apartment. When the doorbell rang, and we headed downstairs to meet our job guy, we both froze as this humongous beast of a man got out of his pickup truck to greet us. My heart was racing, and I could see Abe's subtle expression of someone very close to shitting his pants. But we had agreed to go, even though this guy looked like he could crush us both with one hand.

As we drove to Capitol Hill he told us how appreciative he was for our help, especially at such a late hour, but his wife—HIS WIFE, PHEW! His wife wanted him to rest his back and was a bit angry at him. He had a deadline to meet and therefore sought help. A sigh of relief left our bodies, and we could trust and work with the guy. He had a wife. We walked up to the apartment he was painting, and everything had already been laid out. He had each paint bucket where he wanted it, and everything was taped off and set. He only needed one room painted, not the three already prepped rooms. It was now close to midnight, and he bid us goodnight and said he'd pick us up in the morning. Excited, we painted the room fast—and well. We also decided that since we had time, we'd help him out and paint the rest of the walls he had prepped.

We were just about done with the bathroom as the sun came up. Being 19 meant we could handle staying awake for days on end; we had the energy, and so we painted. The door opened, and our incredible hulk of a man person walked in to find us wide awake. What he saw were three well-painted rooms. He stopped, examined everything, and then broke into tears of gratitude. He couldn't believe we stayed up all night painting. The man cried like a baby for a few minutes as we stood there telling him it was no big deal. He said that it was, and this meant he could take the day off and rest some more. To our surprise, he gave us $350.00 each! We couldn't believe our eyes and thanked him for such a gift. We were back in business and could rule the world again.

Radha, God's Girlfriend.

The next day, with all my riches budgeted for the next month and some to spare, I headed to Westlake Mall to find Alex, the monk, or one of the ladies to get more books. I told Alex I had come into some cash and wanted as many books as he could give me for fifty dollars. He gave me one copy of every book he had, and I thankfully walked away, off to delve deeper into my newfound lust for the Orient. I also met another monk that day, Jayananda, who invited me to a pizza dinner that Wednesday. I asked if it was ok to bring friends and he obliged. When I got back home, Natasha, my roommate from Austria looked at me and said, "Dude, you're glowing!" I was! I was happy to be carrying all these books with me. Now I'd have the afternoons to sit at the waterfront and read as much as I could before work. I invited all of them to the "temple" for pizza dinner the next day. Abe agreed, but Nancy from Pennsylvania and Natasha had other plans. Abe and I seemed to make adventures happen—the paint job was proof —so he was eager to see what this other thing was all about.

I was off work the next two days, Wednesday and Thursday, and so Abe and I wandered about Seattle for a little bit and then headed to the "temple." We thought we'd get there early; after all, these guys extended an invite, and we wanted to at least offer some help in the kitchen. We took the bus from the tunnel under Nordstrom and headed to the University district, got off on University Avenue and then walked for about a mile to the temple address.

In my mind, I had expected an elaborate building in Eastern architecture, with gardens and ponds as we see in Zen garden books. Instead, we walked up to a big house on a corner lot, matched the address with the one we had in tow, and knocked at the door. A monk I had not yet met opened the door, introduced himself, and ushered us in. The meditation hall was a large room, one which, in a regular house setting would be the living room. The space was immaculate and had cool artwork on the walls. We told the monk, Jaya Sacinandana das, that we were invited for pizza dinner that evening, but showed up early to help with any preparations. He thanked us and let us help him in the kitchen with grating cheese. In the sunroom, I saw the lady I had first met, Laxmipriya dasi, tending to some plants. She came in and greeted us, chatted for a few minutes and then again went back to tend to the plants.

Boy did we have questions for the monk that afternoon and evening. It seemed like he gave us a full lecture in the kitchen long before his next talk that evening preceding dinner. The best part was that I didn't have to force the answers to make sense. They just did. I was vegetarian, and so were the monks, but they had a different philosophy on vegetarianism. They recognized the fact that our existence involves one being subsisting on another. Even while walking, he explained, so many living entities on the ground get crushed to death without us knowing. While breathing, we might take in bacteria that die in our mucus. These were deaths we indeed caused but had no control over. The Vedic concept was to limit the violence as much as possible. Plants are also living creatures, but in a lot of cases the vegetables, fruits, or grains gave seed to replant. Animals also gave offspring, but if it came down to choosing to end the life of a cow or carrot, they decided on the carrot.

Furthermore, Krsna, whom the Vedas considered the Supreme Personality of Godhead —he quoted a Sanskrit verse—*krsnas tu bhagavan svayam (Lord Krsna is the original Personality of Godhead)*, only asks for fruits and vegetables to be offered to him. The offering could be as simple as *patram, (leaf) puspam (flower) phalam (fruit) toyam (water)*. But the offering didn't matter if it didn't have a crucial ingredient, *bhakti (love)*. Therefore, their reason for eating a vegetarian diet was because Krsna ate vegetarian foods. "If *Bhagavad-Gita* told us, chicken, steak, fish, or shrimp (he tried to say those words to match the Sanskrit meter, and we all laughed), we'd fill the fridge with all those things. Our goal is to love Krsna, and whatever he requests to eat, that we'll serve him." I could understand the principle of selflessness in their vegetarian lifestyle; they loved Krsna, and according to their text, he likes fruits and vegetables.

Alex asked why they drank milk since we were grating cheese. Jaya Sacinandana explained that Krsna loves the cow, and in the spiritual world where he lives, he tends to billions of cows. God is a cowherd boy, and he likes to drink milk. The cow gives ample milk for both the calf and others. Things got a bit serious when he said that cow killing was the greatest sin humankind could ever commit. The cow is the most useful animal; the bull plows the field for growing vegetables and eats only grass as its pay. Cows give milk, which we use to make many products such as yogurt and cheese. The cow dung provides fuel for cooking, and the cow's urine is highly antiseptic. I wasn't going to be using cow dung or urine anytime soon, but I had heard of different products made from cow urine. We had lots to think about during this conversation, mostly things we'd not heard before in mainstream society.

Reincarnation made more sense to me after I had the experience with Leanna. According to their scriptures, the soul is what animates the body. It has an existence independent of the body. He explained that the physical body changed—as in babyhood, youth hood, and adulthood —but the person inhabiting the body remained the same. I thought about mommy when he said that if you went away from home at age ten, but came back at age thirty, your mom would still recognize you, even though your ten-year-old body looked different from your thirty-year-old one. Alex chimed in that science tells us that the body's cells changed over every seven years, so it made sense that the body changed as well. Jaya Sacinandana then broke down the word reincarnation, before we asked him more questions. *Re- again, in- within, carnis- flesh (like chili con carne)*. It meant, simplified, in the flesh again. My love for breaking things down to their simplest form led me to ask him the meaning of "*Namaste*." Some said it meant, "the divine in me embraces the divine in you." Others gave more elaborate explanations. I wanted the sim-ple, easy meaning of the word. "*Namas*," means *bow*, as in bow and arrow. It also means as the bow does when you pull it to you, *to bow. Te* means *you. Namaste's* simplest translation is "*I bow to you*."

153

Living simply and cultivating higher knowledge clicked with the no encroaching policy I had read earlier in the Isopanisad. I also had the simple-living experience during the civil war. Although the circumstances were dire, we never felt lacking. We had food to eat, clothes to wear, and a place to sleep. And I had the luxury of many books to read. These monks voluntarily chose a simpler lifestyle in a society where many things were advertised as "needs." Their monastery—house—didn't "need" a living room set, but invited me to grab one of the mats in the corner and sit cross-legged. They didn't have many gadgets, like pagers, just a regular house phone. Studying their surroundings, I noticed that things were clean and simple.

The best of the lessons came when Abe finished grating a brick of cheese and chucked the final piece into his mouth. For most, it's a regular kitchen habit, but the monk admonished him. He said, "Normally we don't eat anything in the kitchen during preparation; we want to make it purely and let Krsna taste it first." Abe asked, "How do you know your preparation has the proper taste then if you don't try it?" "Well," Jaya Sacinandana continued, "Krsna is the master of all mysticism, so when you're cooking for him, he guides you as far as how much spice to use." He said that it was a matter of loving exchanges; the beloved wants to cook something for the lover, and wishes that beloved be the first to taste it. Regardless of taste, the main ingredient was love; common sense will tell you not to put a full spoon of salt or pepper in a small dish. He explained that when the food was ready, they made a plate for Krsna and put it on the altar for him and Radha, his consort, to eat. It was an act of offering and giving thanks. Radha? Who's that? Consort?

"Yes, God has a girlfriend, and her name is Radha." He said their movement was known as "Hare Krsna," because they were seen chanting and dancing on the streets, but the chanting was meant to invoke a spiritual presence in a hectic environment. "Hare," in "Hare Krsna" is the female energy or potency of the divine couple. In the west, we have a very male-centered concept of divinity, but in the east, there is a balance. The absolute truth is not limited to a male form. In fact, the absolute can take on many forms or incarnations to fulfill "his" purposes and pastimes. I was intrigued now and wanted to hear more.

He continued to explain that philosophies which depict a lonely God, or a God with just one offspring are incomplete. These philosophies are often projections. Any of us in the room could have as many children as we wanted, or as many lovers as we wished to, but God was limited to just one son; a son he had to use immaculate miracles to beget as if he was hiding from someone. As for us, we didn't like his son's message, so we killed him. The Western philosophies, he explained, portrayed a harsh and angry aspect of God. But there are steps in God realization, and some people need specific sets of understandings to feel fulfilled. I laughed when he said, as far as projection, "if you ask a rat what God looks like, he'd tell you God is a huge rat, and that Heaven is a place with large blocks of cheese and no rat traps."

What an experience that evening was; associating with others who were philosophical without fighting and screaming at the table, talking about topics with calm clarity, and eating good food; I was intrigued. The next day Natasha asked me about my experience the night before and as I told her about the evening, our room filled with the scent of sandalwood. We were both a bit intrigued by the smell; where was it coming from? The outside parking lot didn't smell like it; the halls didn't, neither of us had incense burning. We continued chatting about the temple experience, and then after we stopped talking, the scent disappeared.

Jaycee Kesh Akinsanya

Chapter Twelve

It Burns!

That Thursday evening, I revisited the temple and told Jaya Sacinandana about the sandalwood smell incident. I was interested in hearing what he said and was blown away by his answer. "It is said that Krsna's favorite scent is sandalwood; maybe he was in the room listening to you guys talk about him. Like any of us, God also likes to hear people talk about him." My room? Was God in my room? Yeah right.

As we chatted, I asked why the monks had the tuft of hair on the back of their heads, and he jokingly told me that it was what Lord Caitanya, an incarnation of Krsna, grabbed to "drag" you back to the spiritual realm. At that time, all your karma burned up and you took on a spiritual body. He then explained that actually, the sikha on the back of the head was a "flag" of identification of a specific school of philosophical thought in India.

When I went to work on Friday, the chef that day was in good spirits and teased me a little about my new "Krsna" friends. "Maybe you'll wear those robes too, man, and chant all day and be bright-faced and happy. Those guys are happy every time you see them like they have some species of pot that keeps you always high and happy." We laughed at the thought of me being a monk, but it was something I considered, except I couldn't see myself living my whole life as one. And yes, why were they so happy?

Later that evening when the restaurant was empty, and he was doing some kitchen prep work, he continued to mimic the Krsna chant in the kitchen. I chuckled as I stood at the door waiting for guests. All of a sudden in the middle of his Krsna chant I heard, "Shit! Fuck!" Looking through the window to see what the matter was, I saw that he had chopped into his thumb and there was blood on the chopping board. I was a bit freaked out but stayed until the end of the evening. Luckily there were no customers in the restaurant when it happened. A few people were at the bar, but it was in another corner and had music playing, so I don't think anyone heard him. After work, I went home with my tips and sat in my room, feeling freaked out by the whole hand chopping experience. The chef was obviously absentminded when he chopped into his thumb. Something about this didn't sit right with me. I felt like I had caused him to cut himself because I entertained his mimic of the monks, thus distracting him.

The next day I called in sick, and the manager, a very cool lady, said to me, "Dude, I know you're probably not coming back. I'll bring your paycheck over to the hostel. That was a strange incident last night. You guys were laughing, and then all of a sudden, things got serious. I saw your discomfort as you stood by the door." Indeed I did not feel like going back. No one was rude or treated me wrong at the restaurant. Something just caused me to lose interest in going back. I had about 700 bucks and figured I could coast for a little bit in between jobs. That day went on, as usual, cleaning up the hostel, walking to the Space Needle, and sitting in a park. I didn't have to work now, so I filled my day with things I used to do before my job started. That night, after a nap, around eleven, I woke up with a very high fever. I felt like my body was on fire, and I laid in bed wondering what to do. I didn't feel sick internally, my mind was ok, but my body burned.

Nancy, my roommate, came in and saw that I was up, and we chatted for a second. I asked her if she had a thermometer because I felt like I had a fever. She touched my skin and told me that my skin felt normal, but to me, I was burning up and couldn't understand how she felt a "normal" skin tempera-ture. One by one, other roommates came in, and the same thing happened, each with the same conclusion—my temperature felt fine. Even after a ther-mometer check with a normal reading, my skin still felt to me like it was burning up. And for some reason, I started to think that maybe I was being "dragged" back to the spiritual realm, and my karma was being burned off. Without a second thought, I looked at my roommates and told them that I was going to move into the temple the next day. "Maybe you do have a fever," one of them chuckled. Another hostel worker, Pierre, from Montreal, was in the room and challenged that if I was moving into the temple, could he have my CDs and cool shoes and other stuff. I was quite OK with the proposal and gave away a whole bunch of fancy things that night.

The next morning, I called the temple and asked Jaya Sacinandana if I could come over. I didn't tell him I wanted to move in, nor did I ask his permission. I just showed up with my bag, a yoga mat, and a very excited demeanor. When he opened the door, I told him my plans, and he, seeing my eagerness, just let me. That day I moved into a monastery to live as a monk, robes, tuft of hair on the back, bright face, dancing in the streets and all!

It was all fascinating for me, and I took in the experience like a dry sponge sucking up water. A few monks were living in the house who I hadn't met before moving in the temple. Their house reminded me of home. I didn't find any of their practices unusual. I slept in a room with four or five other people before. I had taken a cold shower before, and I had been trained by mommy to wake up at four every morning. Most of the monks were up getting ready for the morning meditation which began at 4:30 a.m.

Each monk had a service to do as a way of earning their keep. One did

160

managerial work, and another did mechanical; others cooked, and others kept the house clean. A few times a week everyone was encouraged to distribute pieces of literature, as I had seen them doing when I first met them.

The first two lessons I learned at the temple were "know your position," and "no one is irreplaceable." There had to be some form of etiquette in the monastery; some monks had been monks for ten years, or five years and some visiting monks had been monks for thirty or forty years. Learning how to associate with these different levels of monks was necessary, so as not to be too familiar or disrespectful. The monks were kind, and any of them easily started conversations to get to know me, and I inquired about how they became monks. But earning their friendship wasn't automatic; it required time and dedication to the process.

And yes, no one was irreplaceable. Although we all were individuals learning to live a life connected to ancient Vedic philosophy, we were cautioned not to have an air of arrogance about ourselves. As Jaya Sacinandana put it, "If you become proud, and think you're the best cook, or best sweeper, you'll soon find that someone else can do it better than you." And finding out that someone could do it better creates envy in most cases. Monks aren't meant to be envious; they are supposed to engage in loving exchanges with each other and other living beings.

I also learned to distribute spiritual literature with the rest of the monks and had some fascinating experiences. Around a few people, I can be as extroverted as possible, but when a crowd gathers, I tend to become very introverted. Having to go into town was very difficult for me. I loved what the message in the books was saying, and wanted to give it to others, but I found it difficult to be out around people, approaching them and asking for donations for a book. I tried my best to surrender to the process. I told myself that it was perhaps hard for many of the other devotees to be out in public as well. They were my spiritual family now, and so I wanted to earn my keep with them.

To make matters worse, sometimes people on the streets were plain difficult. Some would walk by and mock us; others would point to the yellow markings on our faces and say things like, "You've got bird shit on your face, dude." The marking, called tilak, is made from mud taken from holy bodies of water. A lady walked across the street toward me one day, and pointing to my robes, in a loud voice said, "What are you wearing, man?" "It's called a dhoti," I replied. "You have draws on under there?" "Yes, I do." "Well, let me see em!" "No!" She didn't notice that her loud voice had called the attention of people walking by, and when I said, "No," they all laughed at us.

161

Renee

On one occasion, I stopped a lady who was on her way to catch her ferry after work. She had some time to spare, so she chatted with me. She carried something in her hand that looked like a soft leather briefcase. She asked me what I was doing, and I told her that I was a monk, distributing spiritual literature from India. She said that she was a Christian and that her God was a jealous God, and wanted no other gods being worshipped. I tried to tell her that God was one, and the literature was just another culture's way of viewing divinity, but she stayed on the "angry God, jealous God," train. I opened one of the books, and showed her a picture of Krsna, sitting by the river, playing on his flute. The Vedic concept of God is that he has an ever-youthful form. "This is the Vedic concept of God, mam." She looked at the picture, stared deep into my eyes, and said, "This little girl is your God? I'm outta here." She turned and did a walk away that reminded me of Aunt Esther from Sanford and Son with Redd Foxx.

A few days later, the same lady walked by, this time in a jovial mood. "You're still standing out here, boy? Didn't I tell you God don't like no false Gods?" I sensed the joking in her voice, so I told her not to tell her God what I was up to. I asked her why the happy mood, and she told me it was her daughter's birthday and she was off to celebrate with her. I had a vegetarian cookbook that the Krsna movement printed, called, "Higher Taste." I handed her a copy and asked her to give it to her daughter and wish her a happy birthday. I told her it was just recipes, and some reasoning in the first part of the book, about why we were vegetarians. She accepted the cookbook and told me I was a very nice man. She bid me farewell, and as she left, I said, "Thanks, Renee." She stopped in her tracks and turned toward me.

"What did you just call me?"

"Renee," I responded.

"My name is Tabitha Renee Johnson, and no one knows my middle name. How did you know it?

"Maybe I'm psychic," I said playfully.

"Psychic? You mean, that's not of the devil?"

"I don't think it is. I've been meditating lately, and my intuition has been pretty strong, so maybe I just guessed your name."

"Meditation?"

"Yes. I'm a monk, and we meditate."

"Well, where can I learn that? Do these books talk about it?"

"Some do. The *Bhagavad-Gita* is one of the oldest books and some parts talk about meditation."

"Can I have them? Here's fifty dollars, how many of these books can I have for fifty dollars?"

I gave her a copy of each book I had, remembering a time I had also given fifty dollars for the books Alex had. She gave me a big hug, thanked me for what I was doing out there, and left with her books. I stood bewildered. How in the world did I know her name was Renee? What just happened? Wasn't her God a jealous God?

Of all the people I met in downtown Seattle, there was a young girl, Nora, who took her bus from downtown every day. She would stop and sit and talk with me and other monks for long periods, and then bid us goodbye. She was studying photography and would take my picture while I was out on the street talking with people. Nora and I became very good friends and still are to this day.

Kesh

One day I learned that the teacher of the monks I lived with would be visiting for a few weeks. He had been a Krsna devotee since 1972, was a Jesus scholar, and was writing a book which looked at Jesus from a Vedic perspective. I was eager to meet him. His students, these monks I lived with, made me feel like I was a part of something, and I wanted to meet their teacher. When he arrived that weekend, other Krsna devotees and students of his from Portland and Eugene, Oregon, came as well. He was German, with a Santa Clause belly like my dad's and had a bright smile about him. His name was Prithu Das. When a person received formal initiation into the Krsna culture, they were given a name from the scriptures, and the term "das" was added to their name. "Dasi," the female counterpart, was added to a woman's name. Das means "servant." Krishna das means "servant of Krsna." And Krishna dasi would mean the same, but with the "i" added at the end. It was similar to a Catholic person taking on the name of one of the saints at baptism. I had, in Liberia taken on the name Raphael, after baptism.

Prithu sat on a raised seat, a little elevated from the floor, and leaned against the wall very casually, like someone who had just been traveling for a

163

long time. It was late in the evening when he arrived, and he spoke for about ten minutes. He began his speech with a Bible verse that was very familiar to me: "Like Jesus says in the Christian faith, 'the lilies in the fields neither spin, nor do they weave, yet King Solomon in all his glory wasn't arrayed like one of these lilies. Or the birds, they don't sow, nor do they reap...'" Tears filled my eyes. That passage in the Bible, Matthew 6:25-34, was mommy's favorite passage, and she quoted it many times during the war. Many times. He also spoke about the value of taking up some aspect of spiritual life to bring clarity to one's daily affairs.

When I was introduced to him, the first thing he said was, "Wow! He's so black! Very dark. Are you from Africa? When I was a child, I saw a black boy with his parents, and I went home and asked my mother to make me black. I wanted to be black." Everyone laughed at this, and he encouraged me to continue my study of the Vedic scriptures, "There's much to learn about various topics in the Bhagavad-Gita and Srimad Bhagavatam. We have many books, and you can learn about cooking, astrology, yoga, astronomy, culture, martial arts, so many things." I thanked him, and the night continued.

I asked Prithu if he could accept me as one of his students, and the next fall, 1999, he gave me formal initiation as a Krishna devotee and monk. He named me Jaya Kesava Das, meaning "the glorious servant of Kesava." Jaya, meaning, glorious, reminded me of mommy's name, Gloria. I had made some good friends with the monks, and some nicknamed me JK, Jaya Kesh, and some called me Kesh. Years later after I reunited with mommy, and she heard the name Kesh, she told me that Kesh meant hair, as in a horse's mane. She said since I was born in the year of the horse (Chinese astrology), and had a wild horse nature, the name fit me well. Krsna is known as Kesava because of an incident where he killed a demon named Keshi, who had assumed the body of a horse. I asked mom if I could legally add Kesh to my name, and she said it was my name to do with as I pleased.

A few months later, in December, the temple phone rang one morning, and one of the monks, Deva, picked it up. He then handed me the phone and told me that it was my dad on the line. My dad? How did he even know where to find me? Not even my brother knew where to find me. I wasn't using my pager anymore; I had it in a box somewhere. I picked up the phone and spoke with him. Dad was cordial, and asked me to go and visit my sister Yabo, who had now graduated from Medical School at Rutgers, and was now living in Atlanta. I agreed, but still wondered how he got my number. After I hung up, I spoke with some of the monks, and they encouraged me to reconnect with my dad. They said at least he will be able to see that I was OK and not doing anything negative in my life.

I visited Atlanta for Christmas, and it was nice to see my family. My sister Yabo had just gotten married and had a two-year-old daughter, Sedia. My stepmom, Olive, was also there. Everyone, except my dad, asked questions about my life, and I was happy to answer what I knew about living in the monastery. On Christmas Eve, as we chatted with some other family members who stopped by to visit, someone again asked me about my life, but my dad interrupted. He expressed how he wasn't so happy with me living in a Hindu monastery; our family was Christian. Africans were Christians. I responded that actually, Africans weren't historically Christians and that Christianity came to Africa. I talked about and asked everyone to recall the fact that previously, Africans, in many regions, understood divinity from a different perspective. I wasn't trying to argue about whether there was a "one true God," I was merely correcting the fact that Africans were not initially Christians.

Then came the subject of vegetarianism. My stepmom had been trying to accommodate my diet so that I would have something to eat, since, well, the next day was my birthday. She also baked a rum cake that I am still addicted to. She promised that the alcohol evaporated during the baking process, and the cake was, therefore, ok for me since I didn't drink alcohol. Dad got more worked up. "Your mother raised you with access to the best fish right there by the ocean; the fishermen gave her first pick. Chicken — your grandfather had goats and pigs, and chickens — but now you've decided to eat grass!" He was furious, and I only added insult to injury when I retorted, "Don't forget, I eat leaves and flowers too, dad." My dad's eyes burned with anger; he could have sent me to Hades that day. To top it off, when I said my "leaves and flowers" line, everyone else laughed hysterically. I truly meant it as a joke, but dad wasn't joking. "Well," he said, "Go back to your Hindu people and let them take care of you."

"They've been taking care of me for a few years now, dad. Where were you?" This time I was upset and decided to go to my room, but dad wanted to talk more. I ignored him and turned to my sister and stepmom and said, "If he keeps being this negative, I will leave here, and he won't see me ever again; not even at his funeral." They both asked me not to say such a thing, but I left and went upstairs crying. Later, my stepmom came into the room and consoled me. "You boy, your father's just grumpy sometimes. That's why he lives up there in Jersey by himself." Later that evening, for the first time in a few years — since I left my sister's in Virginia — mommy called to wish me a happy birthday. I was too worked up to chat much with her. I told her what had happened between dad and me, and her response was similar to that of my stepmom: "You boy, your pa is just grumpy, don't mind him."

165

I went back to Oregon a few days later, and told the monk, Deva, who had answered the phone when my dad called, what had happened. He advised me to be forgiving to my dad and said that it's a hard pill to swallow when kids went against the family grain, especially when it came to religion. He understood the Nigerian Yoruba culture of the father being the maker of decisions in the family, and my being in the monastery was not his decision for me. He said the best thing I could do was pray for my dad during my meditations and see what Krsna wanted our relationship to be.

The most beautiful aspect of the life I lived in the monastery was the people with whom I lived. We were all from different backgrounds and had different interests, even in Krsna culture. One lady, Nikunja was a quantum physicist and gave a memorable lecture one night. She talked about discovering the soul through quantum physics. It was one of the most intriguing discourses I had ever heard. In the audience was an older gentleman who was a retired professor from a nearby college. He had also studied quantum physics and was very impressed with Nikunja's lecture. "How old are you?" He asked. "Don't tell me your age, ladies don't tell their ages, but you're no older than my grand-daughter. I've never heard someone give such a clear explanation, connecting spirituality and quantum." We were very proud of Nikunja that night. She was very shy and had been almost commanded to give the lecture that night.

"We were kids back then just looking for the bliss

a ragtag band of transcendentalists."- Michael Cassidy

Nocturnal Capacity

In the Spring of 2000, after living in the temple and learning that I didn't have to be a monk for life, I asked permission to move out and be a regular part of society. That option was available, and I thought the time had come for me to use it. I had immersed myself wholeheartedly, without a plan b, or exit strategy. I wanted the full experience and knew that when the time came – if the time came – I would stop living in the monastery like I would stop eating lunch when I was satisfied. I didn't need any explanations or justifications; when I was ready to move on, I would say so. Years later, mommy would laugh at my attitude of "stopping eating when I'm satisfied," and say, "You waltz to your own music." But I was her son, wasn't I? Wasn't she the one who always said that a person was free to say yes or no at any time in their lives? I gave the monastery a yes time, and now, I was ready to exit the stage.

The experience was magical for me. Through the mixing of regulated eating, sleeping, and recreation, with meditation, study and practical self-observation, I achieved a type of focus that caught one of the monks, Deva, off-guard. The monastery had moved to the Mt. Hood area of Oregon, and we had a small center in Seattle where I would spend most of my time. I was more suited for outreach, so I liked staying in the city. One day, while I sat and studied, Deva called from Oregon, and I answered the phone, "Hare Krsna, how may I help you?" "Who is this?" Came Deva's voice, confused as to who had answered the phone. "It's Kesh," I replied. "Keshi! You sounded different- so focused and mature, very deep." "Me??" "Yes, like you've achieved a calm mental state." We chatted a bit about why he called, and when he hung up, I became introspective, trying to understand what Deva had heard in my voice.

I was calm. I had spent the last few weeks reading "*The Teachings of Queen Kunti*," philosophical thoughts of Kunti, the mother of Arjuna of the *Bhagavad-Gita*. Her ideas were very practical, to the point, and easy to understand. My day, for those few weeks, consisted of early rising at three in the morning, meditation, breakfast, outreach, *Teachings of Queen Kunti* reading, visiting with the other monks who lived at the center and then in bed by eight in the evening. Life was simple, and I set a time for everything I did, and that focus showed even in my voice. I had been in that space before, but this was the first time he caught it and was quite impressed.

What I never revealed to the monks, was the experience of nocturnal emissions that plagued me. The bewilderment that started in my teenage years was still there with me. Even after I learned more about what wet dreams were, a feeling of being contaminated came over me when it happened. In the monastery, I felt incomplete, like one of those well-sculpted statues in Rome that had its penis chiseled off and replaced with a fig leaf. Monastic life called for a level of purity, and although I physically followed the rules, having wet dreams made me feel impure. Like the statue, I felt like people could see my flaw of lost virginity, and although I was genuine in my interactions, I felt exposed and counterfeit. Someone would approach me with a question, and as I would speak, there was a part of me which felt that the person was getting only eighty percent of the answer. My lack of virgin consciousness had clouded the other twenty percent of the response. Philosophically, I knew it was not so, but deep within, I felt it.

One reason I never talked about this wet dream issue with the monks is that I joined them to learn something valuable, not to create a pity party of, "I too, have sinned" guilt. I'm sure each person in that house had their demons. I felt that God already knew what my flaws were, and had still allowed me

167

to access spiritual knowledge, either through Christian means or now, Indian Vedic culture. But, I always felt impure. I needed a healing acceptance of my state of being that I couldn't share with any of the monks.

At the height of my impure/wanting to feel pure, struggle, I gave in and sent an email to Jaya Sacinandana, explaining myself to some extent, using a means I was already flawed at—justification. I tried to explain myself this way, then that way, then the other way, and at one point, I just hit send without writing anymore. I was tense. I felt utterly exposed to this monk, and instead of feeling free, I felt even more covered in shame. I felt sick. For the few days when he didn't reply, I felt emotions flow through me like emotional diarrhea. I was angry at those guys who fooled me into losing my virginity. I was annoyed at the wet dreams which made me feel like I hadn't entirely lost my virginity, yet couldn't go back in time and unfuck that girl. I hadn't focused much on homosexuality while in the monastery, or I probably would have been angry at my friends in Minneapolis too, for perpetuating my focus on sexuality. I felt like the end of my world would come for me and my stay with the monks would end earlier than I wished. Like they were all sitting around some monk roundtable, discussing my email and shouting, "Kick him out! Away with him!"

Then a few days later, and email came from Jaya Sacinandana. It wasn't an email with understanding and forgiveness; with "Oh Kesh, you're a good person." It wasn't some practical solution to my situation. Or maybe it was. It was the full lyrics to Lou Reed's *"Perfect Day."* It was Jaya Saci's, as we called him, way of saying to me, "Man, don't make a mountain out of a molehill." I read the lyrics and heard the music play in my head. I went for a walk on a hiking trail, feeling relieved from this strange burden I bore for years. Not everyone was perfect, and I wasn't either. Just like that, I lay my weight of nocturnal emissions down, never to stress about it when it happened again. It was a combination of the song and Jaya Saci's attitude toward my situation that broke down the guilt wall I felt trapped behind.

Later that week when I went to Oregon to visit, Jaya Saci and a few of us watched *"Brother Sun, Sister Moon,"* a favorite of our gang. I saw the film with new eyes, especially the scene when Francesco saw Giocondo sitting in the alleyway, distressed and begging God to forgive him, a miserable sinner. Giocondo had just stared at a mother in her kitchen preparing dinner, and lusty feelings arose in him when he looked at her moving breasts. Giocondo told Francesco that he could take all the austerities, but would gladly face eternal damnation, for one moment of love. Francesco told Giocondo that they weren't a regiment of priests, for whom the vow of chastity was a discipline; they were a band of men who simply loved God, each according to his own capacity. That scene touched me deeply, and I felt my spirit lift. I could have burst out in tears in the room that day, but I felt happy that I wasn't judged and discussed, and felt like I was around a group of people, all seeking to love God according to their own capacity. I didn't yet know my capacity, but I didn't feel like a disappointment to the monastic life. My friendship and respect for Jaya Saci deepened, as I thought that I could approach him with anything, and feel safe, heard, and valued.

The monks decided to close the small Seattle center and focus on Oregon, as well as Transform an old Greyhound bus into a traveling temple. The lease on the house in Seattle had two more months left on it, so I asked if I could stay in the house for the remainder of the time, while I looked for a place of my own. Deva and Jaya Saci agreed, and when I left Oregon a few days later, I was officially leaving the monastery. I was going without guilt, with no judgment from anyone, and feeling assured that something good would come about for me on my next adventure.

Chapter
Thirteen

Jaycee Kesh Akinsanya

Caffeine

I was once again a member of Seattle social society, no longer in the seclusion of the monastery. I rented a room in a house in the Greenlake area of town, and then later got an apartment in the University District, by the University of Washington. Within a week, I got rehired by Nine West Shoe Company, the same one I worked for back in Minneapolis and began living independently of the monastery, all the while keeping a friendly relationship with the monks. I resumed exploring Seattle like I used to before I moved into the temple, and found new cafes and parks to sit, relax and write.

I discovered Seattle's night scene and visited a few nightclubs because I loved dancing. I hoped to meet a few good friends as I had done in Minneapolis. I did indeed. Jason was the first one. I was dancing, recalling some of the choreography to "*Together Again*" one of Janet Jackson's songs from *The Velvet Rope* that was playing, when he walked up to me and introduced himself. Jason told me my dancing reminded him of a guy, Walter, who came out to dance on Friday nights. It was a Friday, and Walter would be there at any moment, so he'll introduce us. Later, as I danced, a bright-faced, seductively smiling, light-skinned guy appeared before me, dancing, and matching some of the choreography I was doing. We danced together, and people moved out of our way, creating a small circle. I was quite impressed with his moves and dance style, and after the song, I hugged him and complimented his dance moves. He introduced himself to me.

"I'm Walter, what's your name?" "I'm Kesh, nice to meet you, Walter." Jason rushed over to us, recognizing that we had already met. "I knew you two would like each other! I knew it the moment I saw you dance to Janet. You guys have similar moves." I told Walter that I was new to Seattle, for the second time, having just moved out of the temple. We chatted a bit and continued to dance. Later that night a tall, handsome guy climbed on top of the large speaker box and started to dance. He was under the black light and reached into his cargo pants pocket. He took out a folded piece of fabric that glowed under the black light. As the material unfolded, I realized it was two equal pieces of glowing fabric, each held in one of his hands at an angle. He then began to twirl the cloth in the air and dance to the rhythm of the music. To my right, I saw another guy, similar height, on the other speaker box twirling a similar fabric.

I was mesmerized by the movements of the fabrics to the rhythm of the

173

music. I stood, dumbfounded, enjoying every bit of the music. I had to meet these guys and learn whatever it was that they were doing. I approached the first guy after he got down from the box and introduced myself. I told him how fantastic he was with the fabrics and I would love to learn someday. He told me his name, Kevin, and that what he was doing was called flagging and that he'd be glad to teach. Kevin introduced me to his other friend John, who had also come down from the speaker box. They let me try twirling their flags. I had some rhythm but didn't realize that the corners of the fabric had some lead weights sewn into them. My fast twirling caused the weights to hit me a few times.

With a good job down, and a few friends made, another adventure presented itself. A previous encouragement from my eleventh-grade Fashion Marketing Class teacher, Mrs. McDowell, came up and I decided to visit a modeling agency and see if I was still fit for the model scene. I checked out the local Seattle Model Agencies and telephoned a place called TCM Models and Talent. A lady named Liza answered and after my inquiry told me that they had an open call every Wednesday. The following Wednesday I eagerly showed up for open call, but the office was empty. I had come in a bit too early. I was dressed casually; a white polo shirt and khaki chinos from the GAP. I felt awkward in my outfit because it reminded me of my high school uniform. As I stood waiting by the elevator, the doors opened, and three ladies walked out. They had just been to lunch. It was Terri, the owner, with Liza and Melissa, booking agents. They were well dressed and looked like women enjoying their time in life. Terri had a lovely presence that reminded me of mommy. She had the wisdom, and knowledge about the industry that made me trust her immediately. She had been a model herself and knew how to guide young models to take the experience seriously. Terri encouraged me to try modeling with their agency and recommended some photographers to contact and get some photos taken for my modeling portfolio. In a short time, I was meeting photographers for test shoots and going to see clients. My young friend, Nora, who I had met as a monk, also took a few pictures for my portfolio. Now that I was out of the monastery, I also got to hang out with Nora a bit more freely.

Being too early that day was a good thing for me. Terri was a well-respected agent in Seattle, and her models always showed up earlier than scheduled. She had been a model back in her early years and would drive, sometimes up to four hours for a job. She was always early. I learned to show up at least thirty minutes or more before a gig. Back then, if you weren't Cindy Crawford or the other top models, you were a glorified hanger and had to take your job seriously.

174

One of the first jobs I got to do was a photoshoot for Starbucks, advertising their Frappuccino. I had never before drunk a full cup of coffee; I'd always take a sip of mommy's when she drank her morning coffee in Liberia. At Café Wyrd, I also drank tea. When I was picked to be one of the models to advertise the Frappuccino, we had to sit on the sofa and sip the drink through a straw. I did the shoot with a few model friends I made; Alicia, an Asian model, and Aluel, a model from Sudan. After the shoot, I headed straight home and sat on the sofa, thinking about what to do for the rest of the evening. I noticed that my mind was going very fast; some thoughts were slow, some were fast. I thought about my dad, as I looked around the room at the accomplishment I had achieved thus far. My face would be seen in Starbucks stores around the U.S, and in local magazines and other publications. I thought about calling my friends to make plans for the evening, but by the time I got up to do anything, it was one in the morning. I had been sitting on that sofa for about 7 hours straight—in thinking mode. I felt no hunger, no thirst, no need for the bathroom; I was in a time warp.

On Mother's Day of 2001, I gave mommy a surprise phone call. Ah, the beauty of her voice in my ear- full of laughter, accompanied by the usual flowery language of "ass," "jackass," and "damned fool." She was sitting on the porch with friends as usual, and they were eating, drinking, and enjoying being mothers on that day. We talked only for a few minutes because the cost of calling Liberia was more expensive than calling from Liberia to the US. She was thrilled and told me that my call was the best Mother's Day gift she ever received. It didn't seem like we hadn't talked each other in a year and a half since she last called me that Christmas when I fought with my dad. Before that, we hadn't called mommy much when I lived with my sister in Virginia, nor when I lived with my brother and his family in Minneapolis. Mommy and I reconnected, and life was good. We would continue to chat at least once a month after that.

After chatting with mommy that Mother's Day I decided to take my happy feeling down to Seattle's waterfront and go for a long stroll to Gasworks park. At Gasworks Park, I lay on the grass and stared at the blue skies for what seemed like hours. I was happy to be blossoming into myself, and had also reconnected with mommy. It was one of the only days I wasn't with my group of friends, and I took the time to relax and relish what was unfolding in my life.

That month I also got to reconnect with Toye, my brother who left Liberia right before the war. He was away on military duty when I was living with my dad and my sister, and now he was back in the U.S. We caught up on everything. I told him about my experiences in Virginia, Minneapolis, and now,

Seattle, leaving no detail untold. We laughed much, and he promised to visit me when he was on the West Coast.

I later discovered that John, Kevin's flagging buddy was also a model, who had done more international work, and when I hung out with John and Kevin, they introduced me to another lifelong friend David. David was a model scout, and the night I met him, he came out of an SUV, where he had been driving through town with a famous model. David and I immediately hit it off. Neither David nor I drank alcohol; we were busy being scout and model. David's loft downtown became the place at which all of us hung out. David was one of the most meticulous people I had met so far; his loft was spotless, despite the constant visitations from friends. The only other home that I recall being so impeccable was Prince's home in Paisley Park. The cleanliness level was noticeable when you entered either space. I appreciated being able to just show up at David's loft whenever I wanted. It reminded me of my home in Liberia when I would just show up at anyone's house, unannounced. For me, this was a mark of a friendship that could last very long. Even when he was traveling for work, I knew where his spare keys were, and would let myself in. I had no inhibitions around David, we talked about everything and anything, his personality was very easy to be around, and I respected his work ethic. He asked lots of questions and took a genuine interest in my life. He wondered about Liberia and the war, and he asked about my time in the monastery. His memory was freakishly good, and I admired that quality in him.

I now had a core group of friends, all with different careers, and again, connected through music. We would go clubbing at different bars throughout the city. On good nights, the meaning of Sleepless in Seattle came alive in us. We would start at one club, say the gay dance club on Capitol Hill, at around ten on a Saturday night, and then head down to another place called Contour at about two in the morning. We'd dance at Contour until dawn, and then head out to a place called Havana's. Havana's, we nicknamed "Church," opened at six on Sunday morning, and we would stay there until noon or so, and then head to brunch or home. We did all this sober! Just a pure lust for music keeping us up all night.

At one point, I hung out with a girl and her boyfriend, who I went dancing with one weekend, and we did the usual club hop. A few of my friends were out of town, and I met the girl when she came to my store, Nine West, to buy a pair of shoes. After leaving "Church" that morning, we headed to their house to recuperate and wind down, but they put on some good music, and so I continued to dance away. A few minutes later, as they both sat on their porch watching me, she said to me, "I would pay anything to have as much energy as you still have right now. Anything!" Her boyfriend reached into his shirt pocket and took out a small Ziploc bag that had some drugs, perhaps methamphetamines, and dangled it in her face, and said, "We do pay to have his energy, but he's African, they were born to stay up night and watch for lions." The three of us erupted into laughter at his wit, and I continued dancing on for a while longer, before heading home to the U-District.

Sunday evenings were my favorite times for dancing in Seattle. We all assembled at a bar called Re-Bar, which was, and still is famous for its deep house music. There, no one cared about dressing fancy for the night out, or any of the other things we considered before going out on Thursdays, Fridays or Saturdays. We took our night outings seriously and shopped for a new article of clothing almost daily. There were days when I would go to work, and end up at Kevin's house in the evening, knowing that we would all go clubbing. On my way there, I'd stop at Nordstrom or Gap, or whatever other stores, and buy something new to wear that evening. I would wear a piece of clothing at most three times, then drop it off at a local charity store. We partied all week; our weekend began on Tuesday night and ended early Monday morning. There was an activity going on somewhere in Seattle on any given day, and we found out about it and went out to be a part of it. But Sundays were very low key, and everyone just wanted to enjoy the house music. A pair of jeans and a T-shirt was enough on a Sunday night. The accessory which accompanied us, and everyone else I regularly saw in the clubs, was a pair of semi-dark sunglasses. They were light enough to see through at night but dark enough to shade the daylight sun when we left certain clubs at noon or three in the afternoon. My favorite Sunday at Re-Bar was Memorial Day weekend 2001, when a visiting DJ dubbed Dr. Martin Luther King's "*I Have a Dream*" speech, to a groovy house beat. When it played, there was no dancing room on the floor. People jumped to the dancefloor, screaming and cheering.

That Memorial Day weekend, I stayed up so long that when sleep finally caught up with me, it was an event in itself. I had stayed up form Friday night to around four in the morning on Monday. When I got home to the U-district, around five in the morning, I walked upstairs to my bedroom and fell asleep immediately. I woke up around three, Monday afternoon, went down to the kitchen, grabbed a kiwi, and went back upstairs. Next time I woke up was noon on Tuesday afternoon, and saw a half-eaten kiwi next to my pillow. My body felt completely rejuvenated, but my mind had to take some time to process the fact that I had slept away a whole Monday, and half of Tuesday.

Freaky Fanfare

During this time in Seattle—the early 2000s—there was still some stigma about the LGB communities, and some of us were still rebels, sticking it to the man by holding hands in public and what not. I toned it down considerably because I realized that I was now a face that could be recognized in the Sunday papers or other local magazines. But at night in different bars and clubs, I had no problem holding my friends' hands, regardless of the orientation of the bar. One good friend I had, Josh, who was heterosexual, but liked to go dancing at the gay bar, would always get hit on by guys. He didn't take it offensively, but the approach from other men began to cross a line into disrespect. People started to touch him inappropriately on the dancefloor. Josh thought up a plan to keep people away from him without openly saying, "hey, stay away from me." When we hung out at a gay bar, he'd hold my hands, or put his arm around me like we were lovers, and the plan worked. People stopped hitting on him. Except it was terrible for me because I wished someone would hit on me.

An interesting experience I had during my modeling time in Seattle was with a local fan. I was no celebrity, and not even close to doing as much work as many other models did in Seattle. But for a town like Seattle in the early 2000s, I was one of a few black male models, and one of the very few African models. My picture would appear in some of Bon Marche's weekly ads delivered along with the Sunday newspapers. I also did a TV commercial for them, and another summer TV commercial for Nike, and one for a casino. The Starbucks Frappuccino ad was in some Starbucks stores, and I, along with another African girl, Aluel, had landed an advertisement for Finish Line Stores. I had a tiny bit of exposure. One Sunday night while dancing at Re-Bar, a guy approached me and congratulated me. He had seen me in the Sunday papers, the Bon Marche commercial, and the Finish Line store display, and wanted to wish me luck. I felt a bit awkward during the conversation. I liked the attention, but something about it creeped me out as well. There were supermodels I looked up to, but what modeling I had done was not even close to the caliber of work they were doing, and didn't deserve fanfare.

It all came to a climax when this "fan" of mine reached into his cargo pants pocket and took out one of the local Seattle magazines that had just come out with pictures of me and another model, Ryan, wearing designer clothing for a local Men's store that sold high-end fashion clothing. He pleaded with me to sign it, saying that he had been saving some of the papers with me in it. He knew that I came to that bar every Sunday with my friends, and when the magazine came out, he knew where to find me and ask for an autograph. I was a bit freaked out. He knew that I came to this bar every Sunday with my friends to dance. I composed myself and told him that I wasn't on any level to give autographs, and thanked him for the encouraging words of congratulations. He insisted that I gave him an autograph, saying that I may just be starting out, but could never know where it would take me, and he could be the first to have my autograph. I talked my way out of not giving an autograph, and said that when the time came when I was big and famous, I would consider it. But for now, I was just a glorified hanger people paid to put clothes on, not a celebrity. I went back to dance with my friends and could feel him watching me from a distance. Finally, thoroughly freaked out, I made my way to the bathroom, came back out, and left the bar. I ran around the block and out of site hoping that this person wouldn't follow me.

Swoosh!

Between Spring of 2000, and fall of 2003, I was fortunate to land some fun modeling jobs in Seattle as well as in Portland, Oregon. I got to do some work for Nordstrom, Bon Marche, and other stores and designers in the area. A big, lucky break came when the fashion coordinator for Nike wanted to see me. She had seen my composite card, something like a business card, but much larger—8.5" x 5.5"— with pictures of me on both sides, and wanted to know if I could work for some of the shows Nike put on. I was not athletically built; I was fit, but more for runway and print. I doubted that this meeting would go anywhere, but at the end, I landed a few months' worth of jobs. I even got yelled at on my first meeting. I wore socks that had the logo of a Nike competitor, and the lady noticed it as I took my pants off to try on some clothes. How dare I wear their competitor's socks on Nike campus grounds? Maybe she was joking, maybe she wasn't, but I took the socks off and threw it in the basket. On my way home, I stopped at the Nike store and bought all new pairs of Nike Socks, and threw away every other name brand sock in my sock drawer. I didn't want to make that mistake ever again.

I found out that Nike didn't just do clothing for runners, basketball players, or soccer players. They had walking shoes, golf attire, and many other pieces of clothing for different lifestyles. The coordinator liked my look and attitude and signed me up for some work. At the time of my booking, in 2003, they were having some international sales meetings, so a few models were hired to showcase shoes or clothing.

Jaycee Kesh Akinsanya

At the end of one of the international sales meetings, we put on a fashion show like I had never seen. It took a few days for rehearsal, and we had to be on Nike campus very early in the mornings. On show day, a group of acrobatic dancers joined us as well. The room was dark, and I opened the show, dressed in a tracksuit made for nighttime use with reflectors in the seams. The stage looked like an apartment building in the city, and I ran from the top floor, down the stairs, down the runway, which was designed like a city street, and through the crowd. For that scene, I was a young man, waking up early and going for a run in the dark. At the back of the room, I met a few other models who had entered the room running on both sides of the auditorium, and we all ran together to the top of the runway. The lights came on, and we walked down the runway to loud applause from the crowd. The adrenaline was high, and the show was a fun one. The acrobatic dancers ended the event with some jaw-dropping dance displays. One boy did a run across the stage and up the wall, finishing with somersaults and a split.

During the Nike shows, I moved to Portland Oregon because of the many days I spent working for them, as well as the time I had to show up for work- seven in the morning. It would have been nerve-wracking to drive back and forth from Seattle to Portland. I was closer to the monks as well and got to visit them regularly. I also started exploring the Pacific Northwest as much as possible. I hadn't experienced the outdoors as much as I thought I would when Brendan and I arrived in Seattle. I was familiar with some parts of Mount Hood, so I started there, and then moved around to other places like the Olympic Peninsula, and the Oregon Coast. I was fascinated with the Pacific Northwest; every chance I got, I made my way to some new place, and each time, I would think of Brendan, wondering where he was, and if he'd enjoy the scenery. I particularly loved the geothermal springs scattered around that region of the U.S. I practically became enamored with hot springs, carefully studying maps and asking local friends where to find them. I made my way as far down as Stewart Mineral Springs near Weed, Northern California. Because the climate was colder in the mountains, and I was from tropical Liberia, the hot springs were a great way to heat my body up.

I also started working at a teahouse where the owner was very diligent about the sourcing of his teas. He was a very artistic spirit and each of his teahouses, called the Tao of Tea, were designed to fit the location. For example, his teahouse at the Chinese gardens transported you from downtown Portland and placed you in—China. I worked at the Belmont store where the ambiance felt like you were in India. Being there daily increased my desire to visit India.

After several months of working at the Tao of Tea, my eagerness to go to India led me to put in my two weeks' notice. I went to Los Angeles for the Festival of The Chariots, a yearly Krsna festival that took place around the world mostly in the Summer months. The festival was a replica of the original one which takes place in Orissa, India, every year, called Jagannath Ratha Yatra. During that festival, the Deities from the ancient Jagannath Puri Temple are taken out on parade for about two miles to another temple. There is lots of chanting and dancing, food, and sometimes the festival lasts a few days. In LA, the festival happens on a Sunday, and so I decided to arrive on a Thursday. When I lived in the monasteries in Seattle and Portland, we traveled to LA for this festival, so I knew some people who lived there. I met a few new friends this year, and a friend, Radha, and I decided to visit India that fall. My teacher, Prithu, owned a house in Vrindavan, India, so I would have a place to stay. We both got six-month visas, and in conversation, I invited another friend, Nick, to come along. Nick, however, was a little more hesitant, and so to twist his arm a bit, I told him that I had been to India already and he agreed. I have no idea why I fibbed to make him come to India, but he bought a ticket and when the day drew close, we drove to San Francisco to the Indian Embassy to get our Visas.

Chapter
Fourteen

The Sweet Forest

Getting to India came with a test for me; my passport would be expiring in a month, and the Liberian Embassy couldn't get me a passport due to the political situation in Liberia at the time, so they gave me a travel document called a *Laissez Passer*. I got to the Indian consulate in San Francisco a day before my flight. The lady at the counter was very reluctant to give me a visa because she hadn't dealt with a *Laissez Passer* before. She argued that there was nowhere on it to hold the Visa, but I showed her the spot on the piece of paper where the Visa would go. I informed her that my passport would expire soon, and therefore couldn't hold the visa. The embassy required that passports have a six-month validity beyond stay in India.

After about 15 minutes of back and forth conversation, I became very frustrated. With tears welling up in my eyes, I looked at the lady and said, "Mam, I've bought a ticket to go to Vrindavan to see Krsna and Balarama, my flight leaves tomorrow, and I see you are reluctant to give me a Visa. If I cannot go, I won't get my ticket refunded. I will kill myself. It will all be your fault." She looked a bit puzzled and concerned, but told me to come back in an hour. She would find a way to solve the issue. I didn't want to leave the consulate and have my Laissez Passer lost in a pile of documents. But I also didn't want to sit there looking awkward and uncomfortable, so I decided to go for a walk. I strolled around Golden Gate Park and other parts of San Francisco that day in a complete haze; my flight was the next day, and I was desperately in need of a miracle. Nick turned in his passport and visa application easily, and we were told to come back at the same time. When we showed up a few hours later, she had pasted my visa onto the *Laissez Passer*. The lady had a big smile on her face which made me tear up. Nick also got his visa, and we drove down to LA for our flight to India.

In LA that evening, we stayed with a friend who lived close to the Krsna temple. The next day we flew on Malaysian Airlines and arrived about ten hours before our next flight from Kalua Lumpur to Delhi. They gave us an option to go outside the airport and visit the city for a few hours, but I was too afraid to deal with a *Laissez Passer* issue in another country, so we hung around the airport.

The whole plane ride, my mind was disturbed; I feared being refused entry and sent back to the U.S due to my *Laissez Passer*. I would try to think positive thoughts but would get overwhelmed by fear. All I could do was

185

pray. When I got off the plane, and the warm Delhi air hit me, I wanted to just stand at the door of the aircraft in case this was my only time to breathe in the Indian air. I took deep breaths and calmly joined the line for customs. Going through customs in India was much quicker than I had anticipated. The customs officer took my *Laissez Passer*, stamped it, and said, "Have a nice stay." I was elated.

One of the monks I had met in Seattle, Giridhari Das, was there to welcome us at the airport. He had moved to Vrindavan a few years prior. Giri, for short, brought with him a very large garland of pink lotuses that had been made the day before for Radha at the temple in Vrindavan. He placed the garland around my neck as a welcome, and after wearing it for some time, I gave it to Nick, who I felt was more deserving of it. We landed in Delhi late at night, and drove three hours to Vrindavan. I felt the hot air blow against my skin outside the airport, and as we walked toward the car, I offered many prayers in my mind for the safe arrival. I was finally on my way to Vrindavan. We drove through Delhi, as the driver maneuvered his way around cows that were sleeping on the tarmac.

"You know," Giri said, as we drove through the night, "It is said that one cannot by a plane ticket to Vrindavan. I mean, any regular person can buy a ticket to the geographical place, and even drive, visit, and stay in Vrindavan. But Vrindavan, the spiritual place, the spiritual mood, cannot be accessed so easily. Radha has to permit you to come to Vrindavan. She will test, and when she sees your eagerness, she will allow you to enter Vrindavan. There you can associate with highly advanced spiritualists and cultivate spiritual depth."

As I listened, I silently reflected on the ordeal at the Embassy. I had seriously considered taking my life if I didn't get a visa to Vrindavan. The desire to go to India was so intense that I wanted no other option than going to India. I meant every word when I spoke to that lady at the visa counter. I felt like the over partying in Seattle and Portland had depleted me of my spiritual bank account, and Vrindavan was the only place I needed to go for a refill. Now we were driving and getting closer, and the anticipation filled me up slowly.

We entered Vraja Mandala, the region described in the Bhakti Section of the Vedas, as the dawn broke. Giri asked the driver to stop so he could say his morning prayers. The Vaisnavas (worshippers of Krsna or Vishnu) chant a series of silent prayers called **Gayatri**, and one of those prayers honors the sun. *Gayatri* is usually chanted three times a day, at sunrise, midday, and sunset. I sat in meditation with Giri, although I wasn't a monk anymore.

When we finished our prayers, we watched the monkeys play in the distance and laughed at their rascal activities. Monkeys are celebrities in Vrindavan and most spiritual areas of India. The *Krsna Book*, detailing pastimes of Lord Krsna, describes them as the "celebrated monkeys of Vrindavan." Hanuman, the greatest of the monkey beings is worshipped as the greatest devotee of Lord Rama, an incarnation of Krsna. One significance of worshipping Hanuman is to show humans that any creature can be empowered to serve God. Love of God is naturally within the heart of every living entity, and pride, especially in the human body covers that loving tendency. But even Hanuman got proud and was chastised by Lord Rama. During the construction of the bridge that went from South India to Sri Lanka, many humans and animals came to help bring rocks for the bridge formation. Hanuman, it is said, carried large boulders easily—he was powerful. When he saw a spider moving a grain of sand, he laughed, and Lord Rama chastised him. Rama told Hanuman that the spider was also doing real service, according to his capacity. We continued our drive to Vrindavan, which was about an hour or less away now.

When we made a left turn onto Bridavan Road by Chhatikara, Giri told me we were a few kilometers away from the Krsna Balarama Temple, the Krsna movement's main temple in Vrindavan, and my heart could have stopped. I was thrilled. Sanskrit prayers flowed through my mind one after another. Prayers about the beauty of Vrindavan came to me, especially a song that I had learned back in Seattle:

jaya radhe jaya krsna jaya vrindavan
sri govinda, gopinath, madana-mohan

All glories to Radha and Krsna
and the divine forest of Vrindavan.
All glories to the three presiding
Deities of Vrindavan—Sri Govinda
Gopinath, and Madana-mohana

syama kunda radha kunda giri govardhan
kalindi jamuna jaya, jaya mahavan

All glories to Syama-kunda

187

Jaycee Kesh Akinsanya

Radha-kunda, Govardhana Hill,

All glories to the great forest known

as Mahavan, where Krsna and Balarama

displayed all their childhood pastimes.

This prayer contains twelve stanzas, called *"slokas,"* and was one of my favorites to recite because it described the atmosphere of the spiritual realm. I
appreciated the Vedic literature for the detailed descriptions and explanations
they gave, especially on topics of divinity.

I could relate to Krsna, as the concept of the supreme Godhead because
the descriptions of Krsna were personal. He has his mother, Yasoda, his father, Nanda, his Brother, Balarama, cowherd boyfriends, and girlfriends, and
lives in a realm called Vrindavan, which means the sweet forest. Vrindavan
is known as the sweet forest because of the mood of the place. Like we need
oxygen in this material world, sweetness is the oxygen of the spiritual world.
It is the currency exchanged between Krsna and his devotees. And the pastimes are numerous, filled with all the various emotions — anger, greed, lust,
happiness, sadness, chivalry — whatever emotions we feel. The Vedas explain
that Krsna is the source of everything imaginable, and in Vrindavan, with
Vrindavan consciousness, one can access those feelings in their pure essence.

As I learned, the "spiritual realm," or the "Kingdom of Heaven," is lo-
cated in a spiritual sky beyond the visible sky, but can be accessed easily
by one's state of consciousness. Srila Prabhupada, the Krsna movement's
founder, explains that the spiritual realm reveals itself to one who develops
the right attitude to experience it. I learned that we are more than physical
matter bound by time; we are spiritual beings living in various bodies, enjoying or suffering different reactions due to our past desires. God, to me,
wasn't a person who just meted out random gifts and punishments to people;
making one person the queen of England, and another, a starving child in
Ethiopia. There was a deeper thread to be followed if one had the time to
study and understand. The topic of Samsara — reincarnation among different
realms of existence — how we get to these realms, intrigued me. Samsara
wasn't just a cycle of reincarnation on this plane; its included other realms
as well- heavenly realms, earthly realms, hellish realms. According to a person's consciousness, they got "promoted" or "demoted" to a suitable space
with an appropriate body. Astronomy and Astrology also had their places in
the Vedic paradigm. I would often joke that Galileo should have moved to
India; he would have been blown away by studying the Vedas and would have
also lived longer.

The verses which touched me the most, and helped me understand my own life mission of wanting to give beauty to the world through cultivating the human spirit, were the prayers called *Gurvastakam*, or eight prayers glorifying the spiritual master. The prayer starts with the mission of the guru. He (Srila Prabhupada, in this case; the guru is not limited to gender, but qualification), sees the plight of humanity burning in their own unquenchable and insatiable desires, one after another, and comes to give something of immense value — spiritual knowledge — to help give people a meaningful life direction. The prayers describe his attitude and activities; he's happy, experiences spiritual ecstasies, and invites us on a path suitable to help us reach his platform. The guru aims at making more gurus, not just being the one guy who gets all the stuff and then hands it down to the lowly. He prescribes various occupations, knowing the nature of each person so that they can feel like their life purposes and professions match with their spiritual journey. Srila Prabhupada would often explain that no matter the occupation — doctor, lawyer, judge, actor, farmer, butcher — or in whatever vocation one may find oneself. One can add a spiritual aspect, and elevate one's consciousness.

The fourth verse of the *Gurvastakam* prayers explains something that I could relate to, coming from a house that was a social hub. The spiritual master loves feeding people. And he arranges various types of preparations so that people can satisfy their bellies. My mother would always tell me that food is the basis of everything. She would say that if people are fed well with nutritious food, a lot of problems we see today will go away. In her Gloria way of putting things, she would say, "Have you ever seen a man whose gut is full, doing something stupid? No, because the food was good. He's fast asleep digesting it. You just saved him one hour of possible mischief."

So much can be said on the topic of feeding people, and with quality food. As an organic farmer, I've experienced many times in my life, and observed in the lives of others, what eating quality food does. I once grew cauliflower, and when they fruited, the cauliflower head was much smaller than the usual ones in the grocery store. I was a bit disappointed in myself and wondered what I had done wrong. But when I sautéed the cauliflower later, the delicious taste was something unforgettable. I could also feel the energy I got from eating such a nutrient-dense meal that day. Some of my other friends, as well as others I've met, claim that fresh grown fruits and vegetables have helped them in a myriad of ways: improved health, sharpened mental focus, raised academic grades, and even more harmonious communal relationships.

The *Gurvastakam* depicts the teacher as someone who cares about the fundamental well-being of those who come for spiritual guidance. Although the body is material, it should not be neglected, in the realm of exercise and health, when one starts a spiritual practice. The prayer goes on to describe more of the credentials of the spiritual teacher, and how to understand those credentials philosophically.

Tulsi

When we arrived in Vrindavan and drove past the temple to Prithu's house, the adrenaline in me shot up so much, that I thought I would be up for the rest of the day, despite having been traveling for so many hours without sleep. I showered and put on some fresh clothes, and immediately went to the temple. The morning meditation had just finished, but a few people were sitting around in conversation with each other. I spotted my friend Laskmi, a photographer from Los Angeles, and her mother, Devadahiti. They welcomed me with excited hugs, and Devadhahiti noticed how tired I looked. She told me to finish saying my hellos to all my friends who were at the temple, and then get some sleep. I did just that, saying hi to the other friends I saw at the temple, and then made my way back to Prithu's house to sleep. I was in a daze and still hadn't seen my surroundings. It was also this time that I met Krishna and Goura, two brothers from Florida who were also taking some time to study and learn about their Krsna roots. They had been in India for some months now and would be leaving for the U.S in December.

I still hadn't told Nick that this was my first time in India. So I decided I'd just tell him, explaining that I saw his hesitancy and made a move to break the ice. He was forgiving and laughed at what I had to do to convince him. He was happy to be in India, and also glad to have a place to stay while in India; he said it was no big deal. He was ready to explore as much as he could, but now we all had to sleep off the jetlag. Nick's ticket wasn't for as long as mine, so he used his days for lots of exploration.

Six hours later, I woke up to the sounds of parrots and cooing peacocks. The guestroom door was open and a screen door blocked intruders like the celebrated monkeys from coming in. I walked out into the courtyard of the compound, and it hit me. I was in Vrindavan. I recognized the neem trees in the yard; we had neem trees in Liberia also, and use the leaves for medicine. Jasmine and other flowers were blooming everywhere. The monsoon season had passed, and this was like a second Spring. The temperature was perfect, perhaps in the high seventies or low eighties. Vrindavan's climate could be fierce in the Summer. Giri told me that he once watched his rubber slippers melt, and leave prints on the road as he walked to the market. Prithu's court-yard was landscaped beautifully with shrubs arranged in sections where one

190

could sit and enjoy the atmosphere. There were a few guestrooms adjacent to the main house. In the far corner, across the lawn, was a cowshed, and next to the gate was the guard house.

Rose-winged parakeets, a species of parrots, were flying everywhere, but I especially noticed that they were congregating around the screened balcony of the second floor where Giri and his wife lived. On his walk home one day, Giri rescued a baby parakeet and made a cage space on the balcony for its recovery. He said that twice a day, morning and late afternoon, a flock of parrots would come to the balcony and "fill the parrot in" on the daily news around Vrindavan. In the scriptures, parrots play the role of messengers in Krsna's town. They fly over the village and watch for new events, and then report to Vrinda Devi, who is considered the chief engineer of everything that goes on in Vrindavan. Did they tell Vrinda that Radha, Nick and I were staying at Prithu's house? I'm not sure if we were of that much importance to Krsna's town, to be part of the local inner parrot news.

Vrindavan gets its name from Vrinda: *Vrinda (sweet), vana (forest)*. Vrinda assumes the form of the holy basil tree and watches everything from the ground level, while the parrots, her messengers, oversee things from above. While walking around Vrindavan, and other surrounding villages, one can see many shrubs of holy basil growing. In the West, Vrinda, in the form of the sacred basil is known as *"Tulsi."* Tulsi is famous in the herbal medicinal world and yoga circles, but in Vrindavan, Tulsi is the holiest of plants. In most parts of India where I visited, I saw that people grow a Tulsi plant in front of their houses. Tulsi is said to protect and ward off negative influences. When the Tulsi plant is old or dead, the twigs are used for ceremonies or made into necklaces and other jewelry like earrings. The wearer is considered protected from bad energy.

There were peacocks in the yard as well, and you could hear them call from all around the neighborhood. No one owned them, they just freely roamed and flew wherever they pleased. I felt like I was in an open-air zoo, with peacocks walking in the yard or on the roofs of the houses. Now and then, one would shake his tail open, revealing their beautiful famous plumes. I later learned from one of the villagers that peacocks eat snakes, and the plumes weren't just a cute mating outfit, but a defense mechanism. They looked like eyes and would confuse the snake as to how many eyes were watching him. Their spread wings made them seem larger than life to a predator. Peacocks also play an essential role in the scriptures; Krsna loves them and uses their feathers to beautify his turban. A God who likes to dress up—I liked him from the start.

A few hundred feet outside the gates, there were Rousettus bats, also known as Megabats, hanging upside down in a tall tree. Some people know these large fruit bats as "flying foxes." At certain times of the day, their flight for food was spectacular. And there were many varieties of fruit for them to eat. The sky took a different hue, filling with black spots as these bats flew around in search of food. One such fruit, the bael fruit, was just out of season when we arrived but has the most fragrant smell when it is ripe and ready to eat. Most people make a kind of smoothie with the bael fruit.

Because Krsna is a cowherd boy, the cow is very sacred to the residents of Vrindavan, and to most of India. Cows roam freely and are very gentle. At Prithu's house, he had a few cows in the yard, and when I woke up in the mornings for my meditations, I sometimes preferred to sit in their shed. If I had a book with me, I'd go close to one of the cows, lay my head against her, and read to her. Living around cows, I began to understand their significance and holy reference. They were very giving—just as Jaya Saci had explained to Abe and me back in Seattle—and they take very little in return. The whole town of Vrindavan is known to follow a vegetarian diet, and you can see, in their lifestyle, their direct dependence on the cow. They use the cow dung, mixed with water, to plaster their houses. Or the manure is gathered and made into large patties which, when dried, is used as cooking fuel. On my last trip to Vrindavan, the use of cow dung to produce biogas was becoming popular. Known as Gobar, cow dung is collected and put into a mixing tank, where water is added to form a slurry. During the fermentation process, the bacteria created "eats" the slurry and "farts" out methane or biogas, which is then collected in a gas holder until its ready to be used for cooking or heating water. Apparently, the methane content in cow dung gives the highest amount of biogas than other stock such as dry leaves and sugar cane husks. Cow urine is also used in traditional medicinal treatments. It is considered to contain many antiseptic properties.

And then, of course, there were the monkeys. They were everywhere—babies, parents, grandparents—all up to some mischief. They are the ruffians of Vrindavan and are very cunning. They will try to steal everything they can from an unsuspecting pilgrim. I've watched, many times, people get the shock of a monkey jumping up on them and taking something: their purse, glasses, anything loose. They'll then climb up on a roof and try to bargain with the victim; fruit for your item. You learned to imitate the locals and carry a stick with you. Monkeys will back off if they see you have a stick. They pose a significant problem to some tourists, but locals learn to live with them and understand their role in Krsna's playful pastimes. In stories, you'd hear about how Krsna would steal his mother's yogurt, butter, and other milk products and sweetmeats, and distribute them to the monkeys. They would even help him and act as a decoy so she would chase them, while he came in and looted the fresh butter or yogurt goods.

I had a few experiences with the monkeys as well; two are most memorable. I washed my laundry one day and lay my "dhoti," the long sari worn by men in India (think of Gandhi's garb), on the lawn to dry. I then went into my room to put the laundry bucket and other things away. Usually, a dhoti took minutes to dry because of the heat. When I came outside, my dhoti was missing. Bewildered, I looked around and couldn't find it. I then saw my dhoti crawling across the lawn from behind one of the shrub fences. Then it stopped in the middle of the yard, and a monkey poked its head out from under the cloth. I yelled at him to scare him away, he started running toward the fence with my dhoti, and I ran after him. From the top of the wall, he looked down at me, grabbed my dhoti, and tore it as many times as he could. I stood there helplessly trying to find a stick or rock. When I saw one, I threw it up at him, and he ducked but started a loud screech. Within seconds, monkeys were on the roof charging at me. I ran for my life and locked my door very fast.

The next time was when I sat out in the yard eating papaya I had just bought from the fruit stand next to the temple. I had spooned out the first half of the papaya and was eating the second half when a mama monkey and baby came down from the roof walking toward me. I couldn't do a thing! She walked over to me, nonchalantly took my papaya from the table, and hopped away with her baby.

The Bhakti scriptures translated by Srila Prabhupada are very fascinating, especially once you visit places like Vrindavan and see the landscape. The writings are a lovely mix of philosophy and descriptions of spiritual and loving relationships, set in this raw, beautiful place. The mystical component of Vrindavan also intrigued me. Although I never met them—or probably did without knowing if—people said that there are yogis in Vrindavan who can see Krsna's manifest pastimes happening on a daily basis. I thought of it as a kind of curtain or screen that some people had access to; they could roll back the curtain at any time and see what was happening in a different dimension.

Kartika

Our arrival in Vrindavan was scheduled for a few days before the actual month of Kartika began. Nick, who I had invited to come to India, and Radha, my friend, explored Vrindavan separately. For the month of Kartika, I spent a lot of time with the brothers Krishna and Goura, exploring and experiencing everything we could about this holy land of Vrindavan. I had no idea how many people would be in Vrindavan at this time of year. There were thousands of pilgrims who had come to Vrindavan. Imagine Mecca during holy seasons. The Vaisnava tradition was much broader than I had known. The rest of the world know Vaisnavas as Hare Krsnas because of their singing, but to understand the cultural and spiritual depth, Kartika was just the experience I needed. Vaisnavism is divided into four schools, each with a slightly different philosophical focus on divinity. But they are all Vaisnavas, worshipers of Vishnu. Vrindavan is holy to Vaisnavas, and so Kartika presented a beautiful mixture of people from all around the world coming to one place for spiritual gratification. Vrindavan is known as the town of five thousand temples, and exploring these holy sites cannot be completed in one lifetime.

Kartika is considered the holiest month for Krsna devotees, where all your spiritual merits multiply a thousand-fold. It is a time used for deep reflection in a sacred place, so most people familiar with the month go to India at that time. Kartika occurs around the time when the monsoons are over, and a second Spring-like weather occurs. India is thought to have six ritus or seasons: Vasant, Spring; Grishma, Summer; Varsha, Monsoon; Sharada, Autumn (more like a second Spring, on account of how flowers bloom, and how green everything still is.); Hemant, Fall; and Shishira, Winter.

In Vrindavan, I had a very private funny experience as a new friend grabbed my hands and told me he'd like to take me around to see the village. He was Indian and held on to my hands as we walked about the place. I felt very uncomfortable at the beginning. I kept thinking how much judgment and negative talk would be coming from people in Seattle or Minneapolis if they saw us walking hand in hand like we were. I even tried a few times to "weaken" my hands so that it would fall free, but each time I did he held on tighter. Plus, this was Kartika season, which meant that people from the west were visiting at that time. Moments later I snapped back to reality and realized that this culture didn't have the sexualized male macho stigma. You saw men walking together hand in hand everywhere. There was more to human intimacy than just sexuality. Plus, I wasn't in India for sexual reasons; I was there for a spiritual visit. Holding someone's hand was part of his culture, and unfortunately, his pure intentions to just show me around had me tense and uncomfortable, afraid of judgment from others. In later years when the meme culture would flood the Internet, I came across a picture of two guys standing with their hands in each other's back pocket. Below the picture was the phrase, "It's not gay, it's just India."

Sundari

When Kartika was over, Krishna, Goura, Radha and I traveled around India, exploring as much as we could. Radha and I had return tickets booked for December, so we wanted to make the most of our trip and see as much as we could in India. One place we visited was Valsad, Gujarat, where a family, the Missacks, lived. We had just met them in Vrindavan during Kartika, and promised to visit them on our trip. They owned a dairy farm and made milk products, which they brought with them to Vrindavan.

Their mom, who we called "Baby Mataji" (Baby Mother), because of her youthful look, was happy to include all of us in their family breakfasts, lunches, or dinners. Our stay in Valsad was one of the most beautiful experiences of my life. There was a river close to the Missack's home, and we would go there to swim or wade in the water. For my friend Radha's birthday, Baby Mataji and Sundari, the eldest sister— still one of my closest and trusted friends—made a mango cheesecake that tasted like the gods baked it in the heavens and delivered it to us. It felt good to be around such a close-knit family, and it reminded me of home.

When December arrived, and Radha prepared to head back to the US, I decided that I needed more time in India, so I forfeited my ticket and stayed until April 1st, a day before my Visa expired. I had cried to get that visa, threatened to kill myself, and sat for hours on a plane in anxiety—I wanted to suck out every bit of juice left on it. We bid each other goodbye in Valsad, and Radha went back to Vrindavan to gather his luggage, while Krishna, Goura, and I left for Bangalore. Nick's ticket was only for two months, so he departed Vrindavan earlier than we did.

I learned a bit of Hindi and some Bengali to help me communicate with the locals, though my true love is Sanskrit. Sanskrit is considered the mother of all languages and the Vedic literature are written in Sanskrit. When I lived in the monastery in Seattle, I studied and memorized as many of the verses and prayers as I could. Another monk named Dravida Das, who used to be a jazz lover, spent his time learning Sanskrit prayers and translating them into English poetry. Whenever I would meet him somewhere, I would take the time to listen to as many of his prayers as I could, learning the proper meter to chant them.

While traveling on a train one time, an old holy man with the ubiquitous orange cloth, dreadlocks, and bushy gray beard, decided to interrogate me after what seemed like hours of him staring directly at me. He had very piercing eyes that were made more prominent by the clay markings on his forehead and his bushy mustache. In other countries, people stare at you out of curiosity and sometimes, awe. My black skin wasn't a regular occurrence in certain parts of India, and I didn't take offense to the stare down. Finally, he looked at me, and in Hindi, asked, "Kahan se (where are you from)?" I, in turn, replied, "America," but he wasn't buying my answer.

"You have ID? Passport?

I showed him my Driver's license.

"Anyone can make and claim. America mei, kala jan nahi hai. Kala jan West Indies, Africa sei (There are no black people in America, only in the West Indies and Africa)"

When I tried to convince him, he pointed at me authoritatively and exclaimed, "I am telling you, Kala jan America no there!" Case closed. He looked away and was finished with me; the train continued. On another occasion, in Mayapur, West Bengal, as I walked to the foreign exchange office, a father, eager to point out his knowledge to his family, pointed to me and said, "dehko, NEGRO (look, this is a Negro)." They all smiled and looked at me, examining my features.

There was no need to take offense in these situations; the man's family had likely never seen a black man in person. A similar incident happened to a friend on a visit to a remote city in another country; a few brave enough people came up to him and rubbed their hands on him to see if his color would rub off on them. In these sweet corners of the world, you find people eager to know you and understand your difference. Such experiences stem from an excited doubt. Doubting is a function of the intelligence, and experimental inquiry, like asking for my ID, or rubbing the skin of my friend. Doubting gets a bit more blurred when it crosses the line into misgivings. Misgivings often involve an attachment to a concept that one refuses to let go of.

Knock, Knock; Life Calling.

For Christmas, I decided to go to Goa and stay there until the New Year. I found out that Prithu was also going to be there, so I went and visited with him. Christmas was a few days away, and I was happy to be in Goa. From the train station to Palolem, where I would be staying, I noticed a more Christian flair in some of the architecture, as well as more churches than I had seen in India. My driver, a Catholic, told me that Goa was once conquered by the Portuguese, and with some research and more conversations with some locals, I learned that Goa played a significant role as the center of Christianization in the East. A large percentage of the locals were Roman Catholics, descendants from the mid-sixteenth century Portuguese occupation of Goa. I was quite fascinated by the history and wanted to study as much of it, but when I got to the Palolem, a beautiful town on the coast, I became a beach bum and only went back to the city on the day I was leaving.

Palolem was magical. I stayed in a beach shack for about three dollars a night, and would walk the mile-long white sandy beach about three to four times a day. The sea current wasn't very fast, so I spent a lot of time in the blue waters of the Arabian Sea. On Christmas Day, I ordered a cake and took it to where Prithu was staying and visited with him most of the day. He was in Goa on a writing retreat, so I didn't want to disturb him. Later that evening I went to a rave party on the beach, met a few other foreigners and had a grand Christmas celebration. While sitting at one of the restaurants on the beach, I noticed that someone was twirling something around their body in the distance. I recognized, from closer inspection, that it was a fire poi, similar to the cloth that Kevin had in Seattle. But this one is a chain, with a large wick attached at the end that is soaked in fuel and lit on fire. I excused myself from the table for a minute and went to the water's edge to meet the dancer. I had tried fire poi back in Portland Oregon after Kevin taught me how to flag, so the guy agreed, and I danced around a with his poi and got some applause from my friends at the table, and other people who watched me.

The next day, after my birthday, for whatever reason, I felt depressed. It was the end of 2003 and beginning of 2004, and I had just turned twenty-five. Instead of feeling elated, I slipped into a kind of quarter-life crisis mood. I sat on the beach or wandered for what seemed like hours. The wandering was good for me as I weaved my way around the local houses and shops. I was wondering about my future. What to do, where to go. It seemed unprofessional for me to go back to Portland and get rehired at the Tao of Tea. I hadn't left on bad terms, but I couldn't just go back as I chose, and expect to be rehired. I was still interested in modeling but was not ready to just move back to Seattle. I wanted to keep experiencing new places.

I sat on the beach in limbo, wondering what next steps to take. Twenty-five seemed like a huge age, and seemingly, I hadn't done anything valuable in my life. I began to look at my life in terms of what other people were doing with theirs. Friends had gone to university and were perhaps now starting new careers. I had great opportunities so far, yet nothing was sticking, as other people did with their long-term careers. Could I have done well with retail store management? What about modeling? Would I be able to go back to it with focus? Externally, I developed my own poker face, but internally I was fighting an inner war, trying to ground myself and conform to the daily grind, like everyone else.

I was also still deeply missing the aspect of community that I had left in Liberia. The saying, "It takes a village to raise a child," was true for me back

197

in Liberia, and in the U.S, I felt like to be a part of the village had prerequisites. There were certain expectations for acceptance into the American village, and I wasn't quite up to standard. I didn't immediately go to college after high school, nor was I interested in making lots of money to secure my future. I was a black Rip Van Winkle hippie who went to sleep at some point in the California seventies and woke up in mid New Jersey nineties, or the Wandering Jew himself, now in a different body wandering the early 2000s. I felt lost.

I was in need of an actual experience of community; not just the identification with a group of people because we shared the same ideals—philosophical connection, racial roots, or sexual preference. The three puzzle pieces for me, didn't fit harmoniously, and I had found myself being pulled in each of those directions, and mentally coerced to pick just one. I felt like I couldn't be a black, bisexual Hindu, without finding some conflict in one of those areas. Most blacks adhered to Christianity, and sexuality in Christianity—especially involving same sex proclivities—was explicitly frowned on. The Vedic culture was a bit more lenient as far as race and sexuality. Both aspects of identification in a person had to do with their karmic desires from a previous birth. But the institutional part of the Krsna movement was slow in balancing philosophy and practical life.

Most people I knew in the LGBT community weren't so keen on religious affiliation because of how they felt damned to hell, and there seemed, to me, to be a not so secret "preference prejudice" in the LGBT community. If I had directly experienced any sexual "them vs us," it was from guys who I found attractive, who couldn't reciprocate with me because they didn't date black guys, or skinny model guys. Or they were afraid to be labeled as a "chocolate queen (a gay man who dates only blacks), or only wanted to date me because I was black. The whole division, although natural to some extent (people naturally find one person attractive and another, not), became a source of mental distress for someone like me who wanted to know people beyond their external skin color or body type. Some LGBT people took this discrimination too far, and I saw, in various situations, that gay bashing in the gay community was a real issue. I can say for a fact that the gay bashing I experienced the most came from other gay men.

Similarly, the most racial bashing I experienced in my life came from other black people. I was blatantly told, to my face, by another black person, that I was betraying black history because I shopped at the white man's store. It was a funny incident for me, because the store I was accused of deserting my black roots for was called "United Colors of Beneton." Another racial incident from other blacks was when a fellow monk, Jaya Jagannath das and

I, walked around an area of Lake Michigan in Chicago. A few black guys were sitting at a table when we walked by, and one, pointing to us, said to his friends, "Look at these faulty niggas walking over here."

I understood that these incidences were circumstantial, and not all blacks were racist toward other blacks, or all gays of other colors hated me. But these issues existed, and were experienced not just by me. I dug into my "how would mommy handle this" files to help me navigate my way through, and out of my funk. I knew mom wouldn't frown on religious differences. I knew she was a people person, not a "black people" person, or a "particular sexual group of people" person. I was looking for a world I lived in as a child in Liberia, and deeply fighting the one I had experienced after leaving Liberia. Furthermore, I knew the world was diverse, with all kinds of people and people-nesses, and in a sense, I too wasn't accepting them because I deemed what they stood for as unacceptable. I realized, with the guilt that came with it, that I was, in fact, human, just like everyone else.

Perhaps one of the most realistic conversations I had with my mom was on the topic of politics and the LGBT movement. For her it was a matter of common sense and not legislation: "You think God gives a damn who you're sleeping with? And if he does, you think it's the government he'll use to tell you? When was the last time you had the government in your room when you were "jooking" someone? People are too much in their heads, I don't have time for that. If you're going to love, just love. And that whole thing where you have to come out of the closet and tell people you like sex this way or another; who's the counsel God sent along with you when you were born, that now you have to tell them your life like you've done something wrong. Are they paying your bills? People have time to let stuff like that disturb their mental tension."

In Goa, I was coming to terms with a fact that my energy was spread in three worlds, yet I didn't feel a part of any of those worlds. I needed a community of people who would be intrigued by each other's differences, and try to learn about and celebrate those differences. I wished for a village in which the prerequisites for living would be, as Dr. King put it, "the content of their character." In my village, people could come together and show how they could help improve the natural world, and human dignity. I guess I was looking for a world where we all existed with each other without the need to try and "fix" each other.

But although this quarter-life crisis was happening, there was always this calm and steady core—mom's lessons and sayings. An inner voice served as an emotional fill-line for me. No matter how anxious I got about not being grounded, or not fitting in, I reached a point where the voice of mother

199

kicked in and started to reason with me and philosophically look at things from different angles. It angered me because I just wanted to have a freakout and see what was on the other side of my anxiety or depressed mood.

When that mom's voice came up, I reasoned with myself on the beach in Goa; I wasn't hungry, or naked, or homeless. I was not lazy and would give time to whatever it was that I had dedicated myself. When I worked in retail, I was never late and had no complaints. As a model, Terri had standards, and I always worked within the boundaries of those standards. In the monastery, I had studied as much as I could, and did what was asked of me. I kept a friendly relationship with the devotees. I kept encouraging myself that I was progressing, and maybe my life wasn't meant to unfold for me as it unfolded for others. Mommy's favorite lines, "I've got my charge to keep, and my God to glorify, and you've got yours," came back to me. I concluded that I shouldn't judge my life by the lives of others. After all, I did not know what struggles they were going through in their own lives.

My time in India was limited, and that reality was ringing in my mind. I had forfeited my ticket to stay and travel longer, but thoughts of the future outside of India kept coming to my mind. These inner voices were causing me to examine myself. Through a series of emails, a friend, Dan, who lived close to the Krsna community in LA invited me to share his apartment as he needed a roommate, so I considered the prospect. When I had weighed all other options, I repurchased a ticket to Los Angeles. I left India on April 1st, a day before my visa expired. I had immersed myself for six months in India, deepening my spiritual cultivation, and traveling as much as I could. Now I had to face the American world again.

Chapter
Fifteen

Scrambled

My reentry into the U.S was a bit of a journey in itself. I had been in the villages in India, only coming to cities like Delhi or Mumbai for specific needs. As the taxi drove me from LAX to Culver City, where I would be staying, I was in a complete culture shock. Everything was a bit too organized — traffic lights, traffic order. I had to remind myself that I was back in the U.S. The following weekend, I decided to go to Venice beach for a walk to get some ocean air. There were people everywhere, and everyone looked like they had just come out of the gym, or tanning booth. I felt anxious like I didn't fit into that world. When I had visited LA before, it was for the festivals, and I didn't notice Muscle Beach or any of those other places. Now it was all around me.

When I got back home that night, I fell into a state that made me want to go back to India. I was ready to drive to San Francisco and get a new visa if necessary, but then I would also need a new Laissez Passer; it was just too much to think about. On another occasion, as I left Govindas, the restaurant attached to the LA temple, with a few pieces of pizza, I all of a sudden ducked and looked around me, watching out for monkeys who might try to steal my pizza. My return from India had a comical tone to it. Adjusting to the busy life around me was very difficult. I stayed inside for weeks. I'd wake up and go to the temple for the morning meditation, and then go back inside and read a book or two. A friend, Dasi, whom I had met in India, visited L.A a few weeks later, and when she came to see me, I told her my predicament. "Kesh," she said, "the same thing used to happen to me. But learn this technique: when you're in India, be in India, and when you're in America, be in America. Otherwise, it will fuck your system up." With her advice, I started moving around, little by little.

I flew to Seattle for a few modeling jobs that Terri had booked for me and then flew back to L.A. After a few weeks, I looked up some agencies in LA and made appointments to meet some of them. Modeling in Los Angeles proved too much for me. In Seattle, at the time, I was one of a very few black models in my age group. I got a fair chance at work up there, but when I went to see some agencies in LA, I saw that on their model wall were about six or seven black models, similar look, and age as I was. I do not have a competitive bone in my body and was turned off by the mention of the competitive nature of the business in LA. I pursued modeling no further during my stay in LA.

To keep my head straight while I figured out my next life move, I started to work at a local grocery store. I had some money saved up from modeling, but in a conversation with mommy, she advised that I keep working, even if I was doing something two or three days a week. Perhaps she understood my life crisis and longing for direction. She advised me to do something, rather than sit at home and let my idle mind eat away at me. What made my job feel useful was the fact that every evening we would take the groceries that would be expiring in a day or two, and put it outside in a shopping cart, rather than the garbage. Sometimes homeless people would come and take those products.

Then one day, out of the blue, our manager told us that we had to open each package of food we threw out, and pour bleach on it. Milk had to be opened and spilled, and yogurt or sour cream also had to be opened and dumped out. The company was afraid that someone would eat food from their garbage area, get sick, and then sue them. I quit that job two days later. I was already in a limbo state, trying to find a purpose and give back to humanity, and leaving food out for people was the least we could do. It gave me a tiny bit of assuring purpose, like I was starting somewhere, and could make my way from there. But suddenly, such an act as pouring bleach over someone's possible food poured water on my small fire. There was no end to how much people could scare themselves and make everything seem like a liability. I even stopped shopping at that grocery chain after that incident.

Unable to make a concrete decision, I decided to go back up to the Pacific Northwest. I called mommy, just to talk and let some things out. I was feeling quite ungrounded, having come back to the U.S. My disdain for competition left me a bit disinterested in modeling, but I left a small crack in the door, in case an opportunity came up. I wasn't going to try modeling in LA, and if it didn't look promising in Seattle, I'd turn my focus elsewhere. Going back to Seattle would also be a good idea since I was comfortable there, had good friends there, and knew areas like the parks and hiking areas that nurtured my creativity. I sent Terri, my modeling agent, an email asking if I could still do some modeling work. When I heard back from Terri, I felt a bit encouraged. My leaving for India seemed a bit whimsical, but she was understanding and encouraged me to come back to Seattle. She said that I was still young and if I focused, had many years of modeling possible. She reminded that there were ethnic models like Iman, David Bowie's wife, and Tyson Beckford, still working, and they were way older than me.

Pit Stop in the Mountains.

With some time on my hands, I decided to make a quick stop through Denver, Colorado. My friend Walter, from Seattle, lived there now. I hadn't visited him in his new city, so I took the time to do so. When Walter and his friends invited me to go snowboarding with them, I agreed to learn the skill. I had not spent much time in the mountains of America, so I went along. I was quite intrigued by the amount of snow in the mountains, and also by the number of people snowboarding. I had no idea that there was a whole outdoor scene happening in winter. On my first try up, after a mini lesson from Walter and his friends, I did a pretty OK job. Halfway down the easiest slopes, I got excited about how fast I was going and tried to stop myself. I landed on my butt and both wrists. My wrists were in pain, but thankfully, nothing was broken. On the next try, my legs cramped up so severely that I had to take off my snowboard and walk down the slopes. I was done snowboarding for the day and haven't tried it since.

A few days later, Walter found out that his father was in critical condition, and went to visit his family. I stayed in Denver, and when he returned, I decided to stay a while longer and give him some friendly support. After all, he had become like a brother to me in Seattle. Some time passed, and Walter decided to move to Chicago and try out life there. I liked Denver enough and stayed there instead of going to Seattle. Terri understood my situation; she must have sensed my ungrounded restlessness. I felt like I had disappointed her to told myself to not email her anymore about modeling if I wasn't going to follow through with it.

To keep me busy, I started working at a market research company and then at a popular bar. I started as a busser, clearing the tables and doing menial work. From there I got promoted to bar back, assisting the bartenders by making sure they had enough ice and drinks stocked up. My schedule was very steady, so I added different activities to my days. With the new friends I had made, like Jorge, Nico, Jesse, Todd, Travis, Chad, Jake, Pat, and Kim, I'd either go skateboarding, play soccer in the park, or go biking or shopping. I was learning to take my time and relish the flow life was giving me after my return from India. One thing mommy always told me was I had to be patient with myself. In Denver, I felt like I was learning to take mom's advice seriously. In one conversation with her, she mentioned how people cause their own anxieties because of goals they set for themselves, wanting to see those desires manifest overnight. High goals, she thought, were okay, if a person gives themselves the time and perseverance to reach them. "We all have our time, you boy, and when the time comes for you to do something, it will be as clear as day." For now, she told me, take care of the basics like rent and food and such, and wait for life to manifest what was meant for me as my purpose.

After a year of working at the bar, and almost two years in Denver, I got abruptly fired from my bartender job. As I skateboarded in one day to start my shift, I noticed the manager's SUV parked outside the bar with him, the assistant manager, and another friend sitting in it. I didn't understand why they were in the car instead of in the bar, so I waved hello and went inside the bar to get things ready for the afternoon. The assistant bar manager came to me and told me that I was let go of. He explained that Denver was a "hire at will, and fire at will" state, so they didn't need to tell me why I was fired. It felt a bit awkward to me, but I felt no need to ask any further. I figured I would ask one of my co-workers what they knew about my firing. I had seen other bartenders and workers get fired in an instant without reason, then hear the so-called reasoning get talked about in gossip. When it happened to me, I wondered what mine would be. But no one cared to tell me. People's silence made me feel like I had made no friends in Denver, especially not at the bar where I worked. I decided I would leave Denver, and finally go Northwest. For the last few days, I stayed in Denver, I got someone to finish up my lease, give away some of my key trinkets that I didn't want to sell, and hung out a bit with a few good friends.

Years later, I found out from Walter and Jorge that I was accused of stealing money from the bar, and therefore, fired. It made no sense to me. As I tried to analyze it, I also learned that the real thieves were caught, fired, and the bar was shut down. I've deliberately "stolen" two things in my life, both on a dare: A T-shirt from a friend's drawer; we wanted to see if he would notice it since he was a bit of an item collector, and some gouda cheese from a grocery store, on a truth or dare move. I felt quite offended by my friends in Denver; were they working with me and hanging out with me, but untrusting of me? I would have stood up for them if I had heard that kind of rumor.

Bus Tour

It was summer of 2007 when I left Denver, and a few Krsna devotee friends were in New York for the same chariot festival that took place in LA on Venice Beach. I had never been to the New York festival, so I let myself be a vagabond for a bit. After New York, I drove down to Alachua, Florida, for a Krsna youth festival called KULIMELA. The goal of this festival was to bring together and empower Krsna youth in various avenues like spiritual strengthening, healing for those who had experienced some very adverse incidents in the eighties, and career strengthening from others who were established in their careers.

After the festival, I stayed with Nila, Mud, and Datta, friends I had met in LA during the chariot festival, and Goura, one of the brothers I had met in India. They were very level-headed, and their household was a good place to associate with other devotees who weren't monks or nuns. They all attended the University of Florida, and I helped out, cooking for everyone and doing odd jobs. I wasn't set on staying in Florida but was at a block as far as my next steps. I weighed my different options. When I felt a bit stagnating, I would talk to mommy, or a close friend, to discuss my available options. Moving from place to place was something I didn't want to keep doing. I decided to take a pause and stick it out in Gainesville for a while until I felt a definite sense or signal of what to do next.

I later joined up with some Krsna devotees who had been doing a bus tour around the U.S for some years. They lived in the Alachua community, and would, every summer, chaperone some fifty or more youth, sixteen and over, to help with the Chariot festivals around the U.S, Canada, and Mexico. It was a beautiful time to get to know some of these devotees who I had seen at festivals as part of the set-up crew, entertainment, or management. Devotees came from all around the world for this summer bus tour.

The devotees did a winter tour down in Mexico, but I never went with them. To help others understand the Vedic philosophy, they would invite senior monks to travel with and encourage the youth. One monk, Jayadvaita Swami, who was one of the senior editors for the books distributed on the streets, in bookstores, and in libraries, loved to come along for a few weeks on the summer tour. Jayadvaita Swami was an excellent monk to engage in question-and-answer dialogue. He had read the books thoroughly and had a very good grasp of Vedic philosophy. I also appreciated his sense of wit and humor. When I first met him, I was intimidated by how he paid full attention to me as I asked him a question. I felt like he was editing my words as I spoke. Beneath his focused stare, I learned to see a human being on a journey of self-discovery. He was also a traveling monk and had no particular base, which was very attractive to me. However, he also had his editing service which he could work on anywhere, and I didn't have such a service. I knew that he went to India every fall, so I left myself a mental note to ask to travel with him as his assistant while he was in India.

In the meantime, while in the U.S, I started a personal travel scheme, where

207

I would visit some temples and help out with whatever was needed. One such temple was a farm in Tennessee, run by Rama and Murali, two sweet Krsna devotees. I knew Rama's children and Murali's son, and had been with them for the KULIMELA festival in Florida. Rama and Murali were like parents to me, and being on their farm was a relaxing experience. I got to help cook for them, and do some necessary services on their temple altar. This temple farm wasn't new to me; I had visited in 1999, when the Seattle monks were traveling from Seattle and going to the Rainbow Gathering, a hippie festival held deep in different national forests around the U.S. We went to the festival to distribute food. Prithu had a liking for the rainbow people, so he set up a question and answer tent wherever they were.

Rama and Murali took me on many excursions around Tennessee, and Rama told me stories about the native Incas and other tribes of South America. I asked him to take me on a trip to South America one day. He had been to these places, and his explanations and storytelling drew you in and made you want to go to those places. The farm was on a few hundred acres and was about a mile long from the front gate to back gate. While there, a few friends I had met along the way during my travels, would come and visit me. With more helping hands and good company, we helped do some painting, cleaned out some cabins and my friends explored the property when there was nothing to do.

I then traveled to Canada to visit a budding center, and while there, invited two young men who were interested in living like monks, to come back to Tennessee with me. It was getting cold in Canada, and I asked Rama if I could come back to the farm with these students for the winter. Rama was pleased to hear from me, said that they were leaving for India shortly after I arrived, and asked if I didn't mind taking over the temple ceremonies and daily affairs while they were gone. I agreed, and one of the guys, Dustin, and I, flew to Tennessee to stay at the farm. Caleb, the other guy, said he would show up at a different time. Rama and Murali left for India, and Dustin and I stayed at the farm.

Foresight

When the day arrived for us to pick Caleb up from the airport, we drove two hours to Nashville, and upon arriving at the airport, found out that Caleb was a no-show. Trying to be accepting and make sense of it, I told Dustin how dedication to spiritual life was not an easy task. We drove back to the farm and on the way had some enlivening conversations. As we drove along the highway, we saw something burning in the distance, and soon found out that it was a truck on fire. Seeing a burning vehicle by the side of the road sparked another conversation about how, in life, there is a lingering danger at every step. I mentioned how that truck driver, minutes before, was probably driving along without a care, and now, his whole life had changed in an instant.

As I spoke, a vision of my cabin back at the farm, flashed before my eyes. The cabin was burning in flames. I couldn't understand the meaning of it; such a vision had never happened to me before. Or, if it did happen, I didn't pay full attention to it. Then again, within a few seconds of the burning cabin vision, I saw another one, this time involving a letter I had written to a monk I looked up to, informing him that the cabin had burned and we lost everything, but were safe. I pondered the vision a bit more and continued driving and chatting with Dustin.

We arrived at the farm and drove in through the back entrance. From a distance, I saw no fire and felt thankful that it was only my mind playing tricks on me, and the cabin was safe. We turned into the parking lot, and as I turned the car off, a glaring light reflected on the car window. I looked behind, and the cabin had burst into flames. We had just enough time to run into the temple and call 9-1-1 before the electricity went out on the whole farm. I stood there completely out of words as the fire brigade arrived to assess the damage. They figured out that someone had done the wiring improperly, and the blowing wind that evening must have caused a spark. They disconnected the wire and turned the electricity back on. After they left, Dustin and I lay sleeping bags down on the temple floor and settled in for the evening. Before bed, I sat at the computer and wrote an email to the monk, like in my premonition. I told him exactly what had happened—just as I had seen it in the vision—and settled in for the night. I woke up startled every few hours, reliving the unexpected blast of flames. The next day, I emailed Rama and Murali and told them what had happened.

Rumor had it around their community that I had been negligent and burned the cabin down, but the rumor mongers failed to realize that I was away from the farm for about 5 hours that day. Rama and Murali were very understanding of the situation. When they returned from India, I stayed a few more days with them and left to travel around the U.S with Dustin.

Serving the Servant

I later wrote to Jayadvaita Swami, the editor monk who was on the bus tour with us, and asked if I could travel with him for some time as his assistant, and he agreed to the proposal. I was happy to be in a position where I was able to travel with one of the Krsna movement's esteemed teachers, as his assistant. My purpose was to be around others who had spiritual depth and could give me some pointers on how to further blossom spiritually. Association in life is like a crystal; you reflect and absorb the mood of those around you. As a proverb I heard in Liberia went, "Show me your best friend and I'll tell you who you are." I traveled with Jayadvaita Swami mostly in India, and on one occasion, Kenya, Uganda, Tanzania, and South Africa.

It was while traveling from Kisumu, Kenya, to Uganda that we made a stop at Lake Victoria for evening meditation. It was one of the most beautiful meditation experiences. I chanted my *Gayatri* prayers almost in tears. Nothing metaphysical and otherworldly; just the fact that I was sitting at Lake Victoria meditating. It was a culmination of a day's worth of magical experiences. A few hours before, as we drove past the equator line, we saw some Massai tribe members walking along the road, and I flipped. I became very emotional and excited, and Jayadvaita Swami laughed at how taken I was to the Massai people. I told him that I had learned about these people since the second grade and longed to see them one day. The two men who walked along the highway looked very regal, with staff in hand, and a simple orange cloth around their waist. They were slender and wore beautiful embroidered jewelry across their shoulders. I was very excited to see these people who I had read about in one of my library books back in Liberia and also studied in Geography class. Next, we crossed a bridge that went over the Nile River, but this time I contained my overexcitement, silently drinking in the scenery with my eyes. If we weren't traveling with a deadline, it would have been nice to find a pathway to the river bank and take a dip in the river. It was as though these people and places I had longed to see were manifesting one after the other. I could genuinely understand what mommy felt when she saw sites like these. I saw, in my mind's eye, the light come on in her eyes as she talked about these different places. Mom had seen the Nile and the Pyramids when she visited Egypt in 1990.

When I wasn't traveling with Jayadvaita Swami, I would drive around the US in a blue Volvo cross-country station wagon, and speak on the Bhagavad-Gita, or give guidance to friends who asked for it. I had a pretty good line of freedom, similar to what my brother gave me in Minneapolis, and so I took the opportunity to mold myself as a traveling monk. I camped in as many national forests and cool campsites as I could. I was no Massai but felt close to them when I would travel on the open road.

Hi Mama, Hi Toye, Hi Dad.

In the summer of 2009, mommy visited the U.S while I was also there, and not traveling. She was staying with my brother Toye, who I had not seen since 1990 when he left for the US. We had reunited over the phone and would talk regularly, but our busy lives had given us no time to reconnect in person. When Toye called to let me know mommy was visiting, I immediately flew to Atlanta, where he now lived, to see the two of them. I had also not seen mommy in almost fourteen years — since I left Liberia in 1995 — until now at the airport. That year was a significant year for reuniting with my family because I had spent a reasonable amount of time giving counsel to a few families in crisis. I helped save two marriages that year and got to be a mentor for a few youth in crisis. Driving gave me lots of time to contemplate life, and I thought it would be nice also to see my family. If I was keeping other people's families together, I thought it would be nice to reconnect with mine.

Mommy and Toye met me in the passengers' arrival area, and we gave each other big, long hugs. Mommy had a little bit more weight on her than I remembered her. She wasn't obese, but the pressures of war, which kept her weight down when I was in Liberia with her, weren't showing on her body. She looked healthy and happy. The war had ended finally in 2003, and a new President was in office since 2005. She smiled brightly, had that recognizable Gloria gait, and as we walked to the parking lot, we chatted and got caught up on how life was back home. Toye looked very much different from the short big brother I last saw in Liberia. He was built like and had the demeanor of a soldier. Back in Liberia, because he was a few inches shorter, we used to tease him and sing, "shortin', shortin', mama's little baby likes shortin' bread." I think that song caused a lot of sibling fights between the two of us. Now Toye was a responsible man, with a wife and a child.

My sisters were doing well: Chee-Chee was about to graduate college, Calvina would be starting college soon, and Serenna was now married and had a daughter. The house was finished — mommy picked an olive-green color for the exterior — and the trees I had helped plant were all grown and giving fruit. I was now six feet tall, and mommy was still five-foot-two; I teased her about being the short one in the group. Mommy's presence was strong, like the woman I knew and left when I boarded the plane back in Liberia. I could feel her happiness in the car; she was with her two sons and the jokes and remembrances flowed on the ride home. I also found out that she was now divorced from my stepdad, Rupert, although she never told me much detail about the divorce. She was also now an Agriculture Science professor at Cuttington University, 3 hours north of our home. She spent a lot of time up there teaching, and the university provided a house for her.

I got to meet Toye's wife, Chioma, a beautiful lady from Nigeria, and their two-year-old daughter, Vanessa. We spent the weekend reminiscing, gossiping, and recounting my life adventures since I had left my dad and sister. I got a bit emotional and angry at my dad and sister, but mom put their situation in perspective for me. My dad had children who were all grown, at least eight or nine years older than I was, who were away in college or Minneapolis when I arrived in the U.S to live with him. He was trying to be protective, although he didn't know how much freedom and independence mom had given me. She understood that we weren't talking, but urged me to at least give him a phone call. She said time changed people, and I had also matured with the help of the monastery and life travels, so talking with my dad could turn out differently.

As for my sister Cheryl, mom explained that she had her own pressures. She was a young woman starting her career and family life and tried to help my situation with my dad from getting worse. It had been a new experience for all of us, and things didn't turn out right. She joked that both my dad and sister could also be "tight like virgins" in their discipline. I was a young teen-ager needing something they couldn't give at the moment. Mom acknowl-edged that life gave me freedom in other ways like staying with my brother Biodun in Minneapolis, or leaving and being AWOL for the time when no one knew how to get a hold of me.

Mom was the fix-it-all person, but although I heard and understood what she said about my dad and sister, I was adamant about not being around them. My dad thought I was a disappointment, and I wanted to keep it that way. Mom dropped the subject. We enjoyed each other's companies for the rest of the weekend. I taught her and Chioma a yoga class, but they wouldn't let me cook for them. Mom said she was no village girl to eat only damn vegetables. She was "citilized" and wanted some chicken or fish. When I left a few days later, I promised to get in touch with my dad and talk with my sister.

A few months later while driving through Atlanta again, I called my dad, who had now retired and moved to Atlanta, and asked if I could stop in and visit him. I was traveling with two friends, Dustin and Dean, and he said it would be nice to see all of us. When we arrived, dad greeted us outside of his apartment building. He looked thinner than usual but had a happy dispo-sition about him. He welcomed us into his apartment and showed my friends pictures of me as a kid. He had a picture he particularly loved with my sister

Yabo, my cousin Francine, and me. It was taken on the day of Yabo's confirmation at church. I was about four years old and had a cowboy shirt and cowboy hat. I listened as my dad told my friends how I was his favorite son, and how proud he was about what I was doing in my life.

I sat in disbelief. Who was this man, and what had he done with my father? I had never heard of my being a favorite son before. Last, I heard, he was disappointed in me. We talked about spirituality and my traveling as a monk, and all he did was encourage and say how much he prayed for all his kids and our success in all we do. Mom was right; time did change people, and dad was very easy going that afternoon. We hung out with daddy for a few hours, and when we drove away, I called my sister Yabo, now a practicing doctor, and asked her what daddy's deal was. She told me that he had just had a cancer scare, and when people realize they're close to death, they try to make amends and be nicer to people they feel they've wronged. I had no idea about his cancer scare, and laughed with Yabo about daddy being scared to death.

Whatever the scare may have been, it took away a lot of the weight of responsibility my father carried. Being around him felt closer to the dad I knew as a child. At least once a month after that visit, I would call my dad to see how he was doing. We would talk about life, philosophy, and how much he prayed and was proud of his children. My friends must have made an impression on him as well; he called them "good boys." Slowly our bond got better. I would call my dad once a month if even to chat with him for a few minutes. His health was fading slowly, and he would call to tell me what he knew from the doctors.

The bond with my other sister in Virginia didn't reconnect for a while longer. I didn't give her a call like I promised mommy I would, and mommy didn't press the subject. I wanted to take one healing step at a time. Although our bond was cut due to the unfamiliar growing territory, she was still my sister, and I wanted to connect with her slowly and genuinely when the time permitted. When Toye called me to wish me a happy birthday on Christmas Day that year, he did a conference call with Cheryl, and I got to chat with her for about a minute. It was an awkward minute of hello, how are you, and oh good, glad you're happy—the surface stuff; but it was a start in a helpful direction.

Smart Monkeys

As I traveled, I discovered a part of America that I felt I could help. I had learned, from some statistics, that only 30% of Americans had a passport, and even had used it to travel. I understood the workload people had, and the difficulty in finding enough vacation time to experience a place. But there was still America, their home, all around them. With many National Parks, State Parks, and a variety of landscapes, America was, in my opinion, one of the most beautiful places to explore. Most people learned about the travel expeditions of Lewis and Clark and other explorers but didn't take time to get out and see for themselves. With each journey, I would visit hiking trails, hot springs, off-the-beaten-path rivers and lakes, campsites—you name it. I wanted to see firsthand, so that not just what I said about a place, but my excitement could affect someone. Mommy's travel around the world had done the same for me; it was her excited eyes that caught my attention and planted the wanderlust seed in my heart.

During one such travel adventure in 2010, I met Rochelle, my very respected friend and nutritionist who studied at Bastyr University in Seattle, and Dan, an aspiring Yoga teacher and chef. We met in Arizona and sparked a beautiful friendship. They both admired my monastic freedom, and I admired the work they chose to do. With some free time on our hands, we decided to take a road trip up to Seattle and back to Tucson. Rochelle thought her Toyota Camry had the best gas mileage, compared to my Volvo and Dan's truck, so we piled our stuff into the trunk and made our way. I still look back on the many beautiful incidents that happened on that trip, like this one:

We wanted to see Point Reyes Lighthouse and decided to drive there after a late Thai lunch in San Rafael, California. We arrived as dusk approached hoping to see the light beam from the lighthouse. We also thought we would camp out in the area, but learned that we couldn't park overnight along the road. We turned back and tried a few campsites, all too expensive for a short night's stay. We were too lazy to set up a tent in the dark, and also saw a few raccoons in the area. Afraid that they might try to tear into our tent, we decided to sleep in the car. We did, however, pass a Bread & Breakfast along the way with a large parking lot across from it. I said to Rochelle and Dan, "If we don't find a campground soon, let's just call it a night in this parking lot." After a few more searches, we came back to the parking lot. For some reason, I was very adamant about parking next to a red car for the night. As we laid out our sleeping bags and settled in the car for the night, we heard the door of the Bed & Breakfast restaurant slam shut, and out walked a lady to the car, sobbing. She got in, started, reversed, and then drove for about twenty feet; she then turned the car off and started screaming.

The three of us speculated about what could be the matter; perhaps a break-up, or a death in the family? I suggested we go and see what was wrong, but Dan opted to stay in the car and rest. "Rochelle, we're gonna make a new friend tonight," I said. Rochelle, always ready for an adventure, obliged and we grabbed a flashlight and walked toward the car. I tapped gently on the window, and the lady inside opened the door slightly. We could obviously see something was wrong, and so asking "Are you okay?" was out of the question.

"We just wanted to come over and be of any comfort you might need; we're in the car over there. I'm Kesh, and she's Rochelle." She introduced herself as Marinna, thanked us for our concern and said she would be all right. "Since you already have your door open," said Rochelle, "would you like a hug?" Marinna gladly took a hug from Rochelle, and then another from me. By this time, the car door was much more open, and Rochelle squatted next Marinna in the doorway. Marinna, now calm, told us her story:

"It's actually nothing bad; I just attended six-day silent meditation a few miles up the road from here, and it was a most beautiful experience. There where these monks who were so kind, and everyone was very loving. It was all silent, so for those six days, we all said nothing to each other. There were many instances where I wanted to share my realizations but had come to a silent retreat, so I couldn't. After the retreat, I asked my parents to meet me here for dinner and to spend the night at this B&B before going back to the noise and the hustle and bustle of the city. But when we arrived at the restaurant, the chatter and crowd was too much that I couldn't handle it and walked out sobbing. I just don't know how to take all I experienced the past few days back to the city with me."

Rochelle let out a chuckle, and so did I, which caught our new friend off guard. "Why are you laughing?" Marinna asked, and Rochelle, pointing at me, said, "Well, it's funny how there are no coincidences! This guy lives in a monastery, and for whatever reason, he wanted to park next to your car."

This revelation sent our new friend into another sob. "I knew it! I knew it. I could feel your energy as you came close to the car. When I saw your flashlight, I thought, "No please go away. Not now; no more people. But as you came closer, I wanted to open my door and talk with you. I knew it!" She was sobbing, and we hugged again. "I feel very vulnerable and do not know how to handle the busy city right now, what do I do?" She thought that if the small restaurant crowd made her feel so irritated, the big city would be worse.

I told her a story about learning to create a sacred space in oneself that no one can access. The story was about a monkey who lived in a tree on the edge of a lake and a crocodile friend who lived on an island in the middle of the lake. The crocodile would swim to shore every morning and would chat and mingle with the monkey. In the evening, he would bid his monkey friend goodbye, and swim back to his island home. His wife, Mrs. Crocodile, wasn't so pleased that her husband was friends with a monkey who could be a night's dinner. One day she asked her husband to invite the monkey for dinner. She said that the plan was to eat the monkey when he got to the island because he wouldn't be able to swim back to shore. The husband was a bit reluctant about eating his friend for dinner but afraid to anger his wife, he agreed to the plan. The next day he invited his monkey friend as planned, and the monkey said he'd gladly come in a few days.

When the day arrived, the monkey jumped on his crocodile friend's back, and as they swam about fifty feet from shore, the crocodile told the monkey that he was a fool for trusting him. That night he was sure to become dinner for his crocodile family. He told the monkey that they would start by eating his heart. The monkey began to sob and said to the crocodile, "Why didn't you just tell me? I would do anything for you because you're such an honest crocodile. There is one problem, I knew what a good cook your wife was, from what you've told me, and so this morning, as I prepared for dinner, I took my heart and other body parts out to make room for her cooking. If you take me back to shore, I'll just hop in the tree quickly and bring my heart, stomach, and intestines along for dinner." The crocodile, amazed at how lightly the monkey took his plan to eat him, thought it wise to take his friend back to shore for his heart. When they got back to shore, the monkey jumped off the crocodile's back and climbed into his tree. From there, he shouted to the crocodile, "You idiot. Oh, foolish crocodile. Have you ever heard of anyone existing without their heart? Now take yourself home to your wicked wife. We will never be friends from now on." The crocodile angrily left and went back to his island home, where his wife divorced him and went to live on another island. The end. Moral of the story, when you're going to hang with crocodiles, leave your heart at home.

I told Marinna that she could create a sacred space in her house so that when she came home from work, that space could be her rejuvenating spot. I also traveled with a half-man, half lion necklace that was given to me by a friend in India for my protection. I gave her the chain as a gift and told her to meditate on that half man half lion person if she ever felt insecure. Over the years I had given that same kind of necklace to a few different people.

A few minutes later Marina's mother showed up to see how she was doing. "Hi mom, these are my new friends." She was smiling from ear to ear, which left her mother bewildered. "You left the restaurant sobbing to high heaven, and I wanted to come and see how you were doing. It looks like these two have helped a bit." We talked for a few more minutes, and then bid them good night. They walked out of the parking lot and back into the Bed n Breakfast where they had rented a room for the night. We went back into the car and fell asleep. In the morning before we drove off, I left a note on her car windshield, thanking her for sharing her story with us. I also wrote my email for her to keep in touch. About a month later I received this email:

Dear Kesava—

I wake up each morning and put my hand on my throat to see if the necklace is still there. If it were not for this exquisite prayer around my neck, I would believe that I just imagined you up in the throes of my wild sobbing. For I returned the next morning with breakfast offerings, but alas, you were nowhere to be found.

How can I possibly find enough words of gratitude?

Thank you for your fearless compassion.

For knocking on my window that night and embracing exactly what you found there. You said, "That's it, this is why we are all here. To feel it all."

What a gift not to be fixed, but honored. To be heard not advised. To be invited to laugh at the monkeys and the crocodiles and how we all find our way in this world.

My heart is forever wider for that night on the side of the road, your laughter and kindness woven into my every step. I hope I can pass along the gifts you shared with me— and to you may the blessings be returned thousand-fold.

Sending a huge hug out into the universe... to land beside you in your traveling ashram and all those who happen to be traveling with you for the moment.

love,

—

Marinna

Miracles rest not so much on faces or voices or healing power coming from afar off. But upon our being made finer, so that for a moment our eyes can see and our ears can hear what is about us always.

Willa Cather

Rochelle, Dan, and I parted ways after our road trip to Seattle was complete, and I continued to travel to different places, teach, give lectures, and meet new people. Once a year I would go to India for a few months in Kartika for rejuvenation.

Traveling independently enlivened me; It gave me a perspective I had not thought of when trying to work with temples to help develop their outreach: if others were unwilling to empower me, it didn't mean I had no experience of being empowered. In fact, I had a wealth of experience; my mother's standard of raising me was empowerment in itself. I had to tap into that place and use the knowledge and guidance stored within. I understood the Krsna movement's fear of granting independence, due to the hefty price they had to pay in the form of lawsuits and member gripe. Back in the eighties some independent monks misused their privilege of power and did some atrocious things. Their mistakes and misuse of power led to murders, lawsuits, and loss of faithful membership. To counteract and prevent these issues from reoccurring, a lot of rules, resolutions, and regulations were put in place. Some of these rules were necessary, like a crackdown on self-worship and cult following, but others, I felt, could be a bit more lenient. A traveling monk like myself and others, required guidance, like a big brother system where a person had another more experienced person as a mentor.

Chapter Sixteen

Jaycee Kesh Akinsanya

Pull Back

In 2011, almost eight years after my quarter-life crisis in Goa, India, and after trying to connect with people through different avenues, I had to stop and do some sober reflection on how I wanted to give what I had learned in my childhood, as well as in the monastery, to the world. Traveling was working out nicely; I was interacting with unique people. Some of these people I met were very quiet and shied away from visiting large gatherings like temple events. They preferred one on one interactions, and I happened to fit what they were looking for. Others had been jaded by everyday religious institutional politics that they felt dampened their spiritual quest. I came as no savior, but a friend who wanted to know about their lives.

I encouraged activities such as hiking, going to hot springs for a soak, jounaling, and mostly, cooking. Cooking was a big part of my traveling and meeting people. Mom used to say that sharing food was in some ways, more intimate than sex. A cook created pleasure that was nourishing on so many levels. She said that was why people always said that a mother's cooking was the best. The purport was that mothers put loving intentions into their cooking for the health of their families. She enjoyed reading a book called Like Water for Chocolate, which depicted some incidences where people's emotions were transferred into their cooking and felt by those who ate the food. Mom would laugh about how we might all claim to be different, with different philosophies and standards and what not, but when it came to food — good food — all our differences stayed at the door. So above all else, when I met people and stayed with them if even for a night, I volunteered to cook them a meal.

Now I started to wish for something more concrete. I wanted a space to showcase what I was teaching, as well as learning from people on the road. I figured I could have a private space where friends could come and visit me without feeling like they went to a temple. Most of these travel meetings ended in long nights of talking. I empathized with how much people wanted to do to help humanity, but felt like they didn't have an outlet; they felt stuck on a self-maintenance wheel, with not enough oomph to branch out and do something extra. As I traveled like this, I began to see that people had good hearts and good intentions that they could only communicate in conversation. I concluded that I had spent enough time trying to talk about concepts such as community building. Each had a different perspective, but in the end, I wanted to look back at a finished product. That finished product only came about through doing.

I thought up an idea of a community where, say, Rochelle, my friend from Tucson, could act as a nutrition specialist and teach people by taking them out, as she liked to do. They could harvest seaweed and other herbs she knew of in the forest, and then come back and prepare nutritious meals. Dan, my chef friend, who was expert at specialty diets like gluten-free diets, or celiac diets, could have a space to cook for people. Jaymee, another friend, could teach yoga, and make writing retreats with people. We didn't all have to live in the space, but at least we could have such a place for people to use their talents.

I wanted to take people in and "do" community, adventures, and life with them. My mother taught me through her actions; she took in neighborhood children and cared for them as her way of bettering the community around her. She invited people to sit and have a beer, simultaneously creating long-lasting friendships. She was a practical advisor to many, especially as a professor when she would not only teach agricultural science, but help connect her students to job opportunities after college. It was her blend of concept and action that I admired, and in many ways, I felt it could work in my environment. In my reflection, I realized I had to go home to Liberia and visit mom. I could observe and learn from her through a different set of eyes. I would have no teaching obligations or any monk duties. I just wanted to hang out with mommy a bit and go back to my core. For now, I was still traveling and teaching and had just come back to India for some spiritual rejuvenation. I planted the desire to go back home in the back of my mind.

Share Your Good Fortune

India that year was very fulfilling. I invited three young men, Nick, Daniel, and Luke, to stay at a retreat space in Vrindavan, where Jayadvaita Swami and some other Krishna devotees would gather for a month, and immerse themselves in study and meditation. At the retreat space, the senior monks created an atmosphere that invited you in and made you feel like you were a valued part of their group, with access to their counsel at any time. In the evenings when we would gather to read, it wasn't a teaching session, but a learning discussion that anyone could partake in. Anyone could ask questions or present a philosophical thought. The guys I was traveling with loved the setting and took as much advantage of the concentration of knowledgeable monks at the retreat; most of whom were direct students of Srila Prabhupada, the Krsna movement's founder. I thought it would be nice for the senior monks to take a day away from their responsibilities, so we went on an excursion to a holy place one day. Most of the monks who stayed at that retreat space were teachers like Prithu, who had students around the world. The plan turned out successful, and we all enjoyed the outing.

After Vrindavan, we traveled with Jayadvaita Swami to Mayapur, West Bengal, the birthplace of Lord Caitanya, the incarnation of Krsna who Jaya Saci jokingly told me would drag a person back to the spiritual world by their sikha. Mayapur also has the headquarters of the Krsna movement and has a large community consisting of schools, a temple, housing communities, and gardens.

On Jayadvaita Swami's 60th birthday, we had a sweet celebration, and as all of us spoke in his honor, one person read out a letter from his mother. I was baffled by the fact that he had a mother. Some simple human things just didn't cross my mind around some of the monks. They were larger than life for me, and for some reason, hearing about the swami's mother caught me off-guard. When I told another friend about my back-to-reality moment of realizing Jayadvaita Swami had a mother, he laughed and asked, "What, you thought he just fell from the skies or descended from the heavens in his monk garb?"

Another monk in Mayapur who I loved to hear from was a monk named Bhakti-vidya-purna Swami. I made sure I didn't miss a day of any of his discourses which he gave at the local school for boys. The school was built using according to the principles of Vastu, the Vedic version of Feng Sui, with gardens, an open-air kitchen, a stunning temple space, and living quarters. The school was about a mile walk from where I stayed in Mayapur. Every morning, people would gather and sit in their outdoor classroom, and the swami would speak for about an hour. His talks were very enlivening, and he also had a wicked sense of humor that I enjoyed. He told me that during his lectures, when he would make a joke, he could always determine which part of the world the audience was from. If he told an "American" joke, the Americans present would get it and laugh, as the other foreigners sat listening seriously, or vice versa. Luke, Nick, and Daniel enjoyed going to the school and listening to the lectures as well and were amazed at how the swami broke down the Vedic lessons.

We stayed in Mayapur for a month and then Jayadvaita Swami left for South Africa. Luke went back to the U.S while I visited and toured other parts of India with Nick, Daniel and two devotees, Abhi and Chay, from South America. For Nick and Daniel, I hoped it would be a magical experience. I wanted to travel with them like I had gone through India years before.

223

I wanted them to see the innocent realness of India, where nothing about life was hidden from view. In most parts of India, one could find wealth and poverty existing side by side. We traveled mostly along the coast and visited small beach towns to make sure we got some excellent swimming in the warm ocean waters. We also visited some newer places I hadn't seen, especially around the state of Orissa, where Jagannath Puri, the location of the yearly chariot festival, is situated.

In Jagannath Puri, we stayed at an ashram which used to the home of Bhaktivinode Thakur, one of the esteemed gurus in the Vaisnava tradition. The head monk who lived there loved our little traveling party and arranged for us to get Jagannath Maha Prasad every night. In Jagannath Puri, a multitude of preparations are made daily and placed on the altar for offering to Krsna in an abstract deity form. Also residing on the altar with Jagannath, are Balarama, his brother, and Subhadra, their little sister. Again, the Vedic concept of divinity shows that God is not a lonely person; he has a family. When the preparations are offered on the altar, they are then distributed to the general public as "Maha Prasad," meaning the "highest benediction."

Jagannath Maha Prasad is also another abstract, and yet a tangible way of understanding the Vedic concept of associating with the supreme. Not everyone is allowed to enter the temple of Jagganath because of Hindu traditional beliefs, just as non-Muslims are forbidden to enter Mecca. To associate with everyone and grant the experience of love beyond borders, Lord Jagannath invests his transcendental potencies into the food. So anyone who eats Jagannath Maha Prasad is said to be directly associating with Lord Jagannath. We obliged and took in as much of Lord Jagannath as we could in the form of scrumptious daily meals.

Beautiful Yamuna

A few weeks later, while in Srirangam, India, I fell sick due to anxiety. We were now traveling through South India when I got news that one of my mentors, Yamuna Devi, had just died that morning. She was one of the founding members of the Krsna movement, and her voice was immortalized in a song produced by George Harrison of The Beatles. In every Krsna temple, the song called "Govinda" is played in the morning, when the altar is opened, unveiling the deities in their daily outfits. Yamuna's depth in spiritual practice helped her, and those around her, find balance in spiritual exploration. She compiled a cookbook on Indian Vegetarian Cooking, from which she won the International Association of Culinary Professionals (IACP) Cookbook of the

Year. I had learned some cooking tips from her when I got to associate with her. I recalled and relayed my first meeting with her in Vancouver, Canada. A mutual friend and I were talking at the Vancouver chariot festival when Yamuna Devi walked by. I was introduced to her and became utterly star struck and overwhelmed. She reached out and gave me a hug which caused me to sob in her arms. She had a purity and love I had never experienced with anyone else. In later years, to my great fortune, she allowed me to use her meditation beads, the same one that Srila Prabhupada had chanted on at her initiation.

I canceled the rest of the South Indian tour and went back north to Vrindavan where a few other friends of Yamuna were celebrating her life. However, I couldn't attend the ceremony because my body took the news quite heavily. The morning after our arrival in Vrindavan my body was covered in hives. My loss-coping emotions manifested that way and stayed like that for a week. Daniel and Nick were very kind to look after me at that time. I had a week to lie in bed and reflect on my future. I had studied quite a lot about the Vedic culture and how it benefitted human society today. Yoga, Ayurveda, and other aspects of Vedic knowledge were now common knowledge in the West, and I again considered creating a space where people could come and learn about these things. I wanted the environment to be like the one I grew up in: welcoming and nurturing. I would incorporate my mother's inviting nature and show, by my example, how yoga and a simple regulated life worked for me. My thought was to create genuine friends who felt at home in my space, and if the need came up in conversation, I would share what I had learned. I had also gotten the association of some deeply realized Krsna devotees who encouraged my independent traveling and teaching methods.

Lying in bed gave me time to think. It was there I decided I didn't want to be a monk anymore, but would slowly transition myself into a more mainstream life—again. Monastic life had its own set of rules of the trade that wouldn't necessarily work. For example, I couldn't work an outside job as a monk, because the temple took care of my livelihood in exchange for my services. Living as a layman would give me more independence in my outreach, and less dependence on the temples for support. As a layman, I could create a space I felt comfortable with—my own house, living life as I saw fit.

Navel Gazing

In the Krsna community, I was a bit of an independent spirit and butted heads with a few authority figures. I felt capable of teaching independently;

I had the permission from my own teacher, as well as the monk I was traveling with, but in certain areas, the temples I visited felt territorial. I felt an air of subtle, forceful conformity, like a need to centralize the movement and bring everyone to a page where rules of presenting the philosophy could be established. I had no problem with conformity or centralization, but I had a major problem with leaders and teachers not knowing who their students and followers were, and not making an effort to recognize if centralization and conformity fit everyone. For some, it was necessary, for me, it choked my creative spirit. The movement's founder, Srila Prabhupada, had also warned against centralization in a few letters and instructions, and I was feeling the adverse effects of it when I visited certain temples.

What I would always present, when the topic arose, was a need to give people, especially ones new to the Krsna philosophy, a practical understanding of the beauty that was in the books. I felt like I had received that in Seattle, and I had gained lots of appreciation for the Vedas. The monks weren't hardcore and cloistered; they worked hard and studied hard, but found time for associating with each other. We played Frisbee or soccer, took road trips, and watched movies, like Brother Sun Sister Moon, depicting the life of St Francis of Assisi. Living in the Seattle felt wholesome to me.

While visiting some temples, I would hear young novice monks talk about how fallen from grace they felt, or their problems with celibacy, or their problem with an authority figure. I saw the opposite: they were fortunate, with an excellent philosophy to show them how lucky they were. They only had to take some time and study the books to understand their good fortune. I gave a lecture in one temple addressing this fallen from grace mentality. The priests who take care of the altar and ceremonies make a loving effort to decorate the temple, dress the Radha and Krsna deities in beautiful outfits with flower garlands and other accessories. The temple hall was set up in a way that encouraged chanting and dancing, yet I would watch some people mope and "navel gaze," as Prithu called it. Prithu would say that only one being in all of creation was allowed to gaze at his navel because something useful came out of it. That person is Vishnu. When Vishnu looks down at his navel, as the creation of the material universe story goes, a lotus flower sprouts forth, and Lord Brahma, the first created being, is seated on that lotus flower. When we looked down at our navels, we see nothing and become depressed. I addressed the navel-gazing issue. "Krsna gets up in the morning and puts on his best outfit for the day," I said, "And he, God, is eager to come and associate with us in a loving mood. The music is right; the venue is clean and beautiful, yet when the altar opens to us, we stand there gazing at our navels and moping about our various miseries. I'm sure that Krsna knows everything about our situations. He knows where we are weak and where we are strong, and in spite of all that, he wants to love us, and accept love from us. We should learn to cultivate a sweeter attitude when we stand in front of the altar. When we change our inner language, we just might receive the grace we feel so far away from."

As for celibacy, I encouraged some young devotees that it would take time and patience, as Jaya Saci had encouraged me. The world we lived in had sex all around us, and we had to be patient with ourselves. I too had celibacy issues as a young novice back in 1999 with those wet dreams. When I learned the monks were celibate, I became furious at my friends in Liberia who had fooled me into losing my virginity; something, I felt if I still had, could be valuable to me in the monastery. I carried that anger and also felt fallen from grace and unable to take the philosophy fully. However, my superiors like Jaya Saci and Deva, back when I was a novice monk cared, and gave me engagements that made me feel like I was contributing. I would help cook in the kitchen, give lectures, and go to town and distribute books.

Soon I began to relish the philosophy I was giving to others and began to see that Krsna, God, knew everything about me. And in spite of my lack of virgin purity or lack of anything else, I was still given the opportunity to practice spiritual life. I understood what mommy meant when she said people beat themselves up for not being patient enough to see where their philosophical quest could lead them. As for dealing with authority figures, traveling was suitable for me. I could visit a temple for some time, and leave when I wanted to. I had permission to do so. I had seen many authority figures abuse the position they held, and cause discord for the people they were meant to be guiding.

Lastly, the reason I had joined the Krsna movement was to be a part of a missionary movement, sharing the good fortune of Vedic wisdom with others. As the years went by, other members who couldn't live in the temples for life, moved out to start their families and live more secular lives. There weren't many left in the temples to train young novices, and the focus became more on maintaining the temples than missionary work. As one monk put it, as the years went on, the movement formed into a society, but the society stopped moving. I wanted to get a focus on movement, but I felt voiceless and became increasingly disinterested in temple activities

Resolve.

One of the recurring thoughts which flowed in my mind while bedridden in India was the seed I had planted to go back home and get mommy's association. Emotionally, it thought it would be good to take a vacation and reconnect with my family. Hearing from mommy back in 2009, that my sisters were now grown women, that the house had been painted, and the trees were grown and giving fruit, made me a bit nostalgic, and I began to long for home. I tried to come up with different ideas that could take me to Africa more; West Africa, in particular. Jayadvaita Swami was traveling mostly to East and South Africa and was making plans to visit West Africa, so I thought it would be good to travel with him there. I even thought about moving back to Liberia to live. I could ask a few monks to come with me, and we could go and start a center there. But there weren't many young monks available to travel since the temples needed all the manpower they could use for daily temple affairs.

I also got some good encouragements from Prithu. He encouraged me to keep searching and studying and allow the knowledge I was learning to digest into practical wisdom. He told me that sometimes, it was best to give wisdom or expertise in the body of an older person, than a younger person. He gave an example of the redwood and sequoia trees in Northern California. He said that a few hundred years ago, when they were small trees, perhaps no one cared for them. But now they were humongous trees, with age, and everyone went to them. He encouraged me to slowly keep moving forward, and not try to be some big leader. He saw that being a small circle person was more suitable for me, and not a figure with a large crowd following me.

He was right in his observations of my personality. I have a tough time with crowds because I feel like I can't spend enough time with each person. I prefer smaller gatherings where I can focus on a few people, and engage in conversations with them. At large parties, I feel anxious, especially when I greet old friends or meet new people. I feel like our interactions become shallow with small talk, just to acknowledge each other's presence in the room.

After I recovered from my hive outbreak in India, I decided to go back to the US, figure out how much time I would be able to spend if I went back to Africa, and have a definite plan for when I returned. Daniel and Nick left Vrindavan a few weeks before my flying back to America. Some friends invited me to a few weddings and birthday celebrations in the summer months, so I figured April and May of 2012 were two good months to visit mommy.

I came back to the US in early March and made a short road trip from Chicago to San Jose to visit some friends who had just had a baby. I was a bit low on funds, so I decided to sell my Volvo cross-country station wagon, and have a buffer for when I got back. If my plans to open a center worked out, I wouldn't need to travel as much as I did before. I was also planning on being in a city where I could do more walking than driving. I bought a ticket and decided to go to Liberia for six weeks.

Jaycee Kesh Akinsanya

Mama

Japanese Gardens, Kenneth Hahn State Park, Los Angeles.

Walking to the beach, Jagannath Puri, India

Dancing, Chariot Festival. Durban, South Africa

At a friend's home in Govardhana, near Vrindavan, India.

Mommy, Chee-Cheae, and Me at our ELWA home.

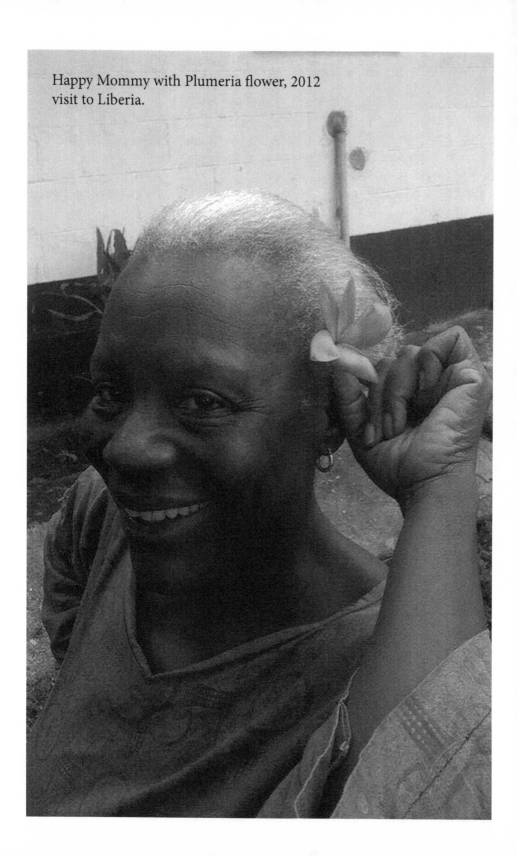

Happy Mommy with Plumeria flower, 2012 visit to Liberia.

Chee-Chee and her son, Vanness

Calvina, my
baby sister

Serenna, expecting her
first child

Mommy and colleagues ,
Cuttington University farm

This page: Mom with colleagues/ students after a symposium.
Next page: Mommy with Melvin, Grace and Crystal
(l-r)
Next Page below:
With Isaac (black and white shirt), and friends at Kpatawee falls.

Oshala Farm
Planting echinacea

Nikko stole my grandfather's Pith hat style.
After work at Oshala Farm.

Hands-free; learned from the war days. Off to plant artichokes at Oshala Farm.

Working in Catherine's garden, U.S. Virgin Islands. This was the morning we woke up to her singing "Bitch Better Have My Money."

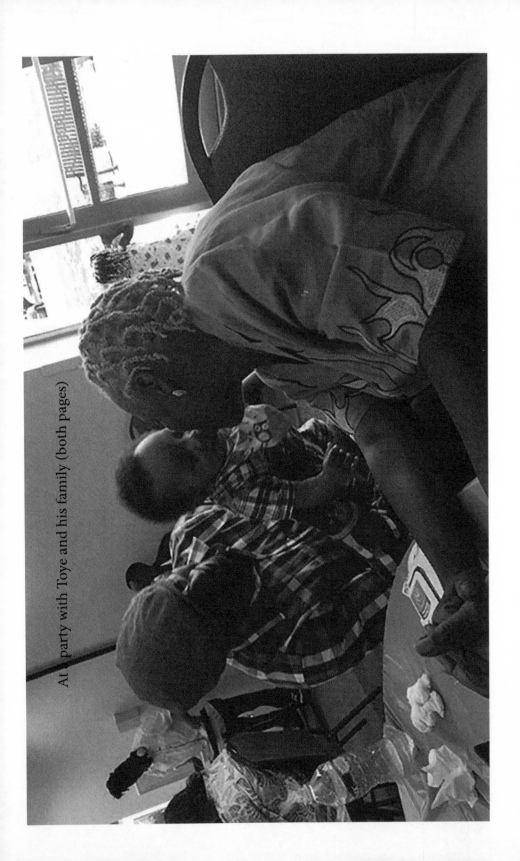

At a party with Toye and his family (both pages)

Mommy and Nikko doing what
they love best: gardening together.
Helping Nikko build a squash trellis

Relaxing her mental tension with a chilled bottle of beer at the farm in Missouri

Virgin Islands shenanigans. Next page:
With our Great Dane, Neil Diamond at
the farm in Missouri.

Mommy dressed in traditional Liberian "country cloth" on her retirement day. (Both Pages)

Last three images:
The moth that landed on my hand after I hung up the phone with
mommy.

When we visited her in Virginia, we went out to have Thai food.
We took this picture for Nikko's Uncle and Aunt, Roy and Rose.
This was one of the last photos of mommy, a week before she fell ill.

Carrying mommy one last time at the commencement of her funeral.

Chapter
Seventeen

Jaycee Kesh Akinsanya

Sister Gloria's Son

It had been seventeen years since I last saw the tropical rainforests of home. As the plane descended, I could see the winding Montserrado River that I watched back in 1995 as the aircraft ascended to the skies. I looked at it with different eyes now; with an appreciation for nature and different climates. Liberia is a country close to the equator and the Atlantic Ocean, so the hot temperature and humid air were the first things to greet me as I stepped off the Brussels Airlines flight. It was mid-April, and there were mangoes on the trees and fresh coconut in the coconut trees. The airport, Robert's International, which was now operational, looked like a small municipal airport like the kind you'd find in a small city like Medford, Oregon. I hadn't flown from this airport before.

Mommy wasn't on the tarmac like she was when I left. Airport meet-and-greet rules had changed. Like other airports around the world, there was now tight airport security, and after I made it through customs, I saw mommy and Chee-Chee waiting for me. The six-year-old Chee-Chee I had left back in Liberia was now twenty-three and reminded me of mommy in her youthful days. Chee-Chee was stylish and had a presence of her own. She was a young woman now. Calvina, my other sister, was away at the University where mommy taught classes.

I had seen mommy just three years earlier at Toye's house in Atlanta, but now she had lost a small amount of weight. She had some dark circles under her eyes and told me her sleep schedule had gone to about five hours a night, hence the circles. Her hair was a bit greyer, and to me, she looked like a woman who had come into wisdom. A few years earlier she looked happy and confident, but now the happiness and confidence had transformed into content and wise. She seemed very relaxed and at ease with life. Her smile, laughter, and joking nature remained. When I was a child, mommy looked larger than life and unapproachable by some; like she had all the answers to life, and knew it, and caused others to be intimidated by her. Now she still had all those answers, knew it, and could be approached for them. I promised her that when she came back to the U.S, we'd have a spa day and relax our mental tension.

Walking out of the airport with my arms around mommy and Chee-Chee, I was immediately thrown back into my mother's natural world of her knowing everyone and being the life of the party. We went to visit a good friend of hers who worked at the Airport VIP arrivals area. "Gloria, if you had told me my Jaycee was coming I would have arranged for him to go right through here without having to deal with customs." It felt good to be back home with mommy's friends. It did take a village to raise me, and I was back home to the village of loving mothers, sisters, brothers, aunts, and uncles. Even the driver was happy to see me, although I had never met him. The weeks that followed were full and strengthening in ways I still haven't begun to digest. Lines from conversations with mom still unfold in my daily interactions; tastes of fresh fruit picked directly from the tree come back to me when my memory reconnects with that time. It was a much-needed time for mother and son connection.

The authenticity that mom was known for was the basis of every aspect of her life. It had not changed; I lived through it, left it when I came to the US, and reconnected to it when I saw her in Atlanta. Now I saw it again back at home. She stopped and talked to every person who knew her, but used my arrival and fatigue as a way to keep the chat short. The drive home was short, about twenty minutes, and I easily recognized places I hadn't seen in years. The trees I had planted in the yard with mommy years before were now grown and bearing lots of fruit: coconuts, palm-nuts, almonds, and cashews. The house now had a fence around it. Looting and armed robbery had gotten out of hand for some time, and so mom built a wall around the house to help prevent people from coming into the yard. Along the fence, mom had made a few pens for pigs and monkeys she kept as pets. Chickens were running around the yard, and the cat had just had a litter of six kittens. Chee-Chee had also just acquired a mutt puppy whom she named "Bloody Hell," because of his love for biting people.

The atmosphere was different at home than I had left it, due to mommy's divorce a few years before. There was more room since Rupert and my step-brothers didn't live there anymore. Chee-Chee had taken over my old room, and another girl, Martha, was staying at the house. Serenna was married and living a mile away on a piece of land which mom bought her as a wedding gift. I stayed with mommy in her room—we didn't sleep at all. We watched "Alias," her favorite TV show at the time, and talked for hours and hours. Like a child, I kept opening and closing cupboards, going through her jewel drawer and looking at old jewelry she had before the war and saved during the war. I was acclimating myself to our home. Most of the pictures in the album had been damaged due to the war, or the intense humidity.

The next day, I resumed wandering the neighborhood, saying hi to everyone I hadn't seen in seventeen years, revisiting the lagoon Chris and I played in as kids and walking the beach as far as I could go. My mermaid rock was still there as well. Chee-Chee walked with me and filled me in on the last few years of mommy's marriage. We talked about everything and enjoyed a lovely walk by the ocean. To my astonishment, parts of the beach had eroded away, as we feared when the Armed Forces cut down those coconut trees during the war. But people were making efforts to plant more trees and slow the erosion process down.

There were more houses in the neighborhood now with a lot of new faces. They all knew me as "Sister Gloria's son," or "mommy's son," and they welcomed me with opened arms. The fishermen had expanded their empire on the beach but now took a different route to the market after mommy put up the fence. Some people heard that I was vegetarian and wanted to cook for me, so mommy instructed them how to prepare traditional Liberian dishes without meat or fish. Back at home mommy, Chee-Chee, and I watched Alias and reminisced about how much the neighborhood had grown in seventeen years.

I also went to the Old Road to walk around my old neighborhood and take some pictures for Facebook. I wanted to keep in touch with my friends who were back in the U.S, and couldn't get through to me via phone. As I walked around the Old Road neighborhood, I felt a bit awkward. Our old yard and the old house looked tiny like it had shrunk over the years. It was a new walking and exploring experience for me, and I tried to make sense of what I was seeing. The swamp took a shorter time to get to, and while there I took a few pictures of the canoes, which looked smaller than when we used to ride in them.

I pondered the new experience as I walked around. Ma Eya had passed away some years ago, and her grandchildren lived in her house now. I introduced myself to them and showed them where I lived 20 years ago, before moving to Duala in 1992. Soon, I had made new friends as I did back then, and they walked around with me through the neighborhood. I stopped at the Dee's residence and greeted Mr. Dee, who told me that his son E.D, my friend, was living in the U.S. I promised to get in contact with him when I returned to America. Finally, I spent the rest of the afternoon with Aunty Zoe, who had built a house next door, where Aunty Kolubah and family used to live. Aunty Kolubah and her family were now living in the U.S as well. Aunty Zoe and I relaxed, chatted, cooked, and reminisced about our lives. I told her all about my travels to India, and living in the monastery, and that I was hoping to go back to the U.S and do more teaching after my break. I went back home to ELWA later that evening, as we were preparing to go to mommy's university campus the next day.

Cuttington

The next morning, mommy, Chee-Chee and I drove three hours to Cuttington University where mommy lectured and had an on-campus three-bedroom house. My other sister Calvina lived there along with Grace, Melvin, Crystal, and Wata; four young children mom had adopted. Calvina too was now a young lady, not the three-year-old baby I left on my way out of Liberia. She had a very welcoming presence about her. I noticed that all my siblings had an aspect of our mom that shone through. Cheryl had mom's "professional' personality, and Toye, whom I called mom's "male version," was equipped with mommy's common-sense and practical nature. I had mommy's traveler and philosophical gene, and Chee-Chee was a replica of mommy's youthful, spirited wild girl personality. Calvina possessed a quality of mommy that I envied the most. She had mommy's "chill." Calvina was very calm and composed and was mommy's right-hand girl around the house now. I told mommy that Calvina was born with "relaxed mental tension;" nothing ever bothered her.

Cuttington University's campus was beautifully situated in the lush Liberian rainforest. Close to mommy's house was a large mango tree, and I arrived just in time for mango season. Picking a ripe mango from the tree brought back a pleasure I had missed for years. This variety of mango next to mommy's house was one we called "German plums;" the external color stayed green even in the ripened stage. They grew in large clusters and to find a ripe one was easy—you just shook the branch—and the ripe mango would fall to the floor. We developed a yummy way to enjoy the mangoes: massage the fruit until it felt tender and juicy inside, then pierce one end and suck out the delicious, juicy pulp. When the mash was all done, peel the mango all the way and suck on the seeds till there was no mango flavor left. Usually, mangos are picked at a half ripen stage before being shipped to US grocery stores. When I bought mangoes in the stores, I could always taste the half-ripened flavor instead of that of ripe mango.

Next to the mango tree was a small garden plot with lots of peppers, okra, watermelon, and jute. I decided to eat mostly fresh from the garden for the six weeks I would be in Liberia. I'd eat traditional Liberian dishes on most afternoons but mostly stuck to fresh fruit and raw vegetables. Another available fruit that I hadn't recently had ripe off the plant was pineapples. We grow a variety in Liberia called "Sugarloaf," which tastes like a few cups of sugar syrup mixed with pineapple essence, and pumped into a pineapple shell. I enjoyed a few sticks of sugarcane as well. My great-grandmother had a sugar cane patch, and when we were kids, mommy would take us to

Marshall, where granny lived, for vacation. At my great-grandmother's I was always sticky from sugarcane juice. When I asked for bitter kola nut, a favorite bitter flavored nut, Calvina, my sister asked why a monk would want to eat bitter kola and get his nuts vexed (get an erection/feel horny). After a good laugh from everyone present, I explained that bitter kola was also used as a tonic to fight colds and improve lung function. Since I came to the U.S, I suffer from constant sinus allergy attacks, and bitter kola helps me.

As I had left it years before, students were sitting around the house doing their homework, watching TV, playing. It was as though Cheryl, Toye, and Jaycee left for the US, and Ansu, Isaac, Fati and everyone else took over. Mom's house was the place to be, and everyone wanted to be there. Calvina's friends would come and hang out, so I got to meet many of them. When she found out I had been a model, Fati, one of the students at CU, and previous Miss Cuttington, engaged me in helping prepare the contestants for the upcoming beauty pageant. In exchange for helping her with the show, Fati cooked me a few traditional dishes.

Isaac, Calvina's boyfriend, took me on excursions around the area. We rode motorcycles, called "pan-pans," through nearby villages. They were called "pan-pans because of the sound made by the horns. We made a trip to Kpatawee Falls, a beautiful waterfall in the region. Kpatawee showed me a more indigenous side of Liberia that I hadn't experienced before. Some tribal people were bathing naked under the falls, and the beauty of the scenery caught my attention. I admired their simple dependence on nature. They lived in a warm area, grew their own food, and had a natural waterfall shower for daily cleansing. While sitting to take a photo in a grassy area on one of the rocks, I suddenly felt a pinch on my inner thigh and realized that I had sat on a fire ant colony. I jumped around and made my way out of the area while brushing the ants away. Their stings burned for a few minutes.

The area was also hilly with a lower temperature, and less humidity than the beach house, so I stayed at Cuttington for most of my trip. Mommy loved the hills; her office and classroom was a half-mile walk, and she taught about three classes a day, so she got her daily exercise walking back and forth to class. She taught agriculture science and agribusiness. Since she hadn't gone to college to become a teacher, and worked for the government in the commerce sector, as a horticulture specialist, she brought in a different dynamic to the academic atmosphere. Her expertise in the business aspect of the subject was one reason she was asked to teach at the university. In front of her office, she had six moringa trees. She wanted to showcase one of the tropical world's most beneficial trees and chose the moringa olifera, a tree known for its many benefits and ability to grow in many regions of the world.

267

She explained that every part of the tree was useful, and a lot of studies were being done to explore its benefits in the medical field. It is a plant used in many culinary dishes in Asia, and in Liberia, most people used the leaves for tea. On the campus farm, there were many varieties of trees and other plants, and mommy was interested in exploring ways of growing local foods to feed people in the rural areas.

Golden Years Revisited

I did notice that something crucial was missing at the house. While mom was teaching, I found some of her old CDs and played a few. Some of the students sitting in the living room had puzzled looks on their faces. This was music from the past, like James Ingram and Teddy Pendergrass. Most of the students at the house were born after 1990 and had never heard much of the artists of the 80s other than the famous icons such as Michael Jackson, Prince, and Whitney Houston. They were used to newer artists like Justin Timberlake, Akon, and others. When mommy walked through the door, they all cheered as she put her purse down and broke into a dance to Luther Vandross. They had not seen her in this light, but this was the mother I knew; this was the missing link to what I knew was home. The icing on the cake appeared when Kenny Rogers' "*The Gambler*" played and mommy and I danced to our heart's content. "The old ma is an old timer oh!" and "Wow, mommy, we didn't know you had all this talent hidden somewhere" were the statements made by some of the kids in the house.

"You mind these heathens," mommy joked, "they didn't get a taste of sweet Liberia. The war spoiled it for them." The war had indeed spoiled it for sweet Liberia. Sweet Liberia was, as mom would consider, a period when Liberia was at her best. Dignitaries such as Queen Elizabeth the 2nd, Emperor Haile Selassie of Ethiopia, and others visited Liberia. Nina Simone and other musicians like Hugh Masekela lived for some time in Liberia. What to speak of Liberia's talent like Fatu Gayflor and Miatta Fambuleh, T. Kpahn Nimley and Zack and Geba. Music and dancing went on for hours into the night, and sometimes even into the next morning. Places like Hotel Africa and Ducor Palace Hotel were hot spots for people from all around the world. The Liberian Dollar was on par with the American dollar.

Although I was very young at the time to know or understand Liberia's history, I shared what I remembered with my siblings and their friends. I talked about Sophie's Ice Cream parlor, a place my dad or mom took us too once a week. My dad loved the fried cassava wedges they served at Sophie's.

There was Diana's Restaurant, Rivoli Cinema, Crown Hill Cinema and many other places for recreation. The beaches were clean and filled with tourists. The roads were nicely paved, and as I recalled, everything looked very orderly.

I glorified our mom with stories my sisters hadn't heard before. I imitated her "younger girl" dance moves which solicited an eye roll from mommy. She used to wear stilettos, and when she was dancing, she'd hold her cigarette-holding hand in the air, and her bottle of beer in another. She'd then make a dance move way down to the floor and back up with a huge grin on her face. Everyone laughed to see me imitate mom. "Where do you think we got our dance moves from," I asked her, as she laughed at how us kids used to spy on her as she was enjoying life.

Even her dress code, although still elegant, had toned down a bit. She wore beautiful dresses with matching earrings, shoes, and necklaces. Aunty Somo, mom's younger sister, shared the funniest memory of going into mommy's closet and taking a pair of shoes and a dress to wear to a party, and how mommy later found out and went to chastise Aunty Somo. Mommy tried to grab her from the back, but Aunty Somo had on a big button-down shirt that she quickly slipped out of and ran away. In the process, mom broke a fingernail, which was more disastrous than the missing dress and shoes. She had long beautiful nails and had an array of nail polish that she used once a week. I would sit at her vanity and color code all the lipsticks and nail polishes. I think, perhaps my first offense to her was when I spilled a bottle of nail polish on her tie-dyed bedspread. I was probably three or four. I didn't get a spanking at that age, but she was upset at the maid for leaving me to my own devices in her room. She had an electric call bell by the side of her bed which she would ring to get one of us to do her bidding.

Mommy used to be a prankster as well. I am de-tickled now, because of the amount of tickling she did to Toye and me. She told us stories of her younger schoolgirl days when she and her friends got in one trouble or another. My favorite story from her younger days, which I shared with the girls, was when mom would have to go to "revival" church services. At revivals, you'd stay at the church overnight, mostly singing hymns and sometimes listening to a sermon. Often, during these revivals, someone would "catch the Holy Spirit," and fall into an ecstasy, shaking, trembling, and rolling around. Mommy didn't like revivals so much and said that she and her friends would feign ecstatic symptoms, beginning with a shake and a tremble and scream, ending with a roll out the church door to freedom.

Mommy enjoyed me telling stories about her younger days, and at one point, chimed in about how her children and the kids these days think they're doing something new or clandestine, and try to hide from grown-up eyes. "I've done everything, and even more, and I know all the signs to look for when young people think they have something to hide. I was young once." Although she admitted, there were a few places where a line was drawn; she thought that in most cases where parents chastised their kids, young people should be left alone, either to learn a lesson or to get an experience out of their system. "I might be sitting in my room playing computer games, but I see everything happening on this campus. I know their girlfriends, boy-friends, everything.

We talked about some of mommy's friends, some now deceased, who made sweet Liberia happen, at least at our house. Some of those friends were in the U.S now, and she kept regular contact with them. Seeing my love for Spicy foods, she brought up Aunty Facia's passion for spicy food: "Man, Tee-tee (Aunty Facia) could eat some hot peppers. She would eat one spoon of rice, and one hot pepper. And her short Bishop self was fiery too! She'd drive that small car around town, and instead of using her horns, she'd yell out the window cussing people in her way. All the Bishops know how to cuss." She laughed, reminiscing about the good old days on the Old Road, in Sweet Liberia.

"And that damned Toye. He could never remember anyone's name to save his life!" Mommy recalled how my brother would forget people's names, and try to speak fast enough so that they heard him say hi when he saw them but didn't quite hear their names. "He would show up from the football field, and we'd be sitting on the porch, and Toye would walk in. The person would say, 'Hi Toye.' And Toye would respond, 'Hi Uncle (gibberish), or Aunty (gibberish).' But Facia always caught him. 'Toye,' Facia would say, 'What's my name?' 'Aunty Fa#$%*' Toye would muddle, and she'd tease and torture him a bit longer before letting him go."

"And don't mess with us Bishop women. Remember how Cousin M picked up the big rock from the road and threw it on Uncle Y's car? He was cheating on her and parked his car by my house to make it look like he was here visiting. But M was a Bishop; we're no fools. She came and saw that everyone else, except her boyfriend, was sitting and drinking, so she took a huge rock and Bam! Right on the car windshield. When Uncle S asked her not to throw another rock, she said if he didn't shut up, she'd throw one at him too." We laughed hysterically at the story. Life was sweet then, and they sucked as much juice out of it as they could. And we kids got the remnants – candy and school report card money.

Correct, that my sisters missed the golden days of Liberia, but they had mommy at home with them. I was living in the U.S relying on the lessons I'd

270

learned from her. They had her present-day wit and common sense. I envied them. But I was there in Liberia at that moment, getting to know my sisters as women. I took as much advantage as I could and hung out in their world; to reaffirm that I had indeed come from a fantastic family. Mom indulged me and let me bring back so many stories of things I noticed as a child or stories she told us of her girlhood. The people around her got to see another side of her – dancing, singing Gloria.

Life had gotten busy, and the music was minimal. Mom relaxed her mental tension now by playing detective games on her computer or watching movies and TV shows. It was the beginning of the rainy season, a season that took me back to my pre-war childhood. As a child, when it rained, I would snuggle under mom's bedsheets and watch The Sound of Music, or Sheena, Queen of the Jungle. I must have watched both of those movies over fifty times. The rainy season lasts for six months in Liberia, and I watched either of those movies once or twice a week. I know for sure that I have seen The Sound of Music over a hundred times so far. Even now, I make it a point to watch it at least three times a year.

I noticed the kids—Melvin, Grace, Chrystal, and Wata—quarters were a little messy and I asked mom why it was so. Our room had to be pristine, though we struggled to keep it so. Mom said she had passed her disciplining age and had reached her "don't give a fuck" age at forty. Now she was sixty-two, and was in her "relax my mental tension age," and couldn't be bothered telling the kids to clean up. It was now Calvina or Isaac's job to discipline everyone. I asked her why I wasn't born at such a time; I would have escaped a lot of spankings.

Talking to mom about the kids' room brought back the incident I had experienced a few days earlier on the Old Road, and I told her how everything looked so tiny on the Old Road. "You've grown up, that's why. You were looking at things from a different vantage point." How could she just pinpoint what I had pondered for hours that day? I had grown. The house and land were the same; my body had grown two feet since I was last on the Old Road. She got a bit philosophical with me in this conversation, and I soaked in her wisdom on change and its effect. "The sign of growth is that your perspective changes. I always feel like as the years go by, and as we learn, we should look at life with newer eyes." She was relaxed on her bed as she spoke, and I sat on the vanity stool in her room, paying rapt attention to her. "Some people stay stuck in how they view the world, yet the world changes every day. I hardly go to town much anymore because it irks me to see friends doing the same old thing they did twenty/thirty years ago. But they have big mouths and want to give 'back in my day' wisdom to the young

271

people around them." She laughed and quoted 1st Corinthians 13:11. *"When I was a child, I spake like a child, understood as a child, I thought as a child: but when I became a man, I put away childish things."* She complained about how people miss out on so much of life because of being stuck in childish pursuits or holding on to ideas that fit a different time and place.

Then she switched to something unexpected, to give a lesson on how some people get used to their situation and fear change. "I'm sure you've seen that movie with Robin Williams and that fine boy. You know, where he's (Robin Williams), a therapist and that guy, what's his name, is good at math. He also plays Jason Bourne." "Matt Damon," I responded. "Yes, that's my boy man, I like his acting." She continued, "But in that movie,"- *"Good Will Hunting,"* I chimed in, "Yes! *Good Will Hunting.* His friend tells him that he hopes to come pick him up one day and he's not home. He wished to find that he's made something better of himself, and not just stick in the same mental space. So, he left for the girl."

I admired how she looked for lessons in everything. My two extra feet of growth caused my perspective to change, and somehow or other she brought the Bible and Matt Damon into the conversation to help me appreciate, and not be bewildered by changes life might bring. It was as though she sensed my struggle for a ride or die situation back in the U.S, and was telling me not to be afraid of change. She was my source of life for sure; I took lessons from many song lyrics, movies and literature, and would try to spice life up with different activities to avoid being monotonous. Traveling as a monk was good for me, from that point of view. It gave me a new situation to experience every time.

Chapter
Eighteen

Mama, Sisters, and Me

We had many conversations at random times. It seemed like life just wanted me to enjoy being home, and if something poignant came up, we talked about it. Mommy wasn't big on dwelling on problems. She was efficient in her approach to issues, knowing what was fixable and what wasn't. She talked about the impracticality of bureaucracy and how it had no face, so no one took responsibility for what went wrong. I chimed in that my spiritual teacher had said something similar about bureaucratic systems: "All they do is say no," which limits the human ability to rise to significant heights.

Mom talked about how people live in a competitive mood, and so don't want other voices next to, or possibly above theirs. She mentioned how my grandfather was a well-respected man, and how she noticed that he did not have a competitive spirit. Mr. Bishop knew who he was and what he could do; when he sat at a table with others, he looked for where his talents could be used, rather than with whom to compete. As I listened, it felt like she was talking about herself. She waltzed to her own music with lots of knowledge and international cultural experiences behind her, but she never advertised it, nor used it as leverage over others.

I told her about my small inner fight with institutional bureaucracy and how I needed to follow my heart and teach without feeling like one part of me was teaching, while another was blocking and fighting institutionalization. Most students I met didn't want to be a member of the Krsna movement; they just wanted to live their lives and apply the knowledge they had. I had a good grasp of the Krsna philosophy and felt it was hindered by more rules and regulations than necessary, which made it difficult for people to grasp the "develop your love for God" concept that was being taught.

"My brother, when you stand for truth, truth will always protect you. Your intuition will always guide and tell you what's right. I don't mean what you like or dislike about a situation, but what's the actual backbone of something." With those words, she took off any guilt or burden I carried. Because I was somewhat alone in my ventures of teaching and had gotten some negative feedback for it, I felt unable to work with full vigor. I could see that mom too stood in a truth that protected her and her "big mouth." She saw things that affected community growth and would bring up those issues without fear. She said what needed to be said to give a situation clarity, and also to provide practical direction as far as how to carry it out. She was never

275

malicious in her address of others and could say sharp words in such a way that would make you reflective, and even thankful that she had spoken to you that way. Whether people took her advice or not, she moved on to the next thing at hand.

Mommy felt she had a place on life's stage and had everything she needed to "keep her charge," and so she lived with authenticity. She had time to be herself, most importantly; then time to be a daughter, mother, sister, teacher, colleague, and friend. In her eyes, and through her example, equality became a reality in how you treated another person, especially one not on the same platform as you. She had time for serious work and made time to relax, and those who understood her mood worked smoothly with her. She trusted that a person could do a job given to them, and if they did, she was alright with them. Once work was done, there was lots of time for social hang out.

One instance, regarding work, that she told me about was when a young professor from a neighbor country was sent to work under her in the Agriculture Department. She had seen his credentials and resume and asked that he go to another department where he might thrive better, but management ignored her request and put this man in her department. When he started work, she called him into her office and told him that she had requested that he work elsewhere but they had sent him to her, so if he did the work required by teachers in her department, they would have a good relationship.

However, one Friday, when she organized a symposium to introduce aquaculture and hydroponics to the curriculum and asked all the teachers to attend, this new teacher didn't show up. The following Monday, as she stood by the doorway chatting with some other professors, the new teacher walked by "with a chip on his damn shoulder." She then took the opportunity to establish a few facts for this new teacher. As he reached ear distance of her, she spoke loud and clear for him to hear. "I say, someone tell this man who just started working here these three things: one, I'm his superior in age, and could be his mother. Two, he works for me in my department, and three, he's in my goddamn country, so he should behave accordingly and get his act together." From that day forward, the new teacher respected and worked with her very well and gained her friendship.

Sweeter than Sugar Days

On Mother's Day that year, I woke up very early and made mommy breakfast, consisting of an array of fresh pineapple, papaya, and mangoes. She thanked me for breakfast and ate just a few pieces of fruit because she didn't like sweet things that much. Mommy wasn't much of a breakfast person; she drank a cup of coffee with two cubes of sugar, and that was about it. Her most substantial meal was at lunch, and she'd snack on something in the evenings.

We sat on her bed and talked about her mom who passed away on Mother's Day in 1979 when I was only five months old. She said her mom didn't suffer, and she wished to leave this world similarly — over and out. We had a connection when it came to mystical stuff, and she would indulge me in "deeper" topics. Whenever she felt troubled about a situation, her mom would appear to her in a specific dream. There would be a circle of people playing music, and my grandma would be the one dancing in the middle. Grandma would dance for a bit, and while looking straight at mommy, she'd fade away. Mom said she'd wake up every time with no anxiety about the situation, as she knew it would work itself out.

She said she had a similar dream when I left my brother's house and did my disappearing act to Seattle, and so she had nothing to worry about as far as I was concerned. About my escapades, when I asked her if she was worried about her son, she looked at me almost sternly, but sarcastically and said, "Son? I haven't seen you as my son since you were eleven. Remember during the war I taught you and Robbie (my stepbrother) how to run the house, make market lists, take care of everything? I see all my children as my friends. I've made five good friends and even step friends." We laughed a bit about her made-up word: "step friends."

It was the truth; because she gave us genuine care and affection, as well as lived with us in a "real" space, we grew up with no inhibitions. She was aware of the world around her. People cussed — she was the queen of it — people drank and smoked; people did all kinds of things because people were people. Once, years before the war, I was probably about seven or eight, she sat on the porch drinking beer with her friend, Aunty Juicy. There were a few others there, including a very puritanical neighbor who lived down the street. Anyone who knew Aunty Juicy knew the reason she was called that, and she and mommy were laughing and talking about certain topics that made Juicy, "Juicy." Our puritan neighbor chimed in, "Gloria, why are you using these bad words around your children?" Mom responded, "They will hear those words in the street if they don't already. So best they hear it from me first."

When we talked about finding love, she said sometimes we have to realize that love is more powerful than any of us, and love grants us an ability to experience "it." We can't dictate love. We can't choose who to fall in love with, and most of the time when we do so, it's trouble in the end. Laughing, she said that is why you see some couples, and you wonder how the hell they are together; it was the reason people say love is blind. Out of the blue, I

277

asked her what if love came to me in the form of a man, and without a second breath, she replied, "Then you 'LOVE' the man." She said it in such a way that sounded like, "Were you not just listening?"

For her it was that simple; love gave itself to you, you chose to accept or reject it. Her discourse of love was very entertaining. I wasn't talking to mommy anymore; I was talking to my friend. Didn't matter the subject, she could just chat away. We talked about my brother Toye being her best friend, and how I had come to see it in a beautiful light. Some people just connect, and that connection, again, love, can grant you experiences in any way shape or form. So Toye was her right-hand man, and I saw, recognized, and through appreciation, relished the fact that no matter what, mommy had a confidential friend. The bucking for son of the day award was no longer a necessity. Mommy loved all her children, and we all had different aspects of her in us. It was such a privilege to have a woman that we all called our friend.

For me, she was more than my friend, she was my light, and my guiding star through life. Many times, in my searching through life, I had asked myself, "what would mommy do right about now?" Being around her meant I could understand anything, no matter how deep, complicated, or obscure. Before Toye left for America, we had our sibling rivalry, like most siblings. He was fourteen, and I was eleven. We fought constantly, and of course, he always won, but there were times I would gain the upper hand. Now I look at my brother and see that I am fortunate to be able to call him so. Same goes for my sisters and step-siblings and adopted siblings; we had such an interesting personality in our lives, and we all looked to her for different reasons.

Mommy and I talked about children that day, and it was the funniest in-depth conversation I had ever had. It started with her asking when I'll give her a grandchild:

"So, you boy, when am I gonna get a grandchild?"

Me: "Chay, mommy, I'm in the monastery, I don't want children right now, maybe when I leave the monastery one day I'll have a child."

Mom: "You boy, just knock one girl up here and then go back to the monastery, I'll take care of my grandchild for you."

My sister Chee-Chee: "Or I can get one of the local girls to cook him a special soup, he'll eat it and fall asleep, then he wouldn't even know he had a kid."

Mom's friend Darlene: "Jaycee, run away, your mom is damn crazy my brother. You better run!"

Me: "But mom, you already have five grandchildren, two from Cheryl

278

and two from Toye. And Serena has one and is pregnant also. Give me to God for one minute, while I learn this lifestyle..."

Mom: "But you're the cute one, I want a grandchild from you too!'

Me: "Look at your damn fool, you're telling me my sister and brother ugly, huh..."

Mom: "I'll say anything to get my grandchild, my brother."

All the while I was laughing so hard my side ached. I told mommy that she could just adopt another neighborhood kid and take care of them and she chuckled and mentioned how these knuckleheads were trying to take her to her early grave. I hadn't heard the phrase "take me to my early grave" in years, and it made me laugh some more. I knew she loved taking care of others, but I had never asked her what she got out of it, so I took the opportunity to do so then. Her wit and practicality were right there in the answer: "I want to live in a peaceful place, you know, and you can never tell what a stupid person will do—because they're 'Stuuuupid.' If I send them to school, at least I'll have peace of mind knowing I have educated people around me. But then some of them get too educated and become "stuuupider."

We laughed some more, and I told her a story I had learned in India about the boatman and the scholar. A young college graduate goes back to his hometown but has to take a boat to his house, so he hires a boatman to row him across. As they row across, the scholar sees some tall grasses growing by the water and asks the boatman what type of grasses they are. "I do not know, I am a simple boatman," says the boatman. "Well, twenty-five percent of your life is wasted- this is the blah blah blah plant in the family of blah blah blah..." The boatman quietly rows on when they come across some fish jumping in the water; "Do you know what kind of fish that is?" "I do not know, sir." Well then, half your life is wasted. That is a blah blah blah fish..." Looking up, the scholar sees a formation of clouds and asks the boatman if he knows what type of clouds they are. The boatman tells him that it looks like it's about to rain, but no, he does not know what clouds they are. "Ah then, three-fourths of your life is wasted. That is a blah blah blah cloud, and it indicates huge torrents of rain approaching; please row faster." Suddenly it begins to rain along with a strong gust of wind which tumbles the boat over. The boatman and scholar surface, and the scholar begins to scream for help. "Swim," says the boatman, "we're close to the shore, just a hundred feet." "I can't swim," screams the scholar, as he struggles to stay afloat. "Well then one hundred percent of your life is wasted," says the boatman." Mom bursts out laughing loudly and says, "See, exactly what I said- stuuuupider with a capital 'S.'"

Later that day, after eating my vegetarian egusi, a dish made with ground pumpkin seeds and sautéed greens (she taught the household how to cook for me), another of mommy's friends came to visit, and we sat on the porch and gossiped, laughed more and talked again about mom's mom. Gloria spoke about her own funeral one day and how she wanted people to come, eat, drink, and be merry. Her friend and I chimed in about how she knew so many people and so there wouldn't be a church able to handle her funeral services.

She then said to us, "Here's the thing, guys. I've been good, I've been bad, and sometimes I have been ugly; so, there's nothing some pastor can stand at the pulpit and say that God already doesn't know about me." To me, she said, "You can say something for a few minutes since you're the monsignor." Then she laughed, and we kept on talking. She wanted lots of liquor and Heineken at her funeral, and lots of food, so when people got drunk and started to cry, they would eat, sober up, and start all over again. "Because we all have to go through that door, you know, and I don't want a bunch of crying people. I don't like funerals because I can't stand people crying." Mommy did not like to see people suffer. She did whatever was in her capacity, to help others. She didn't make a lot of money, but whatever she had went to helping someone else.

I talked about my travels, and how not just the monastery, but some friends who were able to, supported my teaching. One friend, Ron, invited me to New York while he was there doing some work on Wall Street. He usually lived in L.A but was staying at a very prestigious hotel near where the World Trade Center had stood. I didn't know that he was staying at such a place, and when we walked into the hotel, all eyes were on me, in my saffron colored monk robes. People thought I was some high-ranking monk or something. The hotel staff folded their hands as they greeted me while Ron enjoyed the whole scene. I also talked about how other affluent people were quite negative toward me, and sometimes said some nasty things to others about me.

Mom mentioned how economic development has its downfalls and how the culture of distrust becomes very prevalent where too much money is involved. "People forget to see you as a human being; you become a competitor, and this only makes jealousy rise more." One of the things that stuck with me that day was when she said, "You know, people in these countries look at others that way; like we've come to take something from them. What they should see is that we're here to offer them something. Every African, Indian, Chinese—most countries you travel— the people are rich in culture. They show how to live with each other. But we come to the melting pot with our ingredients, yet they don't want us in their kitchen. And in most cases, we're better cooks." She continued, "Young boys and girls grow up and learn a lot about living in their communities. Many cultures have rites of passages like the 'Grebo bush' for boys and 'Sande society for girls.' It's not just something to occupy their time; these are where they learn practical life skills. Imagine if there were an avenue for them to use those skills, the world would truly experience what a 'melting pot' civilization actually means." She was always right on the money and her views corresponded with how she interacted with the world.

It was that day, Mother's Day while chatting with mommy that I decided again that I didn't want to be a monk anymore, and I would transition into a more secular life, move somewhere, and "do my own thing." I wanted to build a community where people felt empowered to express themselves as parts of humanity. I would go back to the US, visit a few friends, attend a few functions, and then see where the energy flowed after that.

Reap What You Sow

Mommy, Chee-Chee and I went back to the city for a few days to get me the new Liberian biometric passport. ECOWAS (the Economic Community of West African States), decided to have a common passport, like an E.U passport, so I had to change my passport to avoid travel issues. At the passport office, a man walked up to mom and greeted her, "Hi, Sis Gloria, what brings you in here today?""Hey, you Jackass, this is my youngest son, and he has to get his passport. And this is my daughter Chee-Chee. Who are all these heathens in line and where are they going that they need passports?"

The man chuckled and said to me, "This woman and her mouth, I don't know how she stays out of trouble!" He asked us to follow him, but mom declined his offer saying that there were "plenty people in front of us."

He insisted and told mommy she was their old ma and had kept a lot of them out of trouble back in the day. He was one of her former students from the university. He wanted to get us out of there quickly. And so it was; I got my passport in an hour, and we headed out to visit Cousin Juanita. Cousin Juanita had just returned from a doctor's visit. She was mommy's cousin and best friend. Everyone called them each other's "other half." Before mom relocated to the Cuttington campus, she and Cousin Juanita hung out every day, and after the move, they would talk at least three times a day. Cousin Juanita was elated to see me and wanted to know all I had been doing. I told her about my travels, and she laughed and said, "Look at this boy, my people; just like his mom. They want to see every continent before they die." She

281

encouraged me to come back to Liberia to teach and even open a yoga studio. She knew a group of women in the city who were into yoga and meditation. Mom joked about how funny it would be to see all the fat, "big butt" Liberian women doing yoga.

After visiting with Cousin Juanita, we went down to the waterside market, like we had done seventeen years before, to buy me some more African trinkets. I wanted a pair of slippers, and as I started to ask for the price, Chee-Chee told me to shut my mouth: "You don't sound Liberian, my man. As soon as you open your mouth, the price will triple. From now on, you do the looking, and mommy and I will do the talking." Chee-Chee was right; shopkeepers were very good at sensing foreign accents. My Liberian accent was not up to par for bargaining. I sounded like an American who had stayed in Liberia for some time and was learning the local dialect.

We then walked around the city for a bit, seeing old sites that I hadn't seen since I left. Mommy wasn't fond of the city anymore; it had become crowded since the war, and she preferred life on the beach, or on campus. CHAMS Lounge had closed a few years after I left Liberia, and Aunty Harriette was now living in the U.S. On our way back to the ELWA house, mommy noticed a new church construction site along the highway, and had something to say about it. "I say, everywhere you turn in this country, a new church has popped up. If they keep it up like this, on Judgment Day, God will come down, see the number of churches per square mile, and just take the whole damn country to heaven. No judgment for Liberia, just straight up to heaven!" Everyone in the car laughed at her witty observation. The driver turned to me and said, "Your old ma can tell the truth in a funny way man. And she can cuss too!"

Six weeks ended too soon, but the sweetness of being centered again and feeling empowered by someone to do something tangible made me feel strong and focused. I had immersed myself in the rich culture of home. I got mommy's wisdom and encouragement, mixed with her humor and nonchalance. My sisters were now women who I got to know for a short time. They had grown under mom's care and the same underlying fabric of respect, but familiarity flowed among all of us. I felt like mommy was subtly saying to me, "You're my son, and I am pleased with you. Continue living as you're living and everything will fall into place."

Harmony

Upon reentering the US, I stayed with some good friends; I'll call them Katie and Kevin, in San Jose and got my head together for my next steps. I brought back some trinkets for friends who I planned to meet in the coming months. I was fired up but needed to let the jet lag settle. Upon arrival at Katie and Kevin's, they suggest that we go out and grab a bite to eat. We went to the local organic grocery store and ordered some pizza. But my body needed to readjust; I had just been eating fresh foods for the past six weeks, and pizza may not have been a good reentry food.

For the next seven days, I threw up everything in my system. I could only have hot water, and if it wasn't at a certain temperature, my body threw it out as well. On day eight I was able to speak a few coherent words with my doctor over the phone who then prescribed me herbal medications to take. My body was weak with sick symptoms I had not before experienced. It wasn't malaria; I had experienced that three times in my childhood and knew its signs. It was gastrointestinal, and my system cleared itself out of whatever the ailment was. On day nine, I had an intense craving for a sprite or tonic water. My friends were afraid to buy me those drinks because they thought it was processed food that had triggered my illness. After giving in and buying me a bottle of tonic water, I drank a glass full and waited patiently for the throw-up moment. Instead, I let out a loud burb, got out of bed and stumbled into the living room to watch TV, all to the amazement of everyone present. Few glasses later and I was outside on the balcony getting some fresh air. The next day I woke up feeling refreshed and cleansed; I showered and went for a walk on the trail.

After I recovered fully, I traveled to the few weddings and events I had previously planned on attending. Finally, I ended up in Tucson Arizona, and by Thanksgiving of 2012, I had rented a house, with the help of a few good friends who saw and wanted to help make my vision a reality. The third time that year, starting with my hives incident in India, my body put me through another test. This time, because of a new venture into new territory, my stomach churned from anticipation and anxiety. I had mommy's encouragement to teach what I had learned in the monastery in a way I felt was palatable, but the step of actually "doing it" made me a little woozy. I was out for three days, alone in a three-bedroom house staring at the empty, unfurnished space. This sickness felt like a trial where my body was asking me if I wanted to do something so bold, or should I just turn back, reenter the monastery and continue, business as usual. I made that conscious choice and told myself that if I were to die in that house, I would have died making a bold decision. I had taken the time to learn about the Vedic culture and its values. I wanted to feel like an independent thinker with something valuable to offer, and not just a religious practitioner afraid to act because of possible pitfalls. If I were to fail, at least I could say I tried it.

Jaycee Kesh Akinsanya

It was a simple start, and I had a simple guideline: clean space, food made with love, and finally, respect for anyone who came through my doors. In fact, I got over my fear of crowds and decided to go to the University of Arizona's campus to meet people and make friends. Soon my little project had people coming around, and things were going beautifully. My mother's words were shining through. I was standing for truth and truth was manifesting the right people and company. Some friends and I made a large garden in the backyard and cultivated and grew as much food as we could.

One friend named, Guru, built an aquaponics system in my backyard. Aquaponics is a blend of aquaculture, raising fish in a controlled space, and hydroponics, growing vegetables in a water filtration system. Usually, nutrition is added to a hydroponics system for the plants, but since the food the plants need is already in the water used by the fish, it becomes an excellent way to blend two cultures. Gardeners usually add fish emulsion to their garden as fertilizer, but in this case, it is all filtered into a grow bed filled with porous rocks that filter out the nutrients and send fresh water back into the fish tank.

I called mommy and told her about the space and the aquaponics system, and she was very excited to hear about what was manifesting. She had visited Washington DC the previous summer and got to tour an aquaponics farm and thought about doing another symposium at Cuttington. At the mention of the word symposium, I told her that she had to include drinks for it to be called a symposium. I had just read Plato's Symposium and described the story to her briefly. In ancient Greece, I told her, a symposium was a traditional part of a banquet that took place after the meal. There was usually drinking, music and conversation. In Plato's Symposium, the topic of discussion was the glorification of Eros, the god of love. Each philosopher at the banquet, Socrates included, had to give a speech on how they understood Eros. Mom sarcastically agreed to include drinks at her symposium and said she'll also tell everyone to come dressed in flowing cloth like ancient Greeks. She'll pretend to be Socrates.

Within a few months of putting myself out there, many people from different walks of life inquired as to what I was doing. Even a fraternity came by, and by the time I could notice, people were coming in to do yoga, tai chi, garden, help cook, etc. We called it the Red Ashram. The purpose was to facilitate people who were passionate (Red) about spirituality (ashram) but wanted nothing to do with institutional politics. People would come, and at the end of the day, people would go. I would close the doors and go to sleep in a now, bit more furnished space. The furniture was simple, and I made the wall art.

My friend Matt had been helping out on certain days like Thursdays when

I would have an open house dinner. Matt was from Ohio, and was attending the University of Arizona. We struck up a conversation one day, and became friends, going out for hikes in the mountains and having good philosophical discussions. Dinners at the house were very simple and casual. We would play music, have dinner, and then talk about whatever topic came to mind. It was a sweet space, and a few friends who didn't feel comfortable in a religious space felt at home there; so much so that we began to have dinners almost every night.

For a few weeks in April of 2013, I started to consider the possibility of having a partner, someone to run the place with. I wasn't thinking someone romantic, just a good friend or two to live with. On one of those nights before bed, I thought to myself how nice it would be to have someone living in the house with me. I had rented the guesthouse to a friend, Cindy, and that helped lower the rent to a certain extent, but she was independent of my space, and so more company was what I wished for. I thought about a few friends like Dan or Rochelle as good fits for the house; they could also teach others from there. But internally I felt that the house would call its residents to it.

Chapter
Nineteen

Hot Like new Love

The next morning, April 11th, 2013, a Thursday morning, I felt this push to go to the campus and hang out for a bit. The problem was that Thursdays were my open house days and I didn't go anywhere. I usually stayed back to make sure the house was made ready for guests. But the feeling remained, and so I talked to Cindy from next door about it. Her response, "Maybe you're meant to meet someone or have a special experience—give it a shot and see." About half an hour later I reluctantly dragged myself to campus.

It was the longest two miles I had ever walked, and when I got there, I ran into my friend, Max, one of the regular attendees at my dinners. Max was adept at playing the guitar; he also looked a bit like Eric Clapton. Usually, after dinners, he would play his guitar, and we'd make up songs to go with the melody. We chatted for a bit, and he played his guitar for some time. Then it was time for him to go to class, and I decided to go back home. I told myself whatever special experience or person I was meant to meet would be there another day perhaps. I got up, grabbed my backpack and turned to leave when a young man walked straight over to me, arms stretched out for a handshake. "Hi, I'm Nikko." He was bright and beaming, and I, in turn, introduced myself.

Nikko was listening to some music and asked if I'd like to hear it. He said he had written the song, so I stood and listened to it. I loved the song and congratulated him on his work. He asked me what I was doing, and I said I was off to get ready for the evening; I had some friends coming over for dinner. I extended the invitation to him, and we exchanged numbers and went our merry ways. I appreciated the way he walked up to me like we had known each other before. I didn't think much about the extraordinary experience Cindy had predicted. My day had only consisted of Max and Nikko, but no seemingly extravagant incident.

That night another friend, Jackson, brought his girlfriend who wanted to see where he had been hanging out. Nikko also showed up. Matt couldn't show up that day to help because he had a math exam the following day. But people were so familiar with the house now that things just went on automatically. Everyone volunteered to help where they could, washing dishes, serving each other, and cleaning up after dinner. Prompted by Jackson with the girlfriend, we chatted about the importance of mothers in society. We discussed how mothers give birth to, and nurture every aspect of humanity.

Jaycee Kesh Akinsanya

The womb, someone said, is the birthplace of all ideas, because, whether an idea is born of a man or woman, both men and women are cradled in a womb. I brought up something I had learned from the Vedas about there being seven mothers: the birth mother, the wife of the Guru, the wife of the Priest, the wife of the king, the Nurse, the cow, and mother Earth. The discussion went on to conclude that to have a peaceful society, we have to try and honor each of these mothers.

During dinner, Matt was usually the one who got up and walked around to everyone, asking how they were, and if they needed anything more. But Matt wasn't there that night, and I noticed Nikko get up, and without effort, do what Matt would have done had he been there. I took note of Nikko's generous mood, and texted Matt, saying that his doppelgänger had come to dinner.

My friend Tyler, Nikko, and I talked a bit more during dinner, as Macen, the son of another regular, Carla, sat between Tyler and me, making funny faces, or rushing over to Guru and having a tickle fight with him. The atmosphere was very relaxed, and we all just sat around talking some more, or getting seconds of the pasta I made that night. We found out that Nikko was on his way to the Coachella music festival for the weekend, and asked him to take as many pictures as possible and keep in touch. Nikko came back the next week and sent me a text asking how I was doing. He asked if he could bring some friends over for lunch and I agreed and said I'd make something from the garden. Random calls and house visits were a common thing at the house; a few friends like Nikko, Max, or Dylan, another U of A student, or Ari, would randomly show up for lunch.

A few friends like Ari, who I met when I first rented the house, would spontaneously spend the night, and Nikko did too. He, though, locked the guest room door (we all could hear it being unlocked when he came out the next morning). Ari thought Nikko's locking the door was a bit out of character for the house. It seemed to us that he wanted to be around us, but the door locking came across as someone from an untrusting environment, concerned about their personal safety. There was nothing wrong with what he did, but it was significant to us as the rest of us noticed it and it came across as awkward.

Nikko let his guard down after a while as he became more comfortable around us. At dinners, we'd mostly talk about the importance of food, especially quality food grown by oneself or a trusted farmer. Food is the fuel for existence, and knowing what goes into one's body, we thought, is important. Some of us considered looking into apprenticeships with organic farmers to learn more about growing food for self-sustainability.

Joy, another friend and regular, was very passionate about seeing the house prosper, and so she suggested that we start something, like a business, to help the house support itself long-term. Nikko was part of this conversation, and mentioned that he had some money saved up, and wanted to donate it to the cause. I was a bit skeptical about taking financial help from Nikko and told him that I had some savings that would last for some months. Nikko was due to move into some new student apartments that were being built but preferred the atmosphere at the house, so he suggested that he could move in and use his savings as rent. It took a bit of convincing to accept Nikko's proposal. I had a few trusted supporters of my project, and so far, things were good, so I didn't see the need for extra funds. After discussing with a few other regulars who were using the house as their space for study, or yoga or whatever, I accepted Nikko's help in running the house.

I told myself to allow Nikko to contribute just as I let everyone else. I think his door locking incident caused me not fully to warm up to him, but as he became a part of the group, I opened up. He had practically moved into the guestroom, and we became great friends. I appreciated how he would check up on me from school with little texts, asking how I was doing, or if the house needed anything. After dinner, some of us went on long walks in the evenings and walked through the Tucson neighborhoods. On one such occasion after talking for a while, Nikko said to me, "I wish I could do one thing right now." I responded, "What would you do if you could do one thing right now?" "Kiss you," he continued. Without a second thought, I agreed, and we kissed. I saw no further than that moment. Nothing was out of sync with me when it happened. I was a free kid back in Minneapolis and had kissed my friends before. There was nothing strange about it, and if it was a wish of his, I was ok with granting it.

For Summer break, Nikko packed up a bunch of his school stuff and drove his car back to Los Angeles. Many of the regulars, like Matt, also went on vacation, so the house felt a bit empty. I missed everyone who was away, but especially Nikko. We had become good friends and talked about everything. Our interactions flowed naturally, so in his absence, I felt a bit blah. A few weeks later, I got to meet his mom, when I visited their home. She had just come back home the night before from a travel engagement, and when she went into the kitchen the next morning, she saw me sitting by the living room window. I got up and greeted her, and complimented her home and how much Nikko resembled her, especially when they smiled. For the few days I stayed with them, Nikko would come into the guest room and wake me up to go and walk around the neighborhood, or drive somewhere and do something for the day.

Jaycee Kesh Akinsanya

Wha...?

In mid-July, the hottest time in Tucson, I went to visit David and a few good friends in Seattle. Rochelle had moved from Tucson to Seattle, so I met up with her, as well as with Nora, my friend, and photographer from the monastery days. We had a good time reuniting and exploring different parts of the city. When I texted with Nikko later in the day and told him that we had gone to see the Chihuly glass exhibit by the space needle, Nikko expressed his desire also to view the works of Chihuly. He said that his dad was a big fan of Chihuly's glass-blown sculptures. Nikko was on vacation with his mom, but with her permission, he joined us for the weekend. We walked around Seattle, went to art exhibits, and ate chocolate form a fair-trade chocolate factory called "Theo." We had fun dinners, met up with David, and his partner Brian, and rowed around in canoes on Lake Washington. On Sunday, we decided to go to see another friend, Gavin, and see if he wanted to go on a boat ride. Gavin was willing and met us at the boat storage parking lot. While all of us hung out in the parking lot waiting for Gavin to pull the boat around, Nikko dropped very unexpected news on me. We had all been talking about some random subject when Nikko continued talking, but added, "Hey I told my mom I'm in love with you. She's a little concerned about our age difference, but that's that. I just wanted you to know." Everyone grew quiet, and looked at me as I stood there with my mouth open, only managing to say, "Wha...?"

All my friends laughed at my dumbfounded facial expression, and I Brian, David's partner, said to me, "Wow, dude, someone shut you up finally!" It was completely out of left field, and it took me a long time to process. Why was he in love with me? Had I given any signals to him? Why did I not see this coming? We were good friends, and I appreciated his company very much, but where did love come in? I felt excited, and I felt afraid. He told his mom he was in love with me? I had twenty thoughts flowing through my mind from then on but decided to enjoy the rest of the evening. My philosophical side tried to analyze the situation for the rest of the weekend. Nikko had shown no "signs" of sexuality around me; it was never something that came up in conversation. His wanting to kiss me a few months back seemed very innocent, especially since it didn't happen again. For a while, I began to panic. I had not started my house project to look for a lover. I wanted to make good friends, and now I feared I was giving people the wrong message.

Now someone was in love with me, and I had no idea what was happening. I called a few good friends, like Goura, whom I had met in Vrindavan, and lived with in Gainesville, and relayed the whole situation to him. "It seems you two were meant to meet each other and be a part of each other's lives,"

292

Goura said, "See where it goes. I wouldn't just ditch it. He could be a gift sent to you for unknown reasons, and not accepting him could be like throwing that gift back to the universe who sent him to you."

Back in Tucson, this uncertain anxiety of my new situation lingered with me for weeks until one night when I went to sleep and had a very vivid dream. Jaya Saci, the monk who trained me up in Seattle, was in my room, sitting next to my bed and we had a question and answer session where he responded to my doubts. In the dream, I asked "why Nikko," and he told me that Nikko and I had both called for each other. We had known each other in previous lives, and at this particular junction in our lives, we needed each other. He brought to light the fact that I had, a few weeks prior, laid in bed wishing for a partner to live in the house. He warned me that some friends would reveal themselves as untrustworthy and try to break Nikko's and my relationship. He said not to worry, but to accept my situation and be happy.

Love the Man

After that dream, my anxiety cleared up, and I began to appreciate Nikko in my life. I started to appreciate the sweetheart he was, and how easy he was to live with. We had a fifteen-year difference, I was thirty-four now, and he was nineteen, and this worried his mom, who told me she didn't want to see Nikko get hurt. It was also the first relationship in my life, and I was coming to terms with my own internal fears and doubts from years ago with Neiman Marcus guy, and internet no-show guy. I had been asked on dates before, but never a formal relationship I was taking the advice from some good friends to give in and experience why Nikko was in my life. To try and not upset his mom, I took on the responsibility of not doing anything to screw up my relationship with Nikko.

Later, while having dinner and talking to some friends about how we met, Nikko mentioned how he had been unhappy with his school situation and was getting anxious and depressed. He started drinking heavily as a freshman and didn't like what was happening to him. He said one night he walked outside and sincerely prayed for a way out of his depression. The next day, a Thursday, while walking from class, he saw me leaving, after hugging Max, and thought that he had to meet me and talk with me. That was when he walked straight up to me and shook my hands. I said nothing but had internal goosebumps. Was Nikko the person I was supposed to meet that Thursday when I dragged myself to campus? Max and Nikko were the only two people I met that day on campus, and Max was already my friend, so I concluded Nikko was the "special" person Cindy had speculated about my meeting.

Mommy, of course, heard about Nikko in every conversation I had with her, and so did my dad. Neither of them questioned my sexuality, nor did they seem to care. I never had to "come out" to anyone. My friend Marc likened coming out to going to confession and asking permission or forgiveness for a committed sin. But no sin is committed by discovering love, and no approval is ever needed to love. As mommy told my Aunt Harriette, "whatever makes Jaycee happy, makes me happy." This new person in my life was a nice complement to me. Our relationship was very playful, and we cooked a lot of food together. Nikko told me how bad my pasta was the first time he came for dinner. He's from an Italian family and knows how to make some delicious pasta. Although the sauce was made well, the pasta, he said was very soft, way beyond al dente. We laughed about my try at pasta, and I learned how to make pasta properly.

Cindy, the girl next door, didn't take my relationship with Nikko so favorably. She spread some rather false rumors around our circle of friends, telling them to stop supporting my project because I was using my sacred space to now live with my male lover, Nikko, whom she had caught me in bed with. Problem with her rumor was when she said she found me in bed with Nikko, Nikko wasn't even in Tucson. I was in bed with no one. The same Cindy, some months after she started living next door to me, made some negative remarks to me about a friend who had shown up drunk at my home one night. For whatever reason, he had been drinking and instead of going home, instructed the cab driver to drop him off at my place. When Cindy saw that I put him in the guest room, she admonished me and told me that having a drunk person in my home would bring down the morale of the sacred space. I told her that my guest wasn't a drunk person, but my friend and that I would risk the morale of the house for a friend in need. Cindy's squabble spread through the community, to the temple, and even to Canada and India, where I received phone calls from people, telling me versions of what they had heard about my bedroom life. The situation also caused friends to stop coming, and our operation came to an almost complete halt. Only two or three friends would come for dinner at random times. This situation sent me into a depression like no other for a few days. All I could do was watch my project fall apart because I allowed myself to "LOVE the man." But Nikko stuck it out through those rare times, and our bond grew stronger.

Nikko's struggle with college, which also affected his grades, subsided when he moved into the house. I set up a study space for him with a fish tank and lots of indoor plants, and his desk facing the window so that he could look outside at the view of the garden. His grades improved exponentially, from a 1.9 GPA to a maintained a 4.0 GPA. The environment, I guess, encouraged him to study better. As with the others who came to dinner, Nikko and I developed strong desires to learn more about farming, and so the two of us decided to look at farm internships with Organic farms around the U.S.

Oshala Love

We sent out forty-two applications to farms and got two responses back. The first farmer was a lady in Washington, and we emailed each other for some time until, after a conversation one day, we stopped hearing from her. The other farm was Oshala Farm in Southern Oregon. Oshala Farm focused on organic teas, herbs, and spices, and was happy to have us intern with them. We decided to go to Oregon and spend the growing season with them. Two weeks after our talk with Oshala, the farmer in Washington emailed us back. The afternoon after she spoke with us, her husband, and farm manager died suddenly, and her whole world stopped. She wasn't planning on having interns that season. We decided to go to Oregon and work with Oshala Farm. We still have the desire to one day visit the farmer in Washington, and maybe even lend her a hand for a week or two.

The experience at Oshala farm was mind-blowing. We seeded, planted and cultivated about sixty varieties of herbs, teas, and spices. I noticed, on a daily basis that working with the soil gave us so much energy. After work when we should have been tired from the fields, we found that we had more energy and wanted to go out and do something in town. The owners, Jeff and Elise, were like parents to us and taught us as much as they could about farming. Elise taught me how to make a variety of health tonics and syrups, and every chance we got we would pick their brains on agriculture topics. Jeff also showed us how to create business plans for owning a farm one day. We also got the opportunity to visit various farms in the area and learn about different growing techniques.

Oshala farm lies in the Applegate Valley of Southern Oregon where a majority of the farmers practice organic and sustainable growing methods. Our stay there, from beginning to end, was a daily philosophical all-you-can-think buffet. Whether we were learning about the fertile soil on the farm, learning to drive tractors, caring for chickens, learning irrigation methods, or how to properly harvest and dry medicinal crops, our minds were filled with questions. The answers, given by Jeff, Elise, or Kenny, the farm manager, were always lively and led to more questions. It intrigued me how all of us on the farm were from completely different backgrounds, but had an appreciation for the land, and wanted to learn more about helping the planet.

Jeff had a long background in Organic farming and fruit production. Elise was expert in herbal knowledge, and I loved watching her stand in the kitchen making syrups or sitting at the table mixing their tea blends for market. Kenny's love was fixing machines, and at any time of the day, you'd find him fixing something or building something, like the seed tray he made to help us quickly seed plants like echinacea or blue vervain. Nikko and I were eager to learn as much as we could, and the week we got there was the week they were harvesting Burdock root. Burdock root went as grew as deep as twenty-four inches or more into the soil, and digging those up helped us build muscle quickly. "Man," Nikko would say, " All my friends who go to gyms and do cross fit should just go work on farms to build stamina and muscles." Something Jeff said that stuck with me was the notion of weeds. At Oshala farm we grew rows and acres of crops that others thought were weeds in their gardens. Crops like stinging nettle, dandelion, dock, and sorrel were produced in large quantities for the herbal market. I begin to consider how much abundance lay at our fingertips if we took the time to learn. Learning about these herbs helped me appreciate the knowledge my parents had about unusual edible plants during the war. I appreciated the fact that people like Elise and Jeff were keeping the knowledge alive and opening their farm to educating others.

We didn't just farm or learn from farmers; we had fun as well. A few miles away was a hotel called the Applegate Lodge, and it would host regular concerts, a few of which we got to attend. Hiking in the Applegate Valley was always rejuvenating, and we often took trips to Crater Lake, the source of the Rogue River, of which the Applegate River is a tributary. We made friends with local vineyards and helped them harvest grapes for their wines. I've never been a big drinker, but occasionally order wines from Sandi, our friend, and owner of Rosella's, a cozy vineyard in the Applegate Valley. Last year, we ordered a case of wine from Rosella's a noticed that year on the bottles was 2014. We were very excited to have wine from grapes we helped harvest, and when we do have a guest who appreciates a good glass of wine, we bring out one of those bottles.

Bloom Where You're Planted.

A year later, after our Oshala internship, another opportunity came up to help another lady in the Virgin Islands. She was a spirited young woman named Catherine and had just bought a three-acre property in the hills on the lush side of St Thomas, and wanted some help developing it into a Bread & Breakfast. Nikko had switched universities and was taking agriculture courses online, so we went to the Virgin Islands for the adventure. Catherine's property was up in the hills and from the balcony, or roof, we could see the Caribbean Sea in the distance. We were only required to do a certain amount of work each day, so we spent a lot of time exploring the island and beaches, and making friends with other young people who were living on the island.

Catherine's property was a beautiful space to work in. With an all-year possibility of growing crops, we planted as much as we could to see what vegetables loved the tropical weather or not. Nikko's love for gardening blossomed in this space. I watched him carefully plot spaces for different crops, and make time-releasing compost, filled with organic matter that would slowly decompose and feed the plants long-term. He planted some caccuzza squash, which had been [assed down in his family for a few generations, over the garage terrace, and when they squashes grew, we had so many that we began to give fresh squash to neighbors, or people who would visit Catherine. I designed a small rock garden for Catherine's space which had a Japanese feel to it. We reciprocated with Catherine's sweetness by making breakfast for her when we could, so that as she ran out the door to work, we were waiting by her car with a breakfast surprise.

One day a friend and local sailor, Tyler, came to our house with a brother and sister, Tomas and Gabriella, who were traveling to different countries around the world. Tomas's purpose was to travel like the Avatar and learn the four elements. He was quite expert at tai chi, and as we got to know each other, he told me about the different places he was traveling to study the elements. What he was speaking about was a bit over my head, because I wasn't familiar with the Avatar culture. But I knew something that was very close to my heart and fate had led us to meet. Tomas said that he and Gabriella were on their way to India to study the fire element (they were studying water in St Thomas), and that he was going to stay in a small village that not many people knew about. I was intrigued and asked him what village. "It's a place called Vrindavan." I began to laugh at the whole "no coincidences" thread that weaved its way through my life. "I used to live in Vrindavan," I told Tomas. I went there almost every year at a certain time of year to rejuvenate and study." Tomas was excited to meet someone who had heard of Vrindavan, and I told him of my experiences, and give him some recommendations of places to go and people to meet. I hadn't been to Vrindavan in three years and hadn't been around the Krsna devotees for two years, so this brought about a feeling of nostalgia in me. Tomas planned to write and publish a book on his world experiences.

After hanging out at Catherine's house that day, and relishing the fact that I knew Vrindavan, we decided to go to all go and explore the Islands together. "Man, can this get any better?" Tomas asked, as Tyler climbed up a coconut tree to pick some fresh coconuts for our day's adventures. "Wait Five minutes," I said to Tomas. Five minutes later, we were at the yard of a French couple who Tyler knew. They had a mango tree laden with fresh fruit, and told Tyler to come and pick as many mangoes as he wanted. Well, he brought us along. As we poked around at the mangoes on the lower branch, we heard the door to the house open, and the owners, an elderly couple, came out to greet us. The man started to speak to Tyler in French, and when I heard them talk, my French automatically came back to me. I joined the conversation and learned, among other things, that the couple were originally from Algeria. With the old man's permission, I climbed the large mango tree— something I hadn't done since 1989— and shook the branches, causing many ripe mangoes to fall. After that mango incident, "wait five minutes" became a regular phrase for us as we experienced unbelievable incidents on the islands.

Mommy was in the U.S that summer, and after chatting a bit, we convinced her to visit us in St Thomas. She hadn't been to the Virgin Islands before, so I thought she could resume her world travels and come and hang out with Nikko and me. When she met Nikko in the Virgin Islands, it felt like they had met before, and without missing a beat, she treated him like I knew she would. As Nikko puts it, "When Gloria got off the plane that night and walked towards us, she stole my heart." A bonus was Nikko's interest in agriculture. He and mom held long conversations about gardening, soil science, permaculture, and everything plant related. Their relationship grew into that dreaded thing that happens—your mom calls to speak with you—only chats for a few seconds, and then asks, "Where's Nik Nik?" And they'd talk for longer. Oh yes, it happened many times.

Mommy also loved Catherine's property, and although I told her she was on vacation and should relax her mental tension, the very next day, at about six in the morning, I woke up to the sound of someone singing "Bitch better have my money, la la la la la ..." I woke Nikko up and told him to listen. He did for a second, and we both burst into laughter. "Rise and shine you jack-asses," she said as she interrupted her rendition of Rihanna's song. When I walked outside, mommy was working in the garden and singing away. "My sisters have contaminated you with modern music," I told her, and couldn't stop laughing as she made hand gestures at me and continued singing, "Pay me what you owe me, don't act like you forgot..."

I told a few friends about being from Liberia, and they always ended up asking about the civil war. It intrigued them that I had been there for the first five years of the whole thing. So, when mommy visited the Virgin Islands, I invited a few close friends for dinner. Gloria cooked and also taught Nikko to make a traditional Liberian rum punch, filled with herbs and spices that you could drink many glasses of, and wake up without a hangover. When, in conversation, the topic of the civil war came up, mom reiterated some things I had told my friends about the war, as well as other things I had forgotten. A friend later said to me that all the while when I would talk about the war, she thought the details were a bit fabricated, but listening to mommy tell of the same details made everything "crystal clear." Another friend mentioned that she now understood why I called mommy "my woman of substance."

"Man, your mom carries a presence with her. She's a powerhouse!"

The Land Speaks

It was in the Virgin Islands while working on Catherine's property that we met another friend, Matt, his wife Marcela, and two-year-old daughter, Luna. They appreciated the work we had done in Catherine's garden and one day Matt mentioned to us that his uncle had passed away and left him some land in Missouri. He asked us if we'd like to check out the farm and see if there was anything we'd like to do with it, as far as farm development. We told him we'd think about it and get back to him. Matt had been at the dinner with mommy and mentioned he was from Missouri; a state mommy was well familiar with. She had gone to Lincoln University in Missouri's capital Jefferson City, and it was also where my brother Toye was born. In conversation, it came up that Matt's now-deceased uncle Glenn had also gone to the same university around the same time as mommy. Whether or not they had met, mom didn't know.

When I told her about Matt's land in Missouri, and the possibility of doing something with it, mom casually said to us, "Well, you guys can go there and listen to the land; let it speak to you." A few days later when Nikko spoke with his uncle Roy, he said almost the exact words mommy had said a few days before: go there, listen to the land and let it speak to you. Our time in the Virgin Islands was coming to an end, and we were deciding to either stay and start a landscaping business or go back to the US mainland and find a farm to work on. Living on the islands was very expensive for us, and we budgeted frugally. Opening a landscape business would render us broke, so we reconsidered Matt's offer and decided to take a look at the property. We told Matt of our plan to go to Missouri, check things out, and listen to the land, let it speak to us.

In January, we arrived at the property. Matt had also flown in to get the house in good shape to receive us. They say a picture says a thousand words, but this property had been understated in the photographs Matt had emailed to us previously. We chatted a bit, had dinner at some local Indian restaurant, and then headed back to the farm for the night. When we got back to the farm, Matt showed us a piece of paper he had uncovered from his Uncle's belongings. His uncle used to journal, and would also write little sayings that he'd put around the house. Matt showed us one such quote that was written in November of 1992 which read, "Listen to the land, let it speak to you. I live by this and will die by this."

The next morning Matt took us on a tour of the farm, and as we walked amongst the trees, I stopped and pointed to one particular tree, mentioning to Matt that he should never cut this tree down. Matt looked at me with a sort of dismay and asked why I said so about that particular tree. I told him that the tree looked cool and felt special to me. Matt then revealed that his uncle had asked him to spread his ashes under that tree when he passed away. In this way, the land began to speak, and we showed our dedication to wanting to farm it by cleaning up the house, picking up debris outside when we found it and making plans to develop the land a bit more. Matt dubbed me his uncle's psychic translator when I moved the dining room from where it was, to a room that had windows on all sides. "Glenn always wanted his dining room there," said one of Matt's aunts who was visiting us that day. Matt just looked at me with a funny smirk on his face.

As the months went by, Glenn's friends would visit the farm, and some would hear the news of his passing. One day, a car pulled into the driveway, and I stepped outside to greet the visitor. "I'm looking for Glenn," the man said, as I then informed him that Glenn had passed away and that Nikko and I were taking care of the property. He told me that as soon as I walked out the door, he felt that he was going to hear such news. The man sobbed a bit, and told me that he had helped Glen build the house; they were very close friends. As we talked, he noticed my slight accent and asked if I was from Liberia. I was impressed with his accurate observation, and he said he had been to Liberia. He went there a long time ago for his cousin's wedding. She was married to a guy named Sam Xyz. I froze up. I told him to hang on as I dialed mommy in Liberia. When mom answered, I asked her if she remembered Sam and his wife from America. She immediately knew who I was talking about. They lived down the street from us, and he was one of the people who used to sit on our porch and drink beer with mommy. He used to give us candy money as well. Mom had also just attended his funeral a few years ago. What a very tiny world we live in! In a small town of one hundred people, lived a man who had connections to my neighbor across the globe. We chatted for a few minutes more, and after he left, I sent out a group text to a few people about the incident. Everyone seemed as surprised as I was. I sat on the stairs dumbfounded for a few hours, trying to wrap my mind around what had just transpired.

Gloria and the Land

That July, Nikko and I got an invitation from my sister Cheryl. Her daughter was graduating high school. It had been 19 years since I last saw Cheryl, but a few months earlier, my dad had asked me to connect with her, so I did. Dad told me it would be good for my consciousness to do so, and he was right. I sent Cheryl a text, and she called me back and had a sweet chat for about half an hour. Nikko and I decided to make a road trip of it because mommy wanted to come and visit the farm for a few weeks before going down to Atlanta to stay with Toye. Mom made it a habit of spending every summer in the U.S, and I was happy about the prospect of hosting her. Max, our friend from Tucson, was visiting us for a month and agreed to house sit while Nikko and I went to Virginia.

The reunion was lovely; not only with Cheryl, but with her husband Curtis, her two kids, who I was just meeting, and a few family members I hadn't seen in years. Mommy's younger sister and my favorite aunt Somo, drove down from Maryland for the graduation, as well as Monica, another cousin I hadn't seen in years. Toye was there with his now increased family of 5, and we all had a good time reuniting and hanging out with mommy. It was the first time in many years – since Cheryl left for America, that mommy was with the three of us in one place. Mommy was very happy. The next day Nikko, mommy and I drove back to Missouri, taking a leisure route from Virginia to Ohio, and then down to Missouri.

Mom immediately fell in love with the farm and would wake up early each morning to tend to the roses and the garden. "I'm no damn vegetarian," she said and had me fish daily in the pond for her lunch and dinner. She would sit on the wharf and clean the fish we caught, then bring it into the kitchen to cook. I countered her "I'm not damn vegetarian" speech by designating a particular pot she could use to cook her fish, saying, "I don't want no damn fish smell lingering in my good pots when this crazy woman leaves here." One of the first things she noticed was Matt's blue pickup truck. Mommy laughed and told me that my grandfather's truck was also blue. Added to my love for dressing fashionably, I was on my way to becoming, as she put it,

301

"Just like your grandpa: his Pith hat, his style, his stance, everything." She told me how happy she was that I was enjoying life. She said that of all the Liberians in the world, she knew only two who were living their lives fully— my stepbrother Robbie, who she said was a socialite and was having a great time at it—and me.

Missouri summers can get very hot and humid, so Nikko, Max, and I slept out in the yard in a large tent that Nikko had gotten as a birthday gift from his mom a month earlier. Mommy slept up in the guestroom but would come out every morning and peek into the tent. "Look at these three heathen knuckleheads, sleeping in a tent like country men. You got a whole house there. Mr. Jaycee, I thought you were from humid, tropical Liberia. You're a cold climate man now?"

Mom would comment on how much food Nikko ate, but how skinny he stayed: "I say, Nik Nik, whereplace all the food going, my man? You eat, eat, eat, but you still dry like bony fish." Nikko had been learning some colloquial Liberian English and understood her. He tried to respond with the little he knew, "You girl, I still growing oh, when I finish I will be fat like my Uncle Roy." Mommy laughed at Nikko's try at speaking like a Liberian. She was also very entertained by his love for Liberian food. She cooked us a few vegetarian style Liberian dishes, all the while cussing us heathens for not putting all the good stuff like chicken, goat, or crawfish in them.

During the day, we'd work out in the garden, and to "relax her mental tension," she'd sit out on the porch with her Heineken beer and listen to Max play his guitar. If he wasn't playing his guitar, Max would do a few hours of yoga, or he, Nikko and mommy would sit and talk about agriculture science, the importance of self-sufficiency and how happy mom was to learn about the growing permaculture and local food movement. She said that although the late President Doe of Liberia was a damn country man, at least he wanted Liberians to be self-sufficient and grow their own food.

Max, a very quiet person, enjoyed being around mommy, but he brought out her joker side as well. One day she sent him inside to get her a bottle of beer from the fridge, and when Max asked me to show him where the beer was, I told him to go and tell mommy her beer quota was met. She hadn't had any that afternoon, and so this was meant to be a joke. Max went out to tell mom, and she, in turn, looked at Max very seriously and asked him where he'd like to be buried. Mom got her beer pronto, and Max is still alive.

On a walk with her one afternoon, she asked if I was feeling more grounded in Missouri, and how I liked the farm and my relationship with Nikko. I was happy with both. The farm was a good space to cultivate what knowledge we had learned, and Matt trusted us with his property and was glad to see that we were enjoying living in the house. Nikko, I told her, had been a good addition to my life the last few years. I fell in love with him because his heart was pure, and his intentions were pure. I told her about my internet experience, and Neiman Marcus guy experience, and how it left me jaded toward relationships, but how Nikko, with his simplicity, helped me feel like I was loveable. For years I thought I wasn't qualified for love, and it scared me when Nikko revealed that he was in love with me. But I took it one day at a time, and the years build up around us slowly. I told mom that Nikko and I would sometimes fight about little things, and sometimes the age difference meant that it was hard for either of us to grasp concepts of topics, but we liked each other company, and naturally want to be around each other. Mom was pleased to hear how I felt and said that life was slowly coming together for me. With patience, she said, everything will fall into place, and I'll be very satisfied with life.

As it was everywhere that she went, when she stayed with us, the neighbors quickly fell in love with her. One neighbor came to drop something off for us, met mommy, and came back the next afternoon with some catfish he had caught. It was a pretty big fish, which he took home, cleaned, and froze for her. After we went shopping at the grocery store and other places around Cape Girardeau, a good friend, Carrie, asked me if the lady who came in with me was my mother. Carrie told me later, "She had such a presence! She walked with authority, like a very wise woman. I love strong women like that." I had seen what they were seeing as a child, and fell in love with mommy for that; but now, it felt like I was just hanging out with my closest friend, driving around with her, and introducing her to my other friends.

I rented an Airbnb house in Jefferson City for a few days, and mommy, Nikko, Max, and I drove there from our farm to visit her old stomping grounds. The home belonged to a fellow gardener who lived next door, and he was happy to meet mommy and hear about our various farm adventures where we lived. He was keen to notice that we all farmed in different climates around the world. Max farmed in Tucson, Nikko and I farmed in Southeast Missouri, and mommy, in tropical West Africa. Our host had some potted papaya and banana trees and kept them inside during the winter months.

Mom gave us a tour of her old college; her dorm, the house where she and Toye lived, and on our way to the Capitol Building in another part of town, she showed us the hospital where Toye was born. As was befitting his royal Toye-ness, he called and made us take pictures of the house and hospital. We were paying "homage" to his importance in this world. Mommy, laughing at Toye's boldness, said that if crazy had a human form, it would be Toye. A few days later we drove Max to St Louis for his flight back to Tucson and then drove back down to our farm.

The next morning, after we arrived, we received news that our cousin, and mommy's best friend, Juanita Neal, had passed away. It was another sad day, but this time, unlike Johnny's passing, mom had a calmness and smile on her face as she reminisced about their friendship. We used to call Cousin Juanita mommy's other half. There was not a day they didn't call each other and talk for hours. I recalled how cousin Juanita had encouraged me to keep teaching yoga and wanted me to bring what I had learned around the world back home to Liberia to benefit my people too. We bought more Heineken and drank to Cousin Juanita's memory. Mommy had just come to the U.S, and didn't go back for the funeral, but planned to have a memorial in the U.S. She said that Cousin Juanita wouldn't want her spending excess money just to go back to a funeral where Juanita wasn't even at; her spirit would be long gone to another destination. She told Nikko and I that wherever she died, she should be buried right there. If it was Liberia, she wanted to be buried in Marshall, where we had a few plots of land. If it was in America, she said to cremate her and not spend so much money on funeral arrangements and taking the body back to Liberia. "I like how the Indian people do it; cremation makes it easy for the family, I think."

Beautifully Orchestrated

When it was time for her to go to Atlanta to stay with my brother, I decided to drive her instead of booking a flight or train. Driving would extend our time together a few more hours. Nikko, mom, our puppy, Kiko, and I drove to Atlanta with an adventure in Alabama involving a stray dog trying to eat our puppy at a gas station. Some customers suggested we shoot the other dog; others suggested we call the police on the dog owner. Mom jokingly said as long as she was alive, we were never driving through Alabama again.

We arrived at my brother's house, and as soon as I pulled into the drive-way, my sister Yabo texted me to call my dad. She said he was fading, and it looked like he was nearing his end days. I told her I had just arrived in Atlanta and would head on over to their house. Mommy didn't want to come because she didn't like to see people sick and suffering. When Nikko and I got to my dad's hospice, he didn't recognize me at first but immediately shouted Nikko's name with a huge smile on his face. Dad inquired about the welfare of Nikko's parents, and we visited with him for a little bit. On a previous visit, he had taken us through the hospice and bragged to the nurse about his handsome sons who had come to visit him.

My stepmom showed up as well and went over to hug my dad. As she turned to go to her chair, she pulled dad's oxygen tube a little, and Nikko admonished her, "You're still trying to be the one who took his breath away, huh?" The room erupted in laughter; so much that the nurse came in because we thought my dad was going to die then and there. I was ready to post on Facebook that my dad died laughing.

The next day before we left for Missouri, I stopped in to see my dad again. He sat up in bed, and as everyone left the room, I asked my stepmom to stay. I told him that he had done amazing things in his life, had raised beautiful children, and should now relax and let God do what was necessary for him henceforward. My dad was shaking, and he listened and nodded to me as a child would. That was the hardest thing for me; seeing my dad, a once influential and respected person, shake with uncertainty. I told him I loved him, and I promised to pray for him. We left for Missouri and early the next morning my sister called to say that daddy was gone. Had I not decided to drive mommy—had I not been guided to drive mommy—I would have missed an opportunity to say goodbye to my dad. We had a rocky start in America, made amends later, and slowly built a sweet relationship which ended, in my opinion, beautifully.

Jaycee Kesh Akinsanya

Chapter
Twenty

Jaycee Kesh Akinsanya

I'm Your Mammy

Over the course of the next year, mom would call from Liberia to chat with us and tell us how excited she was to be retiring the following summer. She would come to the US and hop on over from one child to the next, beginning with my sister. I'd give reports on her roses and the garden, and she and Nikko would chat about his school work. We also got a new puppy, a Great Dane, Neil Diamond, who was born with a diamond spot on his head, and she laughed and said that the real Neil Diamond should leave a diamond imprint in our heads for naming a dog after him. Kiko, I told her, had been given to a farmer friend in Wyoming. Our friend needed a terrier to hunt for rodents, and Kiko had killed a few of our chickens a few days earlier. We were advised that once Kiko had a taste for chickens, he would continue to hunt them. Kiko's mom had killed twenty chickens one weekend, so he had that instinct in him. We were planning on getting a Great Pyrenees who would instinctively protect the chickens, and not eat them. When we got one, we named him Pali, which means protector, or herder, and we sent a picture to mom. She was pleased with him but said that she missed her Kiko.

She also started her famous 3 AM phone calls that would wake me up and keep me up for the rest of the night. I am a very light sleeper, and once I'm up, there's no going back to sleep. The calls went something like this:

Me: "Hi momma, what's up?"

Mommy: "Good morning, Jackass, did I wake you?"

Me: "Yup."

Mommy: "Good, I'm your mammy, I can do whatever the fuck I damn well please.

Me: "I'll get you back."

Mommy: "OK, go back to sleep, I just wanted to call and say hi. Hiiiii, now, Byeeeee."

She'd hang up, and I'll be left staring at the ceiling for the next few hours, unable to go back to sleep.

At other times she'd ask, "Where's that other Jackass, is he asleep?"

I'd tell her yes, and that I wasn't gonna wake Nikko up.

"Disobeying your mother, fine. Byeeeeee."

She loved a good gossip and would also call to tell us some fresh news she'd heard.

When a certain family gave me a bit of a hard time, I called her and asked what I should do about it.

"Tell them to kiss your ass."

Standing order for a "kiss my ass" on one day delivery.

In January 2017, mommy called me and told me that she had gotten sick with a slight bout of malaria and was recovering at home, but was still retiring in the summer. In Liberia, when we got malaria, we drank neem tea and also built a dome style structure and covered it with many blankets. Then we would build a fire in the tent, and place a large pot of water with neem leaves and twigs, and sweat out the toxins. She was making plans and had a dilemma as far as who to visit first. She could come to me, and then go to Cheryl for her birthday, and then Toye's; or she could visit my brother and then sister, then me. We weighed all the options, and she ended up staying with my sister that summer. I planned to pick her up from my sister's and then we'd go to the farm, hang for a few days, and then take a month to drive to the west coast and visit friends and family.

Mom loved a good road trip, and so I made arrangements with friends in Oregon letting them know that we'd be coming soon. I alerted Jaymee in Colorado, Elise and Jeff at Oshala Farm, Paula and Jim in Southern Oregon, and a few other friends, letting them know that mommy and I would be coming their way soon. We'd go to Yellowstone, Utah sights, the Grand Canyon, Crater Lake and other places in Oregon. We would visit Aunty Facia in Sacramento and also stop at my favorite hot spring spots along the way to relax our mental tensions.

As a budding farmer, I don't make much income; I also work for a plaque company, so I was saving every penny I could for this road trip. I didn't want her to spend a thing out of her own pocket. I just wanted her to enjoy the ride.

"Well, can I buy my own damn souvenirs?"

"Nope momma, you'll be my traveling guests, and I'll buy your souvenirs."

"Ah, the promises of a broke ass—I'll bring my own money just in case."

I was in New York with Nikko for Labor Day, when she called me and told me of a lump under her arm; a year before in that same place was a knot, the size of a mosquito bite, but now it was swelling, and she felt some slight pain from it. My sister Cheryl decided to take her for a checkup. But as she told me, it would take more than that to worry her. After she hung up the phone, a white moth flew onto my finger, and for whatever reason, I blurted out to Nikko that I thought mommy was telling me goodbye in the form of that moth. The rest of my New York trip was blurry as I was focused entirely on mommy's health and the swelling under her arm.

On Sunday morning Nikko and I drove down to Virginia to visit her; we were supposed to take her back to the farm with us, but her doctor expressed some concerns about the swelling and wanted to do some tests. We hung out with her that day, took her to dinner, gardened, and gossiped. Mom was in high spirits and seemed like her usual self. I told her about some herbs I was taking, and how thyme was very good for the immune system. We found a nice article on Google, and she read it and was pleased with what it said. The next morning, she was up and about in the garden, and when we got up, she told us she had already had some thyme in her tea. She laughed and said I was now Dr. Kesh, thyme specialist. We picked some sweet potato greens, eggplants, and okra from Cheryl's garden, and then sat and had some tea. We then made arrangements to purchase a train ticket for her to come to Missouri after her checkup with the doctor. During the next week, we texted each other, or I would call for the latest gossip, and then I would count the days remaining until she would come to the farm and hang out with us.

On September 19th the day of her checkup, I called later in the day to see how she was doing, and she sounded a bit sluggish, without her usual perky voice. I assumed they had given her some medicine for the swelling. She told me that they would let her know what was going on in a few days. I had a cold and told her I was resting in bed, and she told me to drink some tea and get some rest. She also asked if I had heard from Catherine, or Matt and his family in the Virgin Islands. Hurricane Irma had just hit the Islands, and mom would call or text to ask about the welfare of our friends who lived there.

On the morning of September 20th, I woke up with an eagerness to continue writing this memoir. I had not written anything for over a year, and so I let my thoughts flow onto the keyboard. Most of what I wrote that day was about mommy and her strength, and how she handled the war situation. I wrote for about 4 hours straight. I got a text from her asking how I was feeling and if I was drinking enough fluids. I said yes, and that I would call her later in the day.

311

Jaycee Kesh Akinsanya

That night, as Nikko and I watched "Suits," our favorite TV series at the time, my brother called me to say that mom had fallen unconscious, was rushed to the hospital. The doctor discovered a ruptured ulcer, and she was in a critical state. He would be flying out the next morning to see her. My sister Cheryl was in a frantic mood, and couldn't talk much on the phone. She said that earlier in the day when she came home, she had decided to get her husband Curtis to convince mommy to go to see her doctor because she looked frail. Cheryl said that mom had stopped eating after Nikko, and I left, and she tried to get her to eat something, but she refused. It was a few minutes later when she heard a thud on the floor—just after Curtis walked in the door after work—and they both ran upstairs and found mommy lying there.

I also looked at flights but couldn't fly out until Friday morning. For the next many hours, I sat and meditated, and tried to talk to mommy. I looked up into the skies and told her that it was up to her to stay or go, whatever she needed to do. I asked that if she wanted to leave, to at least wait till I flew in to be with her.

On Friday morning as my plane took off for Virginia, I fell asleep for a short moment, and in a dream state, mom appeared and kissed me on the cheeks. I opened my eyes and realized then that I was going to say goodbye to her. I arrived at the hospital and met Toye downstairs, and we walked up to the ICU where mom lay peacefully sleeping. I held her hands and told her that I was there and that Nikko said hi. Out of curiosity, I quizzed each nurse that would come in to take care of mommy, and they were happy to answer whatever questions I had. I struck up friendly conversations with them, telling them about mommy and the work she had done in her life. I figured she heard me and would be comforted by the fact that we were there and was very proud of the life she led.

I sang many songs to her while sitting by her bed. As a child, perhaps five, or six years old, she recorded Jesus Loves Me This I Know with me, right before we watched a movie. I sang many of her favorite hymns like A charge to Keep I Have, In the Garden, and many other songs. I also started to sing, Not in Vain, one of the songs on Pastor Momolue Diggs's Gospel Album, but I choked, and stopped. I wanted to be there for my mother, and not give time to my sadness. I knew I would grieve later.

If I can help somebody as I pass along,

If I can cheer somebody with a word or a song,

If I can show somebody they are traveling wrong,

Then my living shall not be in vain.

312

We played her favorite songs, and at one point the head nurse in the ICU came in as I sang to mom. She commended me on my singing and mentioned that a guitarist came around to sing for the patients and she would send him to mom's room so he would play his guitar while I sang.

Nikko also called and I put the phone next to mommy's ears for him to say hi to her. She had been sleeping most of the day, and that evening when I put the phone to her ears, she opened her eyes in recognition of his voice. With her brows, she made an approving smile, and closed her eyes again to relax. Nikko told me after I took the phone away that as he was talking with mommy, he saw a shooting star go by, and knew his Gloria was acknowledging his call and reciprocating with him.

Similarly, when Aunty Somo came to visit the ICU, mommy frowned her brows when Aunty Somo told her that she was going home to Baltimore and would be back the next Thursday. It was as though mommy was saying, "No, Somo Elizabeth, stay with me for these next few days.

As the days went on and mom's bodily functions failed, I sang to her, read to her and talked to her as much as I could. Toye told jokes, talked with her, flirted with the nurses, and played music for her as well. Aunty Somo and Cheryl also came in and talked with mommy, and we all took turns sitting in the hospital. I didn't leave the hospital much. I wanted to be right there with mommy. The doctors would come in and when she was somewhat conscious, try to get her to wiggle her toes and make eye movements. As I sang to her at one point, I said to her, "Isn't your son's voice sexy? I can sing, huh?" Her signature sarcastic frowned brows appeared on her face, and so I told her I would stop singing and that I was mad at her for not liking my singing. I told her if she wanted me to continue singing she should admit my "sexy voice-ness" by wiggling her toes and squeezing my hands. She wiggled her toes and squeezed my hands tightly, so I started singing again.

I carefully monitored the machines and asked questions about numbers I didn't understand, and when I noticed her decreased breathing, I took the opportunity to say my final goodbye. Previously my brother had encouraged me to say what I needed to say to mommy and I told him I had nothing to say to her. This was true for me because I had written about and spoken about mommy almost the entire time I lived in the US. She was my hero and guide in everything, and my friends practically "knew" her from how much I talked about her.

Jaycee Kesh Akinsanya

Give me flowers while I'm alive

Please do not wait

Til I'm dead and gone;

It won't mean a thing to me.

These were the lines of a song I learned as a kid, and I had lived those lines almost every day of my life. I saw the world through my mother's eyes, and the world was a beautiful place. In the midst of human interactions, good, bad and ugly, I saw people all striving for loving experiences. Some of the methods people used, I did not understand, but I too am human, and life has yet to teach me what measures I might take when Mr. Hard Times shows up for me.

There, in the ICU, I harnessed one gift I had given to others I came in contact with—lessons I had learned in the monastery. I had seen a few hospice situations, sat in meditation for a few people who were passing, and had given counsel to those who approached me during grieving periods. But as my mother never pushed any religious sentiments on us, I never felt the need to be a monk for my family; they were my family, and I was their son.

I whispered her last rites into her ears and then talked to her personally. I addressed her as a spirit soul, one who doesn't belong to this world but is just traveling through. I reminded her that her role as mother, daughter, sister, friend, colleague, and any other role she ever played in this life had now come to an end and she must prepare for her next destination. I told her that this was the best time to relax her mental tension. I thanked her for being such a wonderful light to many people, regardless of who they were or where they came from. I told her that I couldn't have asked for a better mother and friend, and thanked God for giving us to each other. I told her that she had kept her charge very well and glorified her God excellently in doing so. Now her God wanted her out of this body. All her life she had desired to go as quickly as her mother did and even that had been granted to her. I encouraged her to focus on her next space, and not on the suffering body she lay in.

Hours before, her breathing was quite troublesome as the symptoms of death showed in her, but after I said these words to her, she became quite calm and rested. My siblings were in the room as well and were asleep, but I fought the arrows of sleep and stayed up, keeping watch. It was around three in the morning when I spoke those words to mommy, and her body lay peacefully. She breathed effortlessly now, and I held and massaged her hands,

314

playing soft music on my phone, which was close to her ears.

Around 6:20a.m, I felt the need to doze off for a few minutes, and so I leaned my head against the wash sink in the room, but something wouldn't let me sleep. It was as though sleep had been coming to me all night, and I refused it, but now that I needed it, it was nowhere to be seen. I sat up again and looked at the monitor, only to see that mom's breathing had gotten significantly lower, and far between. I had seen this before, and so I woke my siblings up to let them know what was going on. The three of us stood around the bed massaging her hands and feet, as I quietly urged and ushered her to take the leap and move on. "You'll be alright, and we'll be alright; it has been a beautiful time with you, but now you must go."

At 6:35 in the morning, she breathed one last time.

I sat on the floor in meditation for a few minutes, and when I got up, my adrenaline kicked in, and I felt fully awake. I called the night nurse over and told him mom had passed on, but when he looked at the machine, it seemed like her heart rate was still up, so he told us that she hadn't passed yet, according to what the monitor was saying. I asked him to check with his stethoscope, and when he did, he let out a sigh, noting that she had indeed passed on.

Now we had to wait for the doctor to come in and pronounce her dead, so I slowly walked around the ICU just to move some energy around my tired body. The night nurse approached me and said how sorry he was for her passing, and how amazed he was at us for being such strong kids. He had tears in his eyes as he spoke. He was the first one to be consoled that morning. He talked about what a good woman mommy must have been to have such strong children.

The morning shift of nurses came in, and as they heard of mommy's passing they each came in to pay their respects. Outside of the room at the desk, I chatted more with one of the nurses who had been in a few days earlier to help care for mommy. We had connected on the topic of organic gardening, and so we talked a bit more as I waited for the doctor. Then he came and did his pronouncing; my sister left to go home, and I decided I would walk back to her house. My brother stayed a little longer in the room, and I took my "sweet Jesus time," as mommy would say, to walk through the halls of the hospital and out the door. Donna, another nurse, came up to me and said, "You've done your mama so proud. Go home and rest, the hard part is yet to come."

As I walked out of the hospital and into the parking lot, all of a sudden, I saw the world through the eyes of an uncertain, scared child. I felt unprotected and very vulnerable as I looked around me. The whole place seemed scary, nothing like I had ever experienced before. It hit me that mommy's view of the world had also passed on with her, and for the first time in my life I felt fear and intimidation; nothing like I had felt when my eyes were first opened to the real world in New Jersey. My giant, on whose shoulders I sat and saw a beautiful world, had set me down and left for a place I couldn't see. I sat on the grass and sobbed like a motherless child. I had always known that my strength and leaning space in life was my mother. She was patient with me as I tried to find my way around things. She gave me no time to mope about my situation, because as she put it to me, it was just a situation, and one can never judge life by a situation.

But now I sat in this parking lot in a situation and had no one to lean on. The scared child told me that the world was ugly and I should just go home. My brother came downstairs and saw me in the parking lot, talked with me for a second, and then I left to walk to my sister's house. It was a blurred walk with stops almost every few steps. My body trembled, tears poured, and my voice was choked up. I didn't give a damn if people walked by me and saw my mourning condition with tears and snot running down my face. I was distressed.

When I woke up from a short nap, my cousin Charles was there and gave me a big long hug. I had not seen him in ten years, and we chatted for a bit. Then Aunty Somo came as well, and we hugged and cried. In my mind, I decided to focus on helping with the funeral arrangements and what not; I would have time to mourn later. I planned to take a long road trip to the places I promised to show mommy; there I would grieve and heal.

Now the phone was ringing with family and friends in shock about the news. No phone call was coherent, as people talked through their tears and shock. Words of wisdom came in many ways, but the ones I remember the most were the words of my Aunty Lois who said, "It's sad that she's gone, but now watch as she orchestrates beautiful things from a different dimension."

Beautiful things started immediately. The priest at my Aunty Somo's church immediately agreed to do mommy's funeral services. He had met mommy a year before at Cousin Juanita's memorial service and fell in love with mommy's personality. When we got to the funeral home, while in the parking lot figuring out some details, the priest, Father Eric, called again. He mentioned that he had two urns that had held his parents' ashes. He wanted to save us money and offer an urn for mommy.

At her memorial, her old high school friends, work colleagues, Aunty Facia, Aunty Harriette, and many other family and friends gathered to pay their respects. They spoke of mommy's influence in their lives; her friendship, professionalism, silliness – everything that made her Gloria. When it was my turn to speak, I sang for her one last time. I wanted her to know how much I appreciated her, and how much I knew that there wasn't much more she could do for me through the hungry years. I sang If I could, the same song she sang to me twenty-four years earlier when I recognized my first feeling of depression. I sang it straight through, and after speaking walked outside and let it all out in tears.

The repast dinner after the services was pretty sweet. People told us how proud mom was of us, and how much she would talk about each of her children. Toward the end of the evening, I walked up to the DJ and asked him if he had any Luther Vandross, Teddy Pendergrass, Smokie Robinson, or such. He told me he did but didn't usually play such songs at funeral repasts. I told him what mommy had told me about how she wanted music, dancing and lots of drinks at her funeral. He said he'll see what he can do. By the end of the evening, we were all dancing our asses off in honor of Gloria.

Now you're reading this memoir and I hope it gave you a peek, through my eyes, into the life of someone who, like all of us, was put on this earth for a reason. She knew she belonged here; she was human, with human tendencies for being good, bad, and sometimes, ugly.

To serve the present age

My calling to fulfill

Oh, may it all my powers engage

To do my master's will.

- A Charge To Keep, I Have

Lazarus and The Power of Mistaken Identities

Jaycee Kesh Akinsanya

A week before sending this manuscript in for final proofreading, type-setting, and formatting, something urged me to look on the internet for an obituary for Brendan, my friend who came with me to Minneapolis. I wanted to know more about his passing, to add to my Seattle chapter. I came across a picture on Google, and the person looked very much like Brendan. He lived in another country, but something told me to send him an email. I wrote our this email:

Hello Brendan,

My name is Jaycee, and I am writing because I had a friend in Minneapolis

named Brendan O'Donnell back in 1998. We rode on a greyhound bus to-gether,

and then after a few days he left Seattle and we haven't spoken since. I am

writing a memoir of my life, and have been trying to contact him. I saw your

photo online, and you have a resemblence of him.

Anyway, just wanted to reach out and see.

Thanks,

Jaycee.

I woke up the next morning and had a reply from this person. Part of it read:

What a wonderful message to wake up to! Good morning, Jaycee. Yes, you have found the right Brendan... I'm so happy you found me and I look for-ward to hearing about your life.

NIkko was startled by the scream I let out. "What's wrong," He asked,"Is everything OK? Did you have a nightmare or something?" But he could see that I was smiling and crying at the same time. "Brendan is alive. My friend Brendan is alive. It was his picture that I saw on the internet." Nikko too was bewildered/ elated by the news. We hung out with a few Brendan's in Min-neapolis, and one had indeed passed away, but not this one, who came with me to Seattle. The miscommunication lay in my friend Togba not giving me a last name. What's in a name? A whole lot. Brendan had also heard of his own passing, but was in a position to correct it. I had no idea where he was, and couldn't be contacted by a pager anymore, because when I moved into the monastery, I packed the pager away in a box.

320

We're reconnecting slowly, with emails back and forth. I can't begin to write about how happy I feel that at least one of the two people who I wanted to read this book, is alive and well. I'm also said aboutt the Passing of the otehr Brandon (Spelled differently too!) and I wish I would have known, to attend his funeral. He was also a writer and a poet, and is definitely missed.

Epilogue

Jaycee Kesh Akinsanya

There are long days ahead of me; its winter now and I feel the world could use some inspiration in these dark times. As mommy would say, our strengths as humans lie in how we share with each other; and in no world, can we look at someone as a competitor as well as a friend. Both positions involve different energies. In her own wit, she would compare love and hate to the penis and the brain: "You know, God gave men two heads to deal with, but only enough blood to fill one at a time. If you're thinking with your lower head, your upper head won't work; and nowadays it seems like men are using their upper heads solely for their lower heads."

We can only begin to love and live with each other when we see our connection to each other. This is something that cannot be done just on an intellectual level. If you meet anyone on the street who's willing to talk philosophy, they'll conclude that we're all one and love is all you need. Yet our very species, so full of love, has a huge lack in the trust department.

From my mother, I've learned that it takes trust and courage to actually love one another. That trust and courage saved us in perilous times, empowered us in times of insecurity, and gave us permission to lift our middle fingers or say, "kiss my ass," when there were no other body parts left for kissing. Gloria saw a world in need, looked within herself to see what she had to give, and gave it wholeheartedly.

As my brother Isaac told me, mommy's funeral in Marshall was very packed. If we had it in the city, it would have been a traffic issue for hours—she knew too many damn people. People would get up to speak at her funeral, but stand stunned. As one lady put it, the words "Gloria," and "death," do not fit in the same sentence. I didn't go to the funeral in Liberia but plan to have a memorial for Gloria on the first anniversary of her passing. In her practicality, she told me many times before that wherever she died, to be buried right there. If it was in America, she said, cremate her body- she liked how the Indian people did their cremation. She didn't want us to stress out and buy tickets for a funeral "I won't be at anyway." So, I stayed in the U.S. Cheryl and Toye went back with her ashes to give Chee-Chee, Calvina, Serenna and the rest of the family closure.

I miss my mother dearly. I spoke to a friend a few days ago about how I wish people could die in such a way that makes them easy to forget, in a "ding, dong, the witch is gone sort of way. But mommy left only laughter and wit. Not a day goes by where I don't notice her wit, or remember something laughable. This is the kind of pain that takes longer to heal. The pain that arises from remembering so much good. So much Laughter. So much light.

I pray this memoir touches the heart of the many who knew her as well as the many who never met her. In reality, I know there are countless mothers

324

out there loving in their own way, and teaching their children what a beautiful world looks like.

I hope this book inspires you to dance to your own rhythm; I hope it inspires you to accept your good, your bad, as well as your ugly, find your platform and stand on it.I offer this memoir as a petal falling at the feet of my glorious expert gardener, who enables me to continue to stand, even as she has laid down her garden tools. Until my flowers wither and my roots can take no more food from the earth, I'll be me, one of those trees she so proudly planted in her garden, and proudly told her friends about.